THE JEW STORE

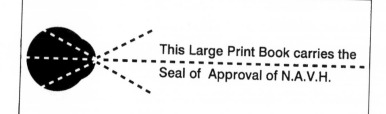

This Large Print Book carries the
Seal of Approval of N.A.V.H.

THE JEW STORE

Stella Suberman

Thorndike Press • Thorndike, Maine

Published in 2000 by arrangement with
Algonquin Books of Chapel Hill

Thorndike Large Print ® Americana Series.

The tree indicium is a trademark of Thorndike Press.

The text of this Large Print edition is unabridged.
Other aspects of the book may vary from the original edition.

Set in 16 pt. Plantin by Rick Gundberg.

Printed in the United States on permanent paper.

ISBN 0-7862-2315-4

For Jack
and
for Rick

For a real bargain, while you're making a living, you should make also a life.

— AARON BRONSON

CONTENTS

Prologue 11
1 The Destination 16
2 Avram Plotchnikoff's New Name . 32
3 A Nice Jewish Girl 45
4 For Better or for Worse 54
5 God's (So to Speak) Country . . . 74
6 Miss Brookie's Cousin Tom 90
7 Xenophobia 98
8 My Father's Fancy Footwork . . . 109
9 Bronson's Low-Priced Store . . . 130
10 Green Eyeshades 142
11 No Picnic 157
12 Opening Day 176
13 In Christ's Name, Amen 199
14 A Gleam in My Mother's Eye . . 213
15 Two Social Calls 224
16 A House and Neighbors 251
17 My Mother's Dilemma 270
18 Seth's New Job 285
19 New York Aunts 304
20 The Bar Mitzvah Question 335

21 Gentiles 348
22 Joey's Homecoming 355
23 Miriam's Romance 367
24 Aunt Hannah's Wedding 380
25 Concordia's Savior 394
26 Miriam's Rescue 416
27 Push Comes to Shove 430

I wish to express deepest gratitude to that most expert of guides, Louis D. Rubin, Jr., who helped me find my way back to Concordia.

Author's Note

Although this is a true story, I have changed the names of the persons whose story it is as well as the names of the town and county in which their story was set. In so doing, I'd like to think I have offered them at least the gesture of privacy.

Prologue

If you leave the main highways and travel on one of the county roads in northwestern Tennessee — which is what I did in August of 1995 — you will see endless cotton fields. I had last seen the cotton fields of Tennessee in 1933, the year my family left the South. Then the fields were small, family-owned, bounded by fences or hedgerows; nowadays they stretch out with no lines of demarcation and have the look of big business. It is, however, still a quiet place, a rural land. I was born there, in the small town I am calling Concordia.

I left the highway out of Nashville and got onto County Road 431 because of a sentimental wish to travel the same road that my parents, my brother, Joey, then seven, and my sister, Miriam, five, had traveled by horse-drawn wagon in 1920 — two years before I was born. Although County Road 431 was then a clay road meandering along, it made its way, as now, west through Weakley County and into the county I have named Banion, of which Concordia is the county seat.

Until this trip I had not been back. A Buddhist text tells us that the elephant is "the wisest of all the animals, the only one who remembers his former lives, and he remains motionless for long periods of time, meditating thereon." This may be fine for the elephant, but Concordia is one of those towns that has been steadily losing population, and I am a woman of more than a certain age. By 1995 I was feeling an urgency to forgo meditating and take a look at the site of my childhood before it or I disappeared. A grandchild told me I was having a "roots emergency," and I guess I was.

I decided on a one-day visit — enough, I thought, to cover a town only six blocks one way and five the other. And I planned not to visit people, only places.

County Road 431 was never very lively. You see the cotton fields, but you need patience to get to the signs — the banion county one and then the one that says concordia town limits. After a church and a graveyard turn up, you are almost immediately on First Street.

First Street seemed little changed from what I remembered. Though no longer cobble-

12

stoned, it is still only three blocks in length, stores on both sides. I went quickly to our old store, which had been in the center block — the Number One location in that day's merchantspeak.

You used to be able to spot our store by the gold letters on the plate-glass windows: BRONSON'S LOW-PRICED store. My father had splurged on those letters. For customer morale, he said, so customers would not feel that "low-priced" meant cheap.

Our store is now Swain's Electronics, one of the few stores on the street that still sells things. Most of the properties that are occupied offer services. Some persevere from my day. The First National Bank, for example, seems as in charge as ever, its brass plaque gleaming perhaps for the ages. At the end of the street the train depot is still operating, if minimally. And across the railroad tracks the church steeple rises into the air, though the church may no longer be New Bethel Baptist.

Bronson's Low-Priced Store was Concordia's "Jew store." There had been none until my family got there, and in those days it was the custom for every small Southern town to have one. A Jew store — and that is what people called it — was a modest establishment selling soft goods — clothing and domestics (bedding, towels, yard goods) — to the poorer people of the town — the farmers, the sharecroppers, the blacks, the factory workers. We were the only Jews among Concordia's inhabitants, of which, when my family arrived in 1920, there were 5,318, counting whites and Negroes.

For us Concordia actually began at the house of Miss Brookie Simmons. As I pulled my rental car up to it and sat looking, it seemed much as it had when I had last seen it and, I have no doubt, much as it had been when Aaron and Reba Bronson and family had pulled up to it themselves on their arrival in Concordia.

Though I was not there on that first day, it doesn't really matter. The story of it, and the events leading up to and following it, have been so often recalled and relived in my family, they have long seemed as much my experiences as the things I remember as having happened to me. My mother and father are with us no longer for the nostalgia sessions that so engrossed us, but Miriam and Joey are still around. Miriam and Joey live up North; I, in the South, though among a mixed population of Southerners and Northerners. Although Miriam has been living up North for many years, her Southern accent is as strong as ever, if not stronger. Joey ("Joe" now to most people but "Joey" as ever to Miriam and me) lost his a long time ago. Mine is still there, more there at certain times than at others: When Southerners are present, my speech is dense with *y'all*s and *mercy*s and much less so when they're not.

Joey and Miriam and I get together as often as possible, and when we do, out come the stories, along with the snapshots and the newspaper clippings and the old store newspaper ads.

Like Banion County and Concordia, most names are not real ones; but what happened and why are pretty much the truth, or, as my father would say, "close enough so nobody argues about it."

Chapter 1

The Destination

My mother always said she'd felt something of a letdown when she first saw the sign reading concordia town limits. They had been riding for three days along rutted dirt roads north and west of Nashville. Somehow she had come to believe that when they got to the town that my father had chosen for their new home — their *destination,* he said — there would be something remarkable about it, something that would set it apart from the other small Tennessee communities through which they had been traveling. But here they were, at the "outskwirts," as my father called it all his life, and what she saw were only more cotton fields, yet another wooden church with a cross on top, one more cemetery. So what should she have expected? she asked herself. An elevated train? Fancy gates?

My mother wasn't exactly overjoyed at being there. Truly, ever since they had left New York City, her mood had been like a thing on her chest, as she used to say. Two years and three months before, the family had ridden the train south to Nashville, where at least there lived other Jewish families, where there was a shul, or synagogue, and the prospect of a glass of tea in the afternoons with the rabbi's wife. Now they were about to enter a small town in Banion County, west Tennessee, fifty miles southwest of Paducah, Kentucky, wherever that was. They were going to try to open a store in a place where they would be the only Jews in town.

These feelings of my mother's were very unlike those of my father. Indeed, in disposition the two of them were very different. She was the one who looked back, fretted, viewed with alarm, often brooded. He lived for the future, crossed bridges when he came to them and not before, hoped always for the best.

In looks, except that they were both small in stature, they were opposites as well. My father's appearance was bright and light, his straight hair "blondish," his eyes famously blue, his smile quickly there. My mother was dark haired and dark eyed, and her smile came less readily.

As they rode toward town, true to form, my father was ebullient, my mother apprehensive. *Oy*, what were they doing here, she was asking herself, herself and her husband and

17

her two children, here among these, as my father called them, "country Tennesseans"? From what she had seen of them along the road, she had already declared them a curious people. Were they not strange, these women who charged out of their houses (in bonnets stiff like iron) to *sweep with brooms* their dirt yards? Whoever heard?

And *oy*, the church spires. As she looked now toward the town, she counted six. Or maybe seven. In such a small town, so many churches? From what she had heard, in the South prayers went to God and to — um — *Jesus,* so why not just one big praying place, come one, come all? The deep gloom all at once upon her, she did what she always did when this happened — put her head in her hands and moved it back and forth, as if tolling it. "Like a bell my head was in those days" was the way she used to describe it.

As the oft-repeated tale went, when, on July 16, 1920, the Bronsons reached the edge of town, there was in the sky a heavy black cloud outlined in cold blue. Within a few minutes the rain began falling. My father pulled the wagon into the graveyard, and my mother joined Joey and Miriam under the tarpaulin, which already sheltered the family's few possessions. My father stayed out in the now-hammering rain and stared at the tombstones. On one a poem started, "So sinks the sun after a gentle day," and he thought it was nice that somebody's day had been gentle, his own not having been gentle by anybody's call.

My father had wanted to go by train; Concordia was a county seat, and therefore the train stopped there. But trains meant fares and freight charges, and with the debt to my grandfather for their trip to Nashville still outstanding, my mother — for whom a debt was, as she put it, "like a growth" — argued otherwise. No, she said, they should think of "a penny saved, a penny to pay back with" and should therefore go by wagon. As if it were a matter of choosing the El over the streetcar to get to 125th Street, my father said.

As the thunder retreated, my father heard its rumble as threats to return if he didn't do right. Understood, he said to himself, but right about what? Out of his choices, of which he had many, he picked the most imminent — a place to stay. The wagon one more night was not an option. But where to look? And where was his *mazel* — his good luck — which should be turning up right about now to point the way?

Suddenly, not from the heavens but from the elm tree, plummeted two boys. As they stood staring at my father, they seemed to him the color and texture of the rain itself.

19

Atop pale hair sat ancient Panama hats, the saturated brims undulating with each raindrop. Pants, perhaps once blue, were streaky white; white shirts, confined by suspenders, were soppy, the long sleeves, buttoned at the wrists, plastered to arms. Feet were bare.

These were the Medlin brothers — T and Erv. As he announced their names, T, the older one and the one who spoke (Erv, six, only gazed), told my father he had been "christened" T.J. but was called T "for short" — as if, my father always said, two letters were too much of a mouthful. T was "near to nine," although my father described him as one of those country boys who might be "near to nine" but were more like "near to" thirty. They were the sons of a cotton farmer and lived "over yonder," T said, pointing to a peeling farmhouse.

T was puzzled by my father's presence. "You be the new Jew peddler?" he asked him.

"Jew yes, peddler no," my father answered him.

It was clear the boy had never before seen a Jew who wasn't a peddler. "Where you bound then?" As we got to know T through the years, we all were aware of his habit of flicking his eyes up when he was doubtful, and he did that now. "And what you got in mind?"

When told that my father was bound for

20

Concordia and had in mind opening a store there, the boy seemed even more confounded. Though we all liked to "do" people, I always thought my father had a true gift for mimicry, and what T said now, according to how my father told it, was, "Danged if I ever heard tell of a Jew storekeeper afore. And, law, in *Concordia?*"

As the rest of the Bronson family emerged from the tarpaulin, T looked them over, commented in an aside to my father, "I see you ain't just the one Jew," and asked if they needed a place to stay. He had something in mind — the home of his "cudden," Brookie Simmons, the one in Concordia who took strangers in, the one who, according to T, "loved company like a darky on Sunday afternoon."

My father had one question — the itchy "How much?" All the money he had in the world was in his inside coat pocket, and it was a slight amount indeed. "She charge much?" he asked T, not comfortable with the question but having to ask it anyway.

It was plainly T's view that everybody in the world except my father knew that Brookie Simmons was the daughter and heir of "Coca-Cola" Simmons, the bottling plant magnate and the town's wealthiest man, and as such she would be little interested in such

21

matters. "You don't know nothing if you think she's in it for the money," he said to my father.

My father had no alternative but to chance it. He asked the boy, "So, you're ready to go, Mr. T?"

"Yessir." T climbed into back of the wagon, and Erv followed. My mother re-seated herself on the perch.

My father flicked the horse lightly, called out, "*Vi-o! Vi-o!* Giddyap! Giddyap! Let's go, you Willy you!" and the wagon was back on the road. Now that they were set for the night, my father felt that he was not mucking around in the yellow mud, which, after the rain, the road had once again become, but that he was gliding along a ribbon of gold silk.

As they neared Concordia, T leaned over from the back to give my father directions. "Left as soon as you hit the cobblestones, Mr. Jew."

The words flew out of her mouth, my mother said later, like a bird from an open cage. "Mr. *Bronson*, little boy."

"Yes, ma'am," the boy answered her.

The house of Miss Brookie Simmons was on Third Street, two blocks from First. It was a little different from the neighboring two-story white frame houses in that it seemed

22

wide rather than tall, with a roof only slightly pitched. Perched on the roof was a little rectangular construction, an attic that had ignored symmetry and simply shot itself off to one side. What the house looked most like was a shallow-tiered, white-iced, sat-on cake.

As the wagon pulled up, everybody except my mother jumped off and started up the concrete walk. After the rain the sun had come out full, and steam was rising from my father's damp wool coat. Also Joey needed a haircut and his black curls hung over his forehead like a bunch of Concord grapes, and Miriam was in a dress wrinkled as if it had been slept in. Well, my mother reminded herself as she sat alone in the wagon, it *had* been slept in. And she thought *oy*, what if my father came back insulted? For the way they all looked. For being in a wagon. For being Jewish.

She gave a long look to the house. It was a house in need of paint, sitting on pilings of cracked, often absent bricks. The steps were scuffed, the lattice under the house broken, the porch floor full of warps and waves. *This* was the house of the daughter of the richest man in town?

Miss Brookie Simmons was out the door before the entourage even got to the steps. Out she came, short and round, a white cotton shirtwaist above, a long navy blue skirt below. Gold-rimmed glasses glinted as she moved; and salt-and-pepper gray hair, cut Buster Brown style with straight-as-pins bangs, swung around.

Plump she might have been, but, according to my father, she was a fast mover. In one quick circuit she had hugged T, shaken my father's hand, run her fingers through Joey's curls, and twisted Miriam's earlobe. Erv's cheek was pinched and a peck planted. The lady seemed as pleased as a hen coming upon unexpected feed. As she went whirling around, she was saying "delighted" over and over, which to my father sounded hopeful. She finally made it plain and said to him, "You can have two rooms, and you can decide for yourselves who goes in which."

My father couldn't decide on the spot who was going in which, but he liked this lady. "How could you not like her?" he used to say. "A lady so busy with such a nice hello?"

She bounded down the steps, and everybody followed. My mother watched her coming to the wagon. *Brookie.* What kind of name was that? The names she missed were more like *Molka, Gittle, Moishe,* which at this moment she feared she might never hear again. When the lady got to the wagon, she laid down a barrage of words, to my mother

24

such gibberish she could only remain mute in the face of it.

The lady finally reached up and tugged at my mother's arm, and in another moment, everybody was going up the walk, Miss Simmons in the lead, a strong flow of chatter in her wake. Joey and Miriam were jumping about, and my father was talking, laughing, being happy. My mother trailed behind. She felt, as she often said, like a shoe run over by many streetcars.

Inside, the house seemed deep and dark. My mother at once thought she smelled the mustiness she had been advised to expect in Gentile houses. Hadn't she heard about a cleaning compound made of pig fat?

Miss Simmons led them to two upstairs bedrooms, furnished identically. My mother's first bit of cheer came from hearing there was a bathroom "down the hall." She had worried that in this country town there would be only outhouses, and she had been remembering them as they had been in the old country — tiny huts in the backyard to which you dashed on hot nights, frigid nights, any kind of nights, for things the house pot wouldn't do for.

After a glance into both bedrooms my mother plunked down on the double bed in one of them. And there she sat.

Miriam was already twirling around, looking, touching. The curtains held her. The bedroom curtains of her memory had been thin and straight, uninterrupted by fold or Xounce, and very unlike these great white billowy things with ruffled edges swelling above their tiebacks.

My father and Joey came in with the trunk, my father dragging from the front, Joey pushing from behind. My father figured my mother needed encouragement. "There ain't nothing to worry about," he told her. "We're doing okay."

How could they be doing "okay," my mother wondered. Everything was in such a *tumel* — a mishmash. She didn't even know how much they were being charged, and when she asked my father, he said he didn't ask and didn't know.

And about being Jewish? Had my father told the lady?

Again no. "You want the first thing out of my mouth should be 'Hello, shake hands with a Jew'?" my father asked my mother. If the boys didn't tell her — and so far they hadn't — he wasn't going to say anything to anybody until they were safely settled.

My father went outside to thank the boys. They were on the walk, already leaving. "Say," he asked them, "ain't it written somewheres that a little child shall lead them?"

"Yes sir," T answered. "Isaiah 11:6."

In the bedroom Miss Simmons was trying to get my mother to come into the dining room. Her words were slow and carefully wrought, as if in this way to ensure comprehension. She said somebody named "Lizzie Maud" was fixing them something to eat.

There was a mention of fried chicken and potato salad. *Potato salad?* That jumbled-up stuff with all the mayonnaise?

In the end my mother didn't go down to the dining room. She pulled back what Miss Simmons had called the "counterpane" — and had pronounced "counter*pin*" — lay down, and went to sleep.

If my mother had gone, she would have been convinced at last that she was in the house of someone with money. The dining room could be said to actually glow with riches: Mahogany gleamed, silver glinted, crystal sparkled.

When my father came in with Joey and Miriam, he always told us, he gave a look to the already-set table, to the silver pitcher in the middle, to the stemmed silver goblets, and to himself said, *oyoy*, could the *poretzim* — the Russian landowners — do better?

After a moment the door between the dining room and the kitchen swung open, and a

27

tall, softly contoured Negro woman came through. In one hand she bore a silver platter of chicken and in the other a crystal bowl of something neither Miriam nor Joey had ever seen before. It was, of course, the potato salad.

Miss Simmons introduced them to each other: She was Lizzie Maud; they were the Bronsons.

Lizzie Maud said, "How do," and my father said, "Likewise."

Miriam and Joey, having never before been in such intimacy with a Negro, stared at Lizzie Maud. The woman was dark, the very color of the room's rich woods. Above full features, kinky black hair was pulled into tiny clusters, each tied with a ragged snippet of white cloth. On her feet were broken-down men's shoes that had metamorphosed into slip-ons. A muslin apron that (no doubt) countless washings had turned into filmy gauze covered her dress. On the apron was a circle of words, which Joey, not yet in school and with the words barely visible, struggled to read. He finally made out "Rambling Rose Flour, Pride of the South."

Lizzie Maud turned back to the door, as if she had forgotten something. When she pushed back through, she had a silver basket of hot biscuits loosely covered with a napkin.

"Be a lots of shuffling of the dishes," she said matter-of-factly.

Into the silver goblets Miss Simmons poured tea from the pitcher. When the tea came out, so did pieces of ice. Joey and Miriam have remembered staring. *Ice in tea?*

Miss Simmons put the pitcher down, and all at once the word *Jewish* was in the air. "Have I got that right?" she asked my father. "Aren't you folks Jews?"

It was out. My father managed a nod. The lady said she thought so, had known it almost at once. According to how Miriam has always told it, Miss Brookie Simmons said, "I confess I had an inklin' when I saw those ravishin' black curls on the little boy and glimpsed a certain look here and there, and I thought, 'Unless my brains have turned to rhubarb after all my years in this town, these people are *Jews.*' " We always expected a quote from Miss Brookie Simmons to be requoted, and in Miss Brookie Simmons's distinctive style, by Miriam. At doing Miss Brookie Simmons, Miriam was matchless.

What finally had convinced her, Miss Simmons was saying, were the accents.

Accents? She heard accents? And she saw *certain looks?* My father was nonplussed. Did my mother and the New York relatives have it wrong when they said he talked "just like a

29

Yankee"? And didn't everybody say that with his light coloring he didn't look Jewish? He didn't fidget over it. The lady was taking the Jewish thing okay, and that's what was important.

She was not only taking it, she was charging ahead. Now she was wondering if my mother hadn't joined them because she was "kosher." "If she's kosher, I reckon she wouldn't touch chicken fried in bacon grease with a ten-foot pole," she said to my father.

How could this country lady know so much about Jewish curls and accents and certain looks and kosher? But so easy was my father feeling, he chose not to ask. Joey and Miriam were eating, my mother was resting, there was a roof over their heads, the lady didn't seem to mind that they were Jewish. He told her not to worry, that my mother had a *rule* to see her through and, very important, one that carried the imprimatur of the rabbi's wife. It was she who had given the word that in an "alien situation," you were allowed to eat nonkosher. "A rule's a rule," my father said to Miss Simmons, "and women don't never hear a rule they don't follow."

"But having to confront this overbearing old lady doesn't help," Miss Simmons answered him.

She wanted to know what had brought

them to Concordia, and my father wondered if the answer would surprise her, as it had the boy. It didn't. She knew about Jew stores, and my father's spirits went soaring when she said Concordia needed one, though they came down a bit when she expressed a "bit of concern" over whether Concordia would take to one.

Joey and Miriam had finished eating long before, and the conversation had lost them at about the same time. My father figured they wanted to go to bed, and he steered them into the bedroom next to where my mother was sleeping. He had it on his mind that my mother hadn't eaten, and he went out to the wagon and got some peaches and cheese. When he came back in, he tried to wake my mother, but she wouldn't wake, just kept on sleeping hard. He sat on the edge of the bed for a moment rethinking the day. How about that *mazel* of his? Like a good sport it showed up just right, led him to the boys and to this house. He wouldn't let himself think of that thing the lady had mentioned — about whether the town would "take to" a Jew store. He got undressed and lay down beside my mother; and though the room was hot, "hot like a boiler was in it," my father said, he put his arm over her and drifted off.

Chapter 2

Avram Plotchnikoff's New Name

My father used to remind me that the small town of Concordia, Tennessee, in which I was soon to be born, was actually larger than the town in which he grew up — Podolska, in Russia. This was his shtetl near Kiev, in the Ukraine. As far as my father was concerned, all the advantages were on the side of Concordia, which whatever its social and cultural limitations, was not like Podolska — a place, he told me with a straight face, where even the field mice ran away, there being so little in the fields to tempt them to stay. It was because *he* was born in Podolska, he often said, that *I* was born in Concordia.

In Podolska he had the added misfortune of being born at the onset of the typhoid epidemic that swept the country in the late 1800s and in due course claimed his mother, father, and grandmother. When his grandfather rose up from his own sickbed, most of the family was in the nearby Jewish cemetery, and he was faced with caring for an infant — my father. I never knew my great-grandfather, but when my father told of him, of a man able to nurture despite new woes heaped upon an already hardscrabble shtetl existence, I grasped even as a three-year-old that he was, as my father said, a mensch, a man who knew his duty and did it. I also grasped why my father knew early on that if a way out was to be found, he had to find it himself.

In his first uncertain steps toward this end, at the age of eight he begged a job from a Jewish merchant in the village. If getting the job might seem a mixed blessing in that a full workday ruled out an education, it should be remembered that in any case there was no provision for public schooling for the Jewish children of the village. Still, there was the cheder, the Hebrew school. But being deprived of cheder was to my father of little consequence, as he would not have traded his job for all the cheders of the world. What served him therefore as education was a bit of schooling in the evenings with his grandfather, enough to get him through the necessities for the bar mitzvah, the ceremony that marked the entry of thirteen-year-old Jewish boys into manhood.

My father's bar mitzvah turned out to be a small event taking place after Saturday services in the tiny hut that was the shul. My father handled the readings competently but found himself hard-pressed in the obligatory speech of gratitude to name people who had helped him thus far in life. In the end he was able to come up with only his grandfather and his boss. For becoming a man, a rite of passage marked by the giving of gifts, my father's entire take was a penknife (from his grandfather), a ruble (from his boss), and a few kopecks from the few others in attendance. Afterward the guests repaired to the dark dwelling that was my great-grandfather's house for tea and sponge cake.

If a conventional education was denied him, an education in salesmanship was fully provided. His boss was a good model, and my father discovered that he was a good mimic. He watched and he listened, and soon he knew better than his boss how to fit the customers, how to banter, how to soothe. It was a talent that came early and stayed late, all the way through the Concordia days, indeed the thing chiefly responsible for the living he made there. In Podolska it is no wonder that with such industry and enterprise he was called a *geborner ferkoifer*, which he translated for me as a "born salesman," an accolade that stuck in his head and occasionally lit up like a storefront sign.

In his middle teens he had his first serious epiphany. It came when business began falling off and his boss turned sour, frequently raising his arms to the heavens and wailing, according to my father, that the country's economy was *farshtunken* (it stank). It was then that my father clapped himself on the forehead (he told me) and connected the country's rotten economy to a transformation in the pogroms: They had become more frequent and worse. "So bad there was no place to hide they didn't figure out," he said.

He then began to listen with a more receptive ear to the talk about America — how it was a land of opportunity (though he couldn't quite swallow the widely held vision of gold-paved streets) and how it was a place where one could live with a reasonable expectation of physical safety. So at sixteen he got from the rabbi the address of some members of the extended family — the *mishpocheh* it was called — who had already cleared out for New York. He then took his savings, said good-bye to his grandfather — who had at any rate been expecting this turn of events — and struck out by train to Hamburg and by steamboat steerage across the ocean. He sincerely hoped his *mazel* was making the trip with him, but of the presence of his *zutz* — a word invented by my father to mean his hustle — he had no doubt.

On the boat his hustle made an appearance immediately, in time to solve the problems of the bottlenecks, the jostling queues at the galley door, which threatened to turn chaotic. My father hatched a plan for taking plates back and forth, clicked on the BORN SALESMAN sign in his head and, through some creative gesticulations, sold the idea to the steward. When his system worked, he was paid twenty-five cents a day — American money! — although it was not net, since he had to split it with the boys he had talked into carrying plates with him. This plan of his and how it had worked so well was something my father talked about a lot, and when in later years Concordia also needed a plan to head off chaos, he again set himself to hatching one, as if he saw himself as the designated hatcher of plans.

Still, at the end of the journey, when he landed in New York and was dumped into the immigration scramble at Ellis Island, his apparatus for problem solving labored in vain. Though in addition to Yiddish my father could speak a little wobbly Russian, the immigration officials were competent in neither, and he was all at once in a muddle, which was on one memorable moment embodied by a man in a white coat coming at his eyes with a small pointed stick. As my father bobbed and weaved, he managed to ask what it was all about of a nearby fellow passenger, who, he knew, had picked up a little English somewhere and might therefore have learned something.

The man had learned very little, only that it was some kind of craziness — *meshugass,* he called it — and that the white-clothed assailants were doctors looking under eyelids for something. The man told my father, "If you got it, you don't go nowhere but back."

My father apparently didn't have it — signs of a communicable disease called trachoma — and he could go forward. This took him as far as a man at a desk who was looking with no discernible enthusiasm at my father's papers. "Name?" the man asked my father.

My father had not even understood the question and so simply stared back.

It came again. "What's your name?"

Some of my father's wits returned. "Droskowitz. Avram Droskowitz."

The official pushed at the papers in a show of irritation, wrote a line on a card, picked up a rubber stamp, brought it down, hard, and authorized the entry into America of a man called Avram Plotchnikoff, a name no doubt already mastered by an official not eager to work on yet another one. It looked as if my father's good luck had not made the trip with him after all.

Actually, it was getting ready to show. As he searched the cavernous hall for help in getting to the *mishpocheh*, there appeared under a stairwell a sign — not an omen kind of sign, but a cardboard one with letters that were unmistakably Hebrew. This was miracle enough. My father put to use the Hebrew letters learned for his bar mitzvah and decoded the words — MIR HELFEN MENSCHEN — as a Yiddish phrase meaning assistance was offered. The man behind the sign, speaking Yiddish, which, my father reported fell on his ears like balm, told him to first take the ferry to Manhattan, then wrote EAST BRONX on a paper, and advised him to take the streetcar that had those words on the front. He wanted to know if my father had any money.

My father held out the coins earned on the boat — several pennies and some dimes.

The man, no doubt surprised, said, "Well, well," took one of the dimes from my father's hand, held it up, and told him to give it to the streetcar conductor and wait for change.

Waiting for change from the streetcar conductor was not a walk in the park (not that my father had ever walked in a park, there being no parks in his shtetl). The conductor, perhaps an early example of the legendary New York streetcar and bus conductors who treated passengers — especially non-English-speaking passengers — as creatures sent to earth for the purpose of vexing them, spat words at my father as if they had been sores on his tongue. But my father had heard angry men before, so he stood quietly until the tirade subsided, got his nickel in change, and sat down.

In the East Bronx he found plenty of Yiddish speakers. They led him to the very apartment he sought, and, after identifying himself to the *mishpocheh* he found there, he followed the poor Russian-Jewish practice and rented the corner of one of the rooms. A few days later he got a job.

It was not a job as a salesman in a store, though he had at first gone looking for such a job. He had looked in the Jewish stores around Delancey Street on the Lower East Side because naturally he could work only in a store where Yiddish was spoken. At the first store he had given the owner a rundown of his experience only to be greeted by scorn. "Forget about it," this owner said to him. "All those years you put in in your pipsqueak town is *bupkis* over here." Just goat dung in America.

The job he got was delivering coal from a wagon, a job for which a grasp of English was a very low priority. But from the first day he knew that as his new name was terrible, so too was his new job. He was never out of the cold, and with the coal dust around his eyes holding fast even after a scrubbing, he knew most surely that this was not a job he would grow to love. Soon he felt burdened by the whole idea of New York. "Too big," he said to the extended family, "and no future here. I feel like I'm walking around in somebody else's coat. It don't fit and it don't keep me warm neither."

After a couple of years, he began to plot a getaway. Daily, in the very early mornings before work, his quest took him down to the docks. He was not choosy; he would go anywhere. He went into one hiring hall after the other, working his primitive English to the limit. He had no luck. The hiring bosses scarcely looked at him.

Desperation looming, he one day plopped down on a bench next to a man he had seen around the docks. He wanted to talk to him, but since he was in New York, he first had to find out if the man would talk to *him*. *"Bist du ein Yid?"* he asked, having some confidence that the man was Jewish, there being, as my father told the story, something Jewish about him. He always declined to say just what this was, but I would guess that it was not the possession of a hooked nose or kinky hair, because he would have discovered that any

40

number of Mediterranean types also showed these characteristics. It was more likely that he saw the look of anxiety and uneasiness unique to the pale, pale faces of Jewish immigrants — the same looks that I saw in my mother's photographs of my immigrant ancestors.

At any rate, when the man said that he was indeed Jewish, my father asked, rather more rhetorically than purposefully, "*Nu,* so what's it take to get a job around here?" The man took this as a serious request for information and after calling my father a "greenie," informed him that he had to slip the hirers some money.

When my father wondered how much, the man said that a five-dollar bill was the least.

My father stared at the man. "So?"

"So I ain't got it yet," the man admitted.

My father had to admit he didn't have it yet either. But he thought that if he skipped meals, he might be able to get it. And before too long he had passed a hirer a bill and was put on a boat going to Miami. Ah, Miami. Good-bye Russia, so long New York. By the time the boat got to Savannah, the air was mild and in fact balmy, the wharves looked warm in the sun, the black men as they unloaded the freight were laughing and calling out to one another, and he decided he didn't have to go all the way to Florida after all, that Savannah warmth was good enough. On the wharf he asked one of the Negroes the way to town. The man looked at him in an interested way and said, "Just walk along the river, look away pretty soon, and you be there."

My father made his way in, assessing the town's size by the number of houses he was passing. He thought with satisfaction that it looked like a good-sized place, meaning that it would have a real shopping street and maybe a job with his name on it.

In a few minutes he found himself on Broughton Street, exactly the kind of street he had anticipated. He strolled up and down it, then went into Whitaker Street, where he made out a sign that said BRONSTEIN'S READY-TO-WEAR AND HOUSEHOLD. He recognized Bronstein as a Jewish name, walked in to see what was what, and after a few words with the owner, got himself hired.

Eli Bronstein was a fatherly man who had lived in Savannah for eighteen years, had raised a family there, and had earned a living almost from his first day. He, like my father, had had an initial stay in New York, had in time soured on the city, and had finally come south with his family and opened a store. In Savannah, while the term *Jew store* was not in common usage, that's what Bronstein's store

42

was, though it was not *the* Jew store, Savannah being big enough to have a couple.

My father at once felt at ease with this man and poured out the tale of his New York woes. Summing up, he said to him, "It was like I had a rotten egg sitting with me the whole time." With Bronstein he spoke a little English here, a little Yiddish there, so that it emerged as a kind of Yidlish.

Bronstein remembered his own bad times in the big city, the chutzpah he found there, the hordes of uncaring strangers. He said to my father, "If you don't watch your rear end, they grind it into kasha." Among his grievances was that at Ellis Island they had put the name Krapchnik on him, a name he got rid of as soon as he came to Savannah. He made it Bronstein, because that was the name of the man who had given him a hand to go to the South.

My father was cheered by this story and decided at once to rid himself of the detested Plotchnikoff. And since Bronstein had given him his first hand in the South — except for the Negro dockhand (name unknown) — he decided to go for Bronstein.

Bronstein's advice to my father was to forget the *stein* at the end. "It tells the world you're Jewish. This is one thing it don't pay to advertise."

43

My father and Bronstein talked it over and decided on Bronson. Bronstein's next idea was that my father should change his first name from the old-country Avram to the new-country Aaron. "Don't worry about it," he told my father. " 'A man of peace' it means either way."

To which my father answered, "You don't remember Avram also was a man lost in the wilderness?"

So it was that in a few days my father stood before a judge, the judge gaveled, and Avram Plotchnikoff became Aaron Bronson.

Chapter 3

A Nice Jewish Girl

When my father arrived in Concordia, he had already learned at Bronstein's how a Jewish merchant operated in the South. The first law was that unlike in New York and Russia, where Jewish stores, in observance of the Sabbath, were closed on Saturdays and open on Sundays, here it was the other way round. He didn't especially care, first because as a born salesman he would do what was required in order to sell, and second because he really didn't take religion seriously.

He really didn't take God seriously either. Though I often heard him make supplications to "God," as the years went on I realized they were coming not out of faith but out of custom. In later years his arguments about the existence of God with my Uncle Meyer, my mother's brother, a man who really loved an argument, were legendary, at least to me. They were not about a God of creation, because both believed this was a subject that defied debate. How could you argue about what got it all started? What were they, *scientists?* they asked, though they agreed also that scientists didn't know what to make of it either. But when Uncle Meyer talked about an intervening power, said things like, "I'm leaving that up to God," my father was quick with the rebuttal. "God has time to put his two cents in?" he would say. Or when Uncle Meyer offered, "God will take care," my father would counter with, "He gives us Cossacks and typhoid epidemics, this is the way he takes care?" Once in trying to explain his views on God to me — a rare occasion — he said, "God is like when those in Russia said America's streets were paved with gold. Did they see? Did they know? Of course not. It was only a rumor agreed on by everybody."

It was also in Savannah that he learned about other Southern customs, so there were few surprises when he came upon them later in Concordia. The thing with the Negroes had been a real eye-opener. Until he had gone to New York, my father had never seen a Negro, while here in Savannah there were more Negroes than whites. In New York, Negroes were to be seen in the houses he delivered coal to, where Negro women worked as domestics; and he had seen them in Harlem when he was going past it on the streetcar. Some place, this Harlem, he had thought then: really a town in its own right and populated exclusively by Negroes. He also came to understand that among the Jewish people he knew, Negroes were spoken of, with a touch of disparagement, as *shvartzerim*.

In Savannah, Negroes also lived to themselves, in ramshackle houses in an area called Niggertown, which was, when my father thought about it, a place pretty much like his shtetl.

When my father spoke to Bronstein about this, Bronstein said he didn't rock the boat. "I'm here for a living, not a crusade," he said. In Concordia it was a question that my father was often called upon to ponder, and though most often he went with "a living," he would sometimes, in ways he felt able, come down on the other side, meaning in personal ways, not in crusades. He never liked the picture of himself out on the parade grounds waving a flag with no troops following. What he did was keep quiet about it and do the best he could, though there was one time when he made a bold statement indeed.

My father settled into Savannah very quickly. He liked his job, he liked Bronstein, he liked his customers. He felt as if he were living on a featherbed.

He even had a friend — Pinchas Shapiro,

nicknamed Pinky — a young Jewish-American man who shared his rooming house and who worked in another Jewish-owned store. Pinky, a chubby young man with very curly dark hair and dark eyes, was born in Waycross, Georgia, and spoke in idioms half Southern, half Jewish; his standard greeting was "How's by y'all?" The two boys got together on their day off and went together to shul on Friday nights.

My father was at first struck by the number of young people who turned up in the synagogue, finding it hard to believe that all these teenagers were so strong in their beliefs. He soon understood that they were drawn there not by religious fervor, but by social needs. Marriage was clearly the dominant goal of the girls' lives, and a Jewish groom sine qua non, so the shul was simply a convenient marriage market.

By no means did the local shul provide the entire pool of the area's young Jews, since the "area" embraced all of Georgia, South Carolina, Alabama, even North Florida. All of the area's eligibles were on lists that were constantly brought up to date and pressed into service for a dozen or so parties each year. Guests came from as far as two hundred miles away, and from these parties a match was often orchestrated.

When I first heard about these lists, I assumed my father must have been at the very top of them. After all, with hair so light it could almost be called blond and eyes blue, blue, blue, how could he not?

Well, on the lists he was, but nowhere near the top. He did well at the parties, but when he took out these girls one on one, it was not a success: His stories did not interest them, and his accent did not fall agreeably on their ears. No, my father was not fighting off the girls with a stick.

Still, after a year he yielded to the badgering of his customers and decided all right, he would see about getting married. There was one girl, Esther Glatstone by name, who seemed responsive, and though it was a feeling he was not sure he returned, he thought to have a preliminary talk with her father.

My father was shocked by the response. Mr. Glatstone liked him, but Mrs. Glatstone didn't. She told her husband, and he told my father, that he was not a catch but just a man to be a clerk the rest of his life.

My father's brain went reeling. Was there a perception in the Jewish community that he was planning to forever be a clerk? Repugnant as the thought was, he finally had to admit it was a possibility: Perhaps at Bronstein's his drive had been becalmed by a sense of comfort and security.

He gave up on Jewish girls. But he was young and he craved a social life, and he was not averse to looking beyond his natural order. Out there in the larger city he found a huge crowd of young Gentiles dedicated to a dynamic social life. In summertime, much of this centered on Tybee Beach, where on Saturdays there were boisterous whiskey-and-oyster parties that lasted until dawn. When news of these pleasure-filled nights filtered through to my father and Pinky, they decided to go after work on Saturday night and try to get invited. They found themselves immediately waved into the group.

After the summer, my father continued to see these young Gentiles, especially the girls, the shiksas, as Bronstein's Jewish customers called them. He was taken on, in fact, as a project by one of the Savannah service leagues, and "Improve Aaron Bronson's English" would have been found among the other projects, like "Raise Money for the Orphanage." The members to whom he was assigned worked with him assiduously. They taught him to read, and then they taught him to write, and then they worked on his accent. "Not 'Mountwernon,' " they would say, "but 'Mount Vernon.' " After a while he began taking these girls out, to a picture show, or to a vaudeville, when one came to town.

Soon his customers wanted a word with him, asking him darkly, "You ain't thinking of marrying a shiksa, are you?"

My father had indeed been thinking of marrying a shiksa, specifically the girl to whom he had been last assigned, the daughter of a city official. She gave him long stretches of time, and when she laughed at his language fumblings, it seemed in delight, not disdain.

The girl's father also seemed to like him, and one day asked him if he wanted a job with the city as a fireman. Bronstein didn't quite endorse the idea but said my father had to find things out for himself. And if my father wanted to come back, Bronstein said, he'd still be there.

The girl's father had another idea: Now that my father could read and write English, he ought to think about becoming a citizen.

An American citizen! It was not something my father had even considered, perhaps because no one had ever mentioned it to him. He had no idea, in fact, whether Eli Bronstein or any of the older Jews of Savannah, were citizens. Somehow this was not something they talked about. Perhaps, like many of the aunts and uncles in my own family, they were fearful of the tests or, being immigrants, they kept as far away from "government" as possible.

My father easily qualified for the two-year residence required in those days for what was called "taking out the first papers," the declaration of intention to become a citizen; the girl taught him what was needed; and then after passing the tests, he stood before a judge, this time to become an American citizen, with the girl's father as a character witness.

In the meantime he had been thinking of proposing. He talked himself into believing that the girl, so interested, so thoughtful, might welcome his proposal. But on a night when they were having ice cream in the drugstore and another girl they knew came in, his resolve was shattered. It was the girl's greeting that did it. "Hello, Pinky," she said to him.

Pinky? Pinky? My father was stunned. Pinky was dark, he light; Pinky was heavy, he thin. The differences were so obvious, how could she have mixed them up? He wanted to laugh, to say she was the silliest of Southern belles. But in his heart he knew the answer: When she saw him, she saw "Jew." If, as the joke went in Savannah, all politicians looked alike, as did Negroes and little boys, then he asked himself, "And Jews also?"

It was an insight. Was the attention these girls lavished on him the same as on a pet, on a plaything? In his need to reject this new perspective, he challenged it again and again. What about Bronstein? Hadn't *he* made it, wasn't he accepted? To this he had no clear answer. He decided maybe there was no answer because the premise was wrong. Maybe it only *seemed* that Bronstein had "made it" when in truth he was merely making a living. And thanks to the Southern tradition of civility, Bronstein would feel rejection only on rare occasions, and when he did, he could run home to his family. So was the answer to have a family? The argument being inconclusive, full of *maybe*s, my father made a tactical retreat and went back to work for Bronstein, saying that anyway he was a salesman, not a fire-wagon polisher.

The customers welcomed him back, and the bedeviling began again. "Look, Aaron," they said to him, "you want you should end up like Markowitz and Leiberman?" — Markowitz and Leiberman being a couple of rich, sixtyish Jewish bachelors known widely as unkempt and miserly. They said that if he didn't see anybody in Savannah who tickled his fancy, he should go to New York and find a nice *Yiddisher maidel.*

At twenty-three, when he could hold out no longer, my father took the train to New York to find that nice Jewish girl.

Chapter 4

For Better or for Worse

My mother came to Concordia by a some-what different route from my father's — one perhaps less convoluted but at the same time more traumatic. It started with my father's cousin Schlomo.

Schlomo had been only a kid when my father had left the apartment of Schlomo's parents — the *mishpocheh* to whom my father had gone upon arrival in New York — to go steaming away to the South; and Schlomo was now selling baby clothes from a pushcart rented from the warehouse of my mother's father, my grandfather.

When Schlomo told my father that the *alter kocker* — a phrase in this case intended respectfully as the "old man," though more often having a scatological intent — had some daughters, my father said, "Talk to him, Schlomo. What can he do to you?"

My mother was at this date seventeen. She had come to America from *her* Russian shtetl at the age of nine, had gone to school for two years, had learned to read and write, and had held two jobs. These were as a stuffer in a toy-animal factory and as a belt turner in a dress plant, neither of which had made much demand on her new skills. Currently she was a "stemmer" in an artificial flower factory, which made no demands either. Despite working downtown she was very, very sheltered; in the ways of the world she was an innocent.

She lived in a big Bronx apartment building with parents, two brothers, and two sisters. The building was almost completely occupied by Jewish families. Although there was a sprinkling of Gentile families, my mother never spoke to them. She most specifically never spoke to the Gentile janitor, her impulse being to run the other way when she saw him on the stairs with his pliers and wrenches.

If her home did not ease her way into the larger world, her job was actually an impediment. This could not be helped. Even if she had wanted to be close to her coworkers, all of whom were non-Jewish (German, Poles, and other middle Europeans), there was her secret: At work she was not Jewish.

She could not be Jewish if she wanted to keep her job. It was a lesson learned in her first job when, during Passover, my mother, aged eleven and trying hard to do right, had brought matzos for her lunch. Naturally the foreman, Szymanski, had fired her, exhausting his lexicon of Jewish insults as he did.

My mother had to work hard to maintain the fiction of her Jewishlessness. It was often on the tip of her tongue to have a conversation with the girls, to share, for instance, surely the most memorable experience in the lives of all of them — the boat trip to America, the two weeks on a floating warehouse packed in with strangers and, in her case, seasickness so bad her clothes hung on her "like from a hook on the wall." But she held back, fearing that some detail might be unique to Jews. So the story of her journey remained untold, like everything else. She would tell us that on those rare occasions when she talked to the girls, she would hold her arms around herself "tight like a bandage" to keep things from leaking out.

Luckily her last name was Malkin, which could be anything, and the girls could not guess. She pretended to be Russian. (This was a real pretense, as she had never once entertained the notion that she actually was.) And then of course she worried that a Russian girl would be hired who would speak to her in Russian, which she could not speak. It was a language, in fact, spoken in her shtetl almost exclusively by the non-Jews. The few Jewish men who spoke Russian bumbled and stumbled — *pfumpfed,* she said — like foreigners.

My mother would also have denied herself cordial exchanges with her sister workers because she would have thought it not right to talk in a friendly way to girls who spoke so freely against the Jewish people. No doubt at those times she not only didn't talk, she tried not to hear.

But when one particular girl spoke — an older girl who was going at night to secretarial school — my mother kept her ears open. When the girl periodically blew a breath up to the ceiling and said, "What a way to make a living. Thank God for me it's only temporary," my mother heard every syllable.

Temporary. It was a comforting word to her, suggesting as it did that whatever the problem, it lasted for only so long. She applied the word to the boat trip, and it fit: The awfulness had been *temporary.* She loved the word. It gave her a modus vivendi, one that she explained to me many times: "You can stand anything," she would say, "as long as you know it is" — and she would carefully enunciate it — "tem-po-rary."

If there was this distance between her and her coworkers, it was but a hop, skip, and jump compared to the one between her and the cleaning people. They were Negroes. In Russia she had never seen Negroes. It's a good guess that most Russians — Jews and non-Jews alike — had never seen them.

The presence of these *shvartzerim* — as the Jewish people she knew, like the ones my father knew, called them — made her uneasy. Naturally she never spoke to them, but she also never *looked* at them except when she was sure they would not catch her. And *oy*, their speech! Like from under blankets.

The other workers acted like bosses with the Negroes, addressing them sharply and rolling their eyes back as if whatever chore the Negroes were doing was being done in the most ridiculous way possible. When the Negroes were near, the girls picked up their handbags from the floor and put them on their laps. My mother was advised to do likewise. "You don't know them like I do," one girl said to her. "Take my word, they'll steal your eyeballs if you ain't looking."

In the flow of manufacture in the flower factory, my mother sat at a table and attached stems to flower heads. From a store of wires, she took one, wound green paper around it, made a "hip" with a twist of extra paper at the end, and then attached the newly made stem to the flower head by means of a length of unpapered wire. When there was a sizable pile of finished flowers, a pale and unspeaking ten-year-old boy materialized and took it away. The work was tedious in the extreme, as the older girl said, "enough to make cockeyed the eyes." Still, my mother actually loved those gaudy-colored, scratchy-paper flowers. When she looked at a finished pile, she somehow managed to see tender blossoms of delicate petals. It was perhaps the first hint of a deep love for flowers, one that reached passion status in the Concordia years.

As for social life, for my mother and her sisters there was the shul and the relatives. Friday night and Saturday morning without fail, my mother and aunts went to the shul. There they sat in the women's balcony and joined in the prayers with the other women. Few of them could read Hebrew, since the cheder, the school where Hebrew was traditionally learned, was the exclusive preserve of boys. The women therefore prayed by rote, though this was not discernible as heads stayed bent over prayer books and pages were turned.

Praying did not mean they knew their religion. This was not only because the cheder was closed to them but also because their fathers were not eager to teach them. Most fathers felt it was not their job, and some shared in the view that it was not necessary for girls to be informed.

I never heard my mother offer an impromptu prayer, though she was keen on ceremonial ones and felt that God was listening. And judging. Her idea was that like the authorities in her family — her bearded father and her superbearded grandfather — God was big on judging. And how did He judge? He judged on the basis of your participation in the religion's rites and ceremonies, its *traditions*.

Afternoon calls to and from their female relatives made up the girls' social lives, though in these visits few social skills were mastered. The girls simply stepped forward for the hello kissing and then sat and listened to the gossip and the old wives' tales — the *bubbeh meisses,* as my grandfather called them — until called upon to help serve the obligatory tea and cake.

Refreshments were certainly looked forward to, but gossip was what the women came for. In my mother's tales of these klatches, it was clear that the women had family matters on their minds. Marital difficulties were openly discussed, the blame most often coming to rest on the husband's compulsive gambling or on his terrible temper. Not so open were the discussions of sexual matters, and it was here that the girls were obliged to decipher code words, head shakes, and tongue clicks. My mother once told me that she and her sisters had had a big moment when they decoded the phrase about a Cossack having "business" with a Jewish girl, which meant he had raped her; though when my mother divulged this, it was with an understanding that no more questions would be asked.

My mother was immediately dazzled by this Aaron Bronson. Most of the girls she knew had only the pool of immigrants to choose from, and a dispiriting pool it was — men with untidy beards, unshaven faces, stained pants and button-shy vests, and voices hoarse from hawking wares on the sidewalk out of a peddler's backpack. And here was my father, fresh from adventures in the South, and *handsome*. His five feet, four inches said "tall" to her, and in truth he had an inch or two on most men of her acquaintance. Surrounded as she was by a people of dark eyes and dark curly hair, she was instantly smitten by eyes blue as skies and hair straight as straight — no twist, no twirl, no spirals — and gleaming as if with sunlight. If she had known the word, she would have called him dashing. Had he stayed in New York like most after being dumped by the boat? No, he had not. "He went to the South!" my mother cried to my aunts, as if penetration of the South was only for explorers in geography books.

On his part, my father clearly found delight in sharing memories of the old country with this young lady who could laugh with him over the frozen bread that had to be thawed in the mouth and the straw beds that made noises in the night like mice, this young lady of the fair skin and the soft dusting of freckles and the lustrous black hair, who praised his English and said, "Just like a Yankee you talk." And wouldn't his heart have leapt up that the nimble hands were gentle and the figure trim and the top of her head went just under his chin? And it's my opinion that it would have been also very gratifying to my father that when he asked my grandfather for his blessing, along with a yes, my grandfather, who had recognized something in my father, said to him, "You ain't a *shlimazel*." A luckless fellow. "You're a man going places."

After my parents' marriage, it was several years before Concordia became something to reckon with. In the meantime Joey and Miriam were born, and though having two children kept my father out of the draft, fatherhood to my orphaned father meant much more than that; for despite the conventional wisdom that you don't miss what you've never had, what my father had never had was a real family, and to say he had not missed one is to misunderstand.

In that long ago time in Podolska, my father had only his grandfather, and he was full of envy for those children who had real families. In his little-boy fantasies of their lives, he had come to believe that no matter what misery descended upon them or, in rare cases, what joy uplifted them, the family shared. He pictured these families at the supper table offering understanding to one another and exchanging stories (even if any humor in them was often black), whereas after his day at his job (which did what it could to save his life, but it could not save everything), all he had was his grandfather's silence (what did this man have to be chatty about?), a wordless meal, and the shuffling sound of his grandfather making for bed immediately afterward. No, my father had had his fill of "no family," had had it up to here.

Though the fact of Joey and Miriam went a long way toward softening things, it could only go so far, and soon the feeling that he must leave New York came to my father strongly, especially when he was at his job selling produce from one of my grandfather's pushcarts, as that was another New York job he would not come to like if he lived to be a hundred. He was now fluent enough in English to have perhaps gotten a job as a clerk even in a non-Jewish store, but now he didn't want it. Selling in New York might make him a hostage to New York, and, perhaps unbeknownst even to him, in his head the South had been waiting all along.

It would be two more years before he would try to implement his idea of a return to the South. This was for my father a long time to stay put when everything in him was telling him to go.

When he at last he began to try to sell my mother on going, he had no inkling that the South would mean a country town in the most isolated part of Tennessee.

According to my father, each year the strain of New York weighed more heavily. Every evening when he walked home from the subway and looked toward the window of his apartment, except for the prospect of seeing the family, nothing about it beckoned. He saw it as a place that even on a sunny day was dark, with a smell always from somebody in the building cooking cabbage. Whenever he looked toward his apartment, he said he wanted to yell *Gevalt!* — an outcry of alarm that in this case, meant, Let me out of here!

It was time — past time — to renew his acquaintance with his hustle. He started slowly, telling my mother that his job with the pushcart didn't feel right, that it wasn't a salesman's job. "Selling from a pushcart ain't selling; it's arguing," my father said to her.

What had once seemed to my mother adventurous now seemed foolhardy. The South? That place down there full of strangers and terrors?

Trying hard to sell her on taking a chance, my father quoted her an old shtetl saying: "If you don't want to risk tearing your shoes, you got to sit at home." He told her how friendly people were in the South and how she'd find friends.

Shoes? Friends? Right now my mother didn't care about shoes, and she didn't care about friends. Anyway, in her milieu, there were no friends, only relatives and *mishpocheh*.

My father cast about for a city where there would be if not *mishpocheh* then at least Jewish people. (Why Savannah wasn't this city was always puzzling to me until one day, while listening once more to this story, it came to me that my father had chosen not to go back to Savannah because of the girl he had almost proposed to.)

He remembered that Nashville had been talked about as having a big Jewish population, and he thought it probably also had a synagogue and maybe even a kosher butcher. He asked my mother if she could see herself in such a town.

One night, after hours of tossing and turning, my mother agreed that maybe, maybe she could see herself in such a town — Nashville, with its promise of shuls and rabbi-blessed chickens, and even a cheder for Joey. Her secret hope, however, was that because they had no money to make such a trip, it would all turn out to be just talk.

My father had already worked out the money part. He said my mother should ask her father for a loan.

"What do you think of this?" My mother had an invisible presence, an unseen third person she often spoke to, as if she were a performer on stage speaking in an aside to the audience. She spoke to this presence now. "He not only wants me to go somewhere I don't want to, he wants I should ask my papa to lend the money besides." All right, she would talk to my grandmother and *she* would talk to my grandfather. My mother had the hope that her sister Sadie, who would certainly be in on it, would come up with a way to nix the thing.

What she was depending on most, however, was the idea of family oneness. She had some confidence that my grandmother would feel that leaving the family to go to such a far-off place would be too foolish to even think about. My mother saw my grandmother giving a dismissive wiggle of her hand, signaling an end to the discussion.

Together with my brother and sister, she climbed the five flights to my grandparents' apartment. As they climbed, they passed the doors of families my mother had known since she had arrived in America, all of whom had at one time or another come under the microscope of the women.

On the second floor, for example, behind one of the four doors on the landing, lived the Bloombergs, a family characterized as living from hand to mouth because of a father capable of losing his entire paycheck in a game of pinochle on Saturday night.

But above them were the Nussbaums, the shameful Nussbaums, the ones who turned up most frequently in the women's talk. The Nussbaums were spoken of as *badlach*. (I have never heard this word used except by my mother and members of her klatch, and it may have been concocted by them. Possibly they put *bad,* or bath, together with *lach,* or lack, and came up with "bathless ones.") The Nussbaums were considered low-class Jews in all manner of ways but chiefly because the Nussbaum housekeeping was judged sloppy in the extreme. It was a *shandeh*, the women said, especially a *shandeh feur der goyim*. A shame, especially before Gentiles. The women clung to the hope that the building's Gentiles would not discover that a Jewish family had a dirty house. How disgraceful if they should know (and say "dirty Jews" among themselves) that the Nussbaums' drinking glasses smelled of herring and that their beds were infested with bedbugs — the abominable *vantzen*.

On the fourth-floor landing she gave a special knock on Aunt Sadie's door, and then went on up the last flight, to the fifth floor. My mother tried to pick Miriam up in case she might be tiring, but Miriam fought against it. Joey was running ahead, trying to produce sparks on the marble steps with the new taps on his heels.

As my mother told the story, she was already sitting at the kitchen table, a glass of tea in front of her, when Aunt Sadie came in. Aunt Sadie had to be in on everything, my father would always say, "like without her nose in it, the world can't turn."

My Aunt Sadie was not a favorite of my father's, chiefly because of this. As the oldest child, she perhaps saw her role as family protector, at which she indeed had had a lot of practice. When the family had first arrived in America, she had been the one to go out and see what was what and to get the family settled. Now, even though everyone had moved out from under her wing in one direction or another, she clung to her old power base as adviser and arbiter. "As boss," my father said.

When Aunt Sadie came into the room now, Miriam was lying on the floor under the spidery gray enameled legs of the stove, pretending to be drinking from one of her old bottles that my grandmother still had. My mother knew her sister would have something to say about a three-year-old child playing like this, but Miriam had already made it clear that she was in charge of herself. She was, as they say nowadays, firmly inner-directed.

The house would have been quiet. My grandfather would have been in his pushcart warehouse for hours; my mother's younger sister, my Aunt Hannah, in school; and her brother, Uncle Philip, the youngest in the family, in school as well. My mother's older brother, my Uncle Meyer, was married and no longer lived at home.

Aunt Sadie sat down. She glanced at Miriam and, to my mother's surprise, only shrugged. Aunt Sadie perhaps sensed this was to be a special, and intense, convocation and was saving her arguments. My grandmother brought her a glass of tea.

My mother was working on a way to open it up. Finally she got out that my father wasn't happy. A few words, a lot said.

To give time for this to sink in, she took a sip of tea. My mother, of course, drank tea in the European-Russian-Jewish manner: The glass went to the mouth with a finger curled around the spoon to keep it from flopping into the eye, and then, as an economy measure, the tea was sipped through a fragment of a sugar cube held between the front teeth. My mother finished her sip and repeated to my Aunt Sadie, "He just ain't happy."

If my father wasn't crazy about Aunt Sadie, she returned the favor. Miriam and I have always agreed that Aunt Sadie's antagonism toward my father was not without its envy component. Vetted or not by a matchmaker, my father obviously had an appeal that her Izzy didn't, her Izzy having come directly from the immigrant pool.

Aunt Sadie said now to my mother, "If it makes him happy to be happy, so let him be happy."

Even in later years it seemed never to have occurred to my mother that what Aunt Sadie had said was ridiculous, though she said she *was* perplexed. So she answered Aunt Sadie only, "So who don't it make happy to be happy?"

After everyone had been served, my grandmother would have come to the table with her own glass of tea, moving leisurely, in an easy flow. My grandmother was never in a hurry. In the taking of tea there was a gentle sliding into her chair, a thoughtful spooning of a dollop of jam from the pot on the table, a letting fall of the jam into the glass, a slow stirring.

At this small klatch, my grandmother would, as always, be in a black long-sleeved shirtwaist top and a black floor-length full skirt. She was a little woman — perhaps "minute" is the better word — who seemed overwhelmed by fabric.

My grandmother neither spoke nor understood English. When English was spoken around her, she waved her hands about her head as if brushing off spider webs. In her presence, therefore, a rapid shuffle went on between English and Yiddish.

With my grandmother at last sitting, my mother gathered herself to tell it all. Out it came: My father didn't like New York, didn't like selling from a pushcart, wanted to go back to the South.

Aunt Sadie was a "spitter." In Yiddish with its gargling chs and exploding sibilants, she was a-splash, and even in English she sent forth sprays. "To the *South?*" she said, moisture molecules flying.

My grandmother clapped her hands to her face, and my mother's heart leaped up at what might be a promising sign. My grandmother, however, was showing not horror but interest. She had brought to mind a family story about a nephew, Zelig — my first cousin once removed — who had left New York to go to Cleveland and who, according to his mother, my Great-aunt Tillie, was doing well there. "Cleveland," my grandmother repeated.

Aunt Sadie responded with a no-nonsense "Cleveland, schmeveland" and asked if my father wasn't just trying to get my mother to go out and work for him. My mother immediately envisioned one of my great-aunts, a woman in her sixties who still set out daily with a pack on her back to peddle soft goods — whatever she had picked up cheap — to pushcart vendors. Did Sadie think this was what my father wanted her to do? Did she think my father was lazy, of all things? "He's just a man likes to do what he likes to do," my mother answered.

Aunt Sadie said she knew all about the South (though it's a good guess that she knew almost nothing) and all of what she "knew" was bad. First of all, she "guaranteed" that my mother would not like it there, even if it turned out the place they chose had a confirmed Jewish population. "The Jews they got there I can imagine," she said to my mother. And *oy*, the Gentiles — the goyim — my mother would have to associate with, "the hilly-billies, the yokels."

As my grandmother poured fresh tea, no doubt taking the usual pains to pour against the spoon so that the glass would not crack, she had a word for her daughters. Little in stature and underlanguaged though my grandmother was, she knew her imperatives. "Go, go with your husband," she told my mother, while my mother's heart bumped around. "Be a warm stone in his pocket on a cold day." Where, my mother wondered, where was my grandmother's outrage at somebody leaving the family?

My mother snatched at her one remaining hope, that maybe my grandfather would object. Maybe *he* would be the one to keep his daughter and his grandchildren from going God knows where.

My grandmother only scoffed. My grandfather would lend the money, of that she was sure. After all, she said, when they had left Russia, had they not left behind a father, three brothers, and four sisters? "Tell Aaron not to worry," she said to my mother. "Pa will lend."

Chapter 5

God's (So to Speak) Country

When my father used to describe how he felt after my grandfather agreed to lend the money, he'd say "I was on top of myself." He immediately sat down and wrote a letter to Bronstein, who wrote back — in a letter penned by his son — confirming that Nashville had plenty of Jews and that the rest of Tennessee was "wide open."

Miriam and Joey have said that they were wildly excited by the prospect of a trip on a train and that my father, though not *wildly* excited, having been on a train before, was nevertheless pretty well fired up. Of course my mother was neither wildly excited nor fired up, only acutely anxious. She was clinging to a single mandate: Food must be taken along. Dining-car food would be too dear, and could you expect kosher? Of course not.

The day before the two-day journey, she gathered together two large brown paper grocery bags. Except for a few things that would be eaten the first day, edibles had to be spoilage resistant. Into the first-day sack went fried fish, tomatoes, and boiled chicken; into the second-day one hard-boiled eggs, as well as jars of borscht, eggless (because raw eggs spoiled) and with an extra infusion of citric acid, or, as it was called, sour salt — among thrifty Jewish housewives, the traditional substitute for expensive lemons and also dimly understood as a spoilage retarder. In both bags were jars of already brewed tea and coffee, canned salmon, and a can opener. Matzos and fruit were strewn throughout.

My father had scheduled the trip for a Sunday because my Uncle Philip, who attended the College of the City of New York all week and on some Saturdays but not Sundays, would be able to transport them to the train. My uncle carried the family and their belongings from the Bronx to Grand Central Station in a rented wagon behind a rented horse. When the protracted, complex trip was over, my uncle said for my mother to try to relax, to try to enjoy the new experience. "Think of yourself as lucky," he said to her. My mother thought of herself as nothing of the sort and could barely summon up the energy to give her brother a good-bye flutter. After that she did a "plunk-down" in her seat, and stayed there, becalmed and listless.

Still, if her body was becalmed, her head was beset by strong winds. She felt, she used to say, that everything was topsy-turvy, or, in her way of saying it, "topsy-mopsy." Only "tem-po-rary" came through clearly, and she clung to it, to keep from being blown away.

They arrived in Nashville in mid-afternoon and walked into town. My father's objective was, as in Savannah, to spot a store owned by Jews. They moved on to Church Street.

From the first step, my father felt he was returning to where the very air was life-sustaining. "Celebrate! Celebrate!" he cried to the family.

Celebrate? My mother answered that what with two days on the train and now the schlepping, they were lucky that instead of dead they were just tired.

My father faked outrage. "What am I hearing? In the South, tired ain't allowed, only peppy! You hear me what I'm saying?"

If my mother thought it was a schlep, my father treated it as a promenade and as a way to get out the kinks from the train trip. He said to my mother, "Listen to your muscles. They're saying, 'Hoo-boy! Thank you, lady!'"

My mother always said she didn't hear her muscles, she heard only my father. He was floating along, lost in admiration for the buildings, the stores, the merchandise. When he came upon a store with a black marble foundation, he seemed overcome. Peering in at the window displays, he awarded an accolade: "Merchandise the finest," he said. It was as if fervently expressed enthusiasm would at last convince my mother of the soundness of the decision to come here. He finally summed it up: New York stores were not better; there were just more of them.

On the next block he glanced up at a sign that said GREENGLASS HABERDASHERY, flicked his head, and they went in.

Greenglass Haberdashery was a store for the better class. There was carpeting on the floor, lamps instead of overhead lights, buttery billfolds and hand-crafted fedoras on display. Barney Greenglass, as well turned out as his store, greeted the family and proceeded to what protocol demanded: New Jews in town were to be taken immediately to meet the rabbi and his wife.

At the rabbi's house, there was a welcome and refreshments. My mother told herself — and was surprised when she did — that if non–New York Jews were like Sadie had said, at least they knew from a nice glass of tea and a good piece of honeycake.

The rabbi's wife was full of the authority

that came from being the rabbi's wife. She instructed my mother on important things: the location of the little store that sold kosher meats, the particulars of the shul, and where there was a room to rent.

The room was around the corner in the apartment of the Moskowitzes. It was furnished in the same spare way as the family's bedrooms in the Bronx, though this one, since all members of the family would sleeping there, had, besides the dresser and double bed, a cot, four straight chairs, and an enameled-topped table. My mother never failed to describe the mattresses as "thick like a piece of matzo is thick."

At the end of the hall was the bathroom, here serving two families, not six, as in the Bronx. At last an improvement, my mother thought.

There were "kitchen privileges" (which my mother had never heard of and always called "kitchen preventleges") that allowed her the use of the coal stove at certain hours and one very small corner of the icebox. But they were to eat in their room, on the table there.

The next morning they had a little breakfast with the Moskowitzes, with the Moskowitzes' food — "as a favor," Mrs. Moskowitz said — and afterward my father left to see what was what, Joey and Miriam went outside in the hope of finding other children, and my mother returned to the room to unpack. She was soon feeling the old heaviness. She tried to retrieve the bit of cheer from yesterday at the rabbi's house, but it was impossible in this dark room with the torn window shades; and in another moment she was calling yesterday's sentiments foolishness and going about her work through eyes full of water.

Greenglass in the meantime had taken my father around to Edelstein of Edelstein's Ladies, Gents, and Children. As soon as Edelstein and my father had shaken hands, Edelstein wanted to know if my father was looking for something to do.

My father said, "Naturally," and Edelstein said, "So stop looking already, you got a job."

Edelstein's Ladies, Gents, and Children (which also sold domestics) was on the street around the corner from Greenglass's. Unlike Greenglass's it sold to the poorer people. It was, then, a store like Bronstein's in Savannah and, also like Bronstein's, not the only store of its kind in the city and not called a "Jew store." Still, it was in Nashville that my father learned the term and came to understand how it was used in small towns like Concordia.

Edelstein's was a very busy place, and my

father could see that Edelstein was making money there. He figured that if he kept his eyes open and his step lively, it was not out of the question that Aaron Bronson could be a Charlie Edelstein someday.

After only a few weeks, Edelstein took my father on a buying trip to St. Louis, something that added to my father's "education and sal-es-man-ship," as he told my mother, giving the latter word his patented four-syllable pronunciation. But my father had something else in mind: He wanted Charlie Edelstein to know that he wanted a store of his own.

This was a three-alarmer for my mother. She was just getting used to everything, and now look.

She once said to me, "What could I do but make believe it could never happen?" She shoved my father's plan into the pigeonhole marked "Maybe Someday," then into "It Could Never Happen," and went back to settling into Nashville. To her surprise, she was finding the settling "a little not too terrible," the best part being the afternoon visits with the rabbi's wife (where she saw the other Jewish women as well) and the Friday nights at the shul.

The shul experience in Nashville was the same as in New York, except the building was smaller. Seating was the same: My mother sat upstairs with my sister; my father and brother with the men downstairs.

My parents got to know a good number of shul-goers and after services accepted invitations to visit. Soon my father said he and my mother should take a turn. My mother thought this was right. If everybody did it, why not them? "Could I let them call us greenhorns?" she asked me, knowing that I knew the answer was a definite no.

Then came the problem of dishes. The Moskowitz-provided dishes were heavy, dull yellow, chipped. Could she serve on them and let people think they were *bodlach?* she asked my father, as an image of the Nussbaums sprang into her head. No, she could not. So she went out and bought her own two sets of dishes. These dishes, bought before I was born, remained our best for all the years I was at home; and when I left and came back to visit, there they still were — a set with roses for meat meals, and a set with violets for dairy ones.

My mother enjoyed the get-togethers. After the guests had left, she would always say, "It ain't like *mishpocheh,* Aaron, but at least they're Jewish people."

And my father would always answer, "So was I wrong?"

Miriam remembers that her nightly ritual of those days was to get my father's Camels and newspaper from his coat pocket after supper. On one particular night after she had performed this ceremony, my mother departed from hers — which was to immediately take the supper dishes to the kitchen after everyone had eaten. Instead, my mother sat down with my father at the table and gave him the long stare. This was a stare we all knew: It signaled a serious discussion on the way. Tonight it was about something the rabbi's wife had said. "She was talking to me today," my mother said to my father.

"This is news?" I have no doubt that my father lit up his cigarette and opened the paper, as this was always his prediscussion maneuver. "Of all people she don't seem to have no trouble talking," he said to my mother.

My mother could not deny that the news of the Jewish community, admonitions, advice, and recipes flowed from the rabbi's wife in a serene — and uninterruptible — stream.

This time the rabbi's wife's advice was they should take a place with two bedrooms, that it wasn't right that they should all sleep in one room. She had recommended the rooms at Mrs. Feinberg's that had been vacated when the Goldmans moved to St. Louis, where Goldman had taken a job with a wholesale house.

My father demurred. He always had his ear to "the street," as the uptown was called among those who toiled there, and he had noticed something astir among the Jewish merchants, something he sensed had to do with him, and whatever it was, he didn't want to create a distraction. "Why should we go moving around like noodles slipping off the plate?" he said to my mother.

This from my father? My father who was always ready for something new? Who couldn't take a walk without coming back with an unfamiliar brand of soap, a newfangled brush, a different-shaped noodle? Who would say, "Let's try it, Reba, it could be just what you're looking for," as if my mother had been beating the bushes looking for just such a thing?

On this occasion my mother argued no more. If my father said "Wait," it was all right with her.

The wait wasn't long. The next Sunday morning my brother opened the door to a company of six black-suited men. When they came into the room, an air of grave mission came in with them.

My father got himself busy with smiles and handshakes. My mother, instantly apprehensive, nodded briefly to each and reached out to draw Miriam close, as if they would serve as protection for each other. Miriam felt no need for protection, being only too keen for whatever was to come.

Joey stationed himself in a spot that promised good viewing. He has remembered thinking that the men looked not just grave, but downright lugubrious, as if they had just come from a funeral that had further diminished the "old-timer" Jewish population.

Joey, it turned out, was quite wrong. Despite appearances, the men were happy, extraordinarily happy, and they were about to make my father happy as well.

The drama began when a man stepped in front of the contingent and announced himself as Mr. Pomerantz. Gripped tightly in Mr. Pomerantz's hand was a long roll of paper, which he waved about. In a series of complex moves, he spread the paper on the enamel table, put the salt shaker at one end, the pepper shaker at the other, the sugar bowl in the middle. At last seeming satisfied that the paper was holding, he propelled my father's head over it, stuck his own forefinger on a spot on the map, for that's what the paper was, and advised the assemblage that he was calling my father's attention to the northwest corner of the state of Tennessee.

Northwest corner? State of Tennessee? My mother knew she was in the state of Tennessee, but *northwest corner?* What was this *northwest corner?* Was it something she shouldn't like the sound of?

Pomerantz held his finger on the map for some seconds, up around the northern rim of the sugar bowl. My father looked at the spot. He made out the name "Concordia."

Pomerantz affirmed this. "There it is — Concordia." He squinted his eyes. "A town you got to have good eyes to see."

My father waited. He knew a disclosure was coming, and finally Pomerantz disclosed it. Pomerantz said he had it "absolutely, positively, no mistake about it" that a shoe factory was going to open up in that little town, in that "Concordia."

My father floated a little smile, weighting it with a touch of puzzlement. It was his trademark look for projecting innocence. "So what's it got to do with me?" he asked Pomerantz.

Pomerantz's hands went up for silence. He was clearly getting ready to deliver the blockbuster he had in his possession. And a blockbuster it was. Pomerantz drilled his eyes into my father's and revealed the awful truth: There was as yet no Jewish "dry goods" in the town.

Pomerantz stood waiting, waiting, for my father's expression of shock. If my father was not shocked, he was something better — joyous. The men were talking a store here, and for him. Still, to prolong the drama, to give the men their money's worth, he thought to produce his most elaborate shrug, as if to say, So what does it have to do with me?

Pomerantz took on the look of a witness to heresy. "Do you know, young Mr. Aaron Bronson, do you know what it means for a town to be without a Jewish dry goods?" His tone was baleful. "What do goyim know from small dry goods? From small ready-to-wear? Groceries, yes. Furniture, maybe. Hardware, definitely. But small dry goods? *Never!*"

My brother could stand it no longer. This seeming inability on my father's part to grasp the obvious was proving too much for him. He ran to my father's side. "Don't you understand, Papa? Mr. Pomerantz is . . ."

My father just put his hand on Joey's shoulder, squeezed hard, and Joey stopped talking.

And now Pomerantz came out with it. "Young Mr. Aaron Bronson," he said, "this is a proposition that fits you to a T."

My father didn't have to tell me that euphoric as he was, he would find it very hard to resist a joke. And sure enough, "No, it don't," he said. "The pants is too long in the rise." He didn't expect a laugh and didn't get one, so he shook his head in a sober way and told the men what they already knew — that he had no money for such a venture.

Pomerantz told my father not to excite himself, that the merchants of Nashville had been keeping "a eagle eye" on him. My father, he said, was in for "oh, boy, some surprise." And then, with deference due a potentate, Pomerantz introduced "Mr. Morris Cohen, owner of Cohen's Department Store in the Number One location in uptown Nashville."

Cohen began with words of wisdom. "Pomerantz is right," he said to my father. "Only Jews know small dry goods. . . . Now big dry goods, that's another story." At this point in retelling the story, my father would describe Cohen's big sigh, as if Cohen had brought to mind his competition, the posh Chappell's Department Store.

Cohen now locked my father in his sights. In a voice so authoritative that in the room only the sounds of respiration dared make themselves heard, he declared that he, Morris Cohen, was prepared to take care of my father's money problems. He waved a letter about. "When the wholesalers in St. Louis read in this letter that Morris Cohen is behind you," he said, "they'll treat you like you was Diamond Jim Brady." He then put the letter into my father's hands.

And soon afterward, it was over. The men had fulfilled their mission, my father had the promise of a store. The men filed back out past my father, congratulating him. "Like Papa was the bridegroom," was the way my mother told it.

But there was no bride. My mother could not bring herself to stand there and receive congratulations. She saw what had happened not as my father did, as a chance, but as a venture fraught with peril. If, as she had been hearing, there were no Jewish merchants in this "Concourse" (the Grand Concourse in the Bronx took precedence), then there would be no Jewish people either. She took to wringing her hands. "Are you sure this is what to do?" she asked my father.

My father at this point clicked on his BORN SALESMAN sign and basked in its light. "Yes, I'm sure," he answered my mother. Indeed he "guaranteed" it.

The point was, of course, that if they stayed in Nashville, there would be no store for my father. "Do you think" — and here my father always gave what I took to be a flawless impersonation of Pomerantz — "Mr. Morris Cohen, 'owner of Cohen's Department Store in the Number One location in uptown Nashville,' is in-ter-es-ted" — as my father famously pronounced this word — "in me getting a store in Nashville?" It was a question he himself answered with a wry "Forget it."

No, the Nashville men had a whole different idea, and it was for my father to open up a new market for the big St. Louis wholesale houses. And why were the Nashville merchants so concerned about the welfare of the big St. Louis wholesale houses? Because, my father would tell us, the big St. Louis wholesale houses were where the Nashville merchants had big investments.

And thus, soon after that day, in an old wagon bought cheap because it had been lying useless in Mr. Morris Cohen's backyard since his image went high-toned, behind a horse named Willy bought for close to nothing from the blacksmith shop, with a bag of sponge cake and peaches from the rabbi's wife to supplement the foodstuffs my mother had already gathered, and armed with the celebrated Cohen letter, my family set out on the three-day, two-night trip to Concordia.

Chapter 6

Miss Brookie's Cousin Tom

In the bedroom at Miss Simmons's, according to how Joey has remembered it, he woke up first, got Miriam up, and together they went into the other bedroom and shook my father — who came awake, he always said, with the store on his mind. They did not wake my mother. My father put the peaches and the cheese on the dresser where she couldn't miss them, and they all went downstairs to the kitchen, where Miss Simmons was sitting with a cup of coffee. Lizzie Maud was there, at the coal stove, and almost immediately a plate of food appeared on the table. Joey and Miriam stared. What was that twisty stuff on the side of the eggs? My father had eaten bacon in Savannah and knew that it brought on no dread disease. "Eat, children, eat," he said. Attempting a Southern effect, he added, "These are some great vittles," which, despite the drilling from the girls in Savannah, emerged as "gray twittles," and Miss Simmons looked startled before she caught on.

After breakfast, my father wanted to ask *Miss Brookie* — the lady had requested that he call her that, and he was trying to keep it in mind — for help in finding a store, but she had first wanted to take them on a tour of the house. They had seen most of it, but the living room, the "front room," as it was called in Concordia, was as yet unexplored.

The furniture in the front room was what Miss Brookie referred to as her "Victorian afflictions" — hard-framed crimson sofas lacking in the slightest give and chairs that she said were not the usual easy chairs but *un*easy ones. These she had inherited, along with numerous small, curvaceous mahogany tables, from her parents. Hanging on the walls in heavy gold frames were paintings by "minor Italian masters," which, she said, nobody in town considered fit viewing, for the reason that they weren't what folks were accustomed to — what they were accustomed to, according to Miss Brookie, being pictures of Jesus with his eyes rolling up toward heaven. Her comment on this, my father said, was, "And mercy, what he's looking at ain't anything I'm prepared to discuss." Miss Brookie, as we found out, could use the vernacular as well as anyone in town, and it seemed to please her to

91

use it whenever she was particularly "outdone," as she would put it.

On this day, the more Miss Brookie described her things, the more bewildered my father became. Victorian afflictions? Minor Italian masters? Maybe it could be interesting, my father thought, but not right now. No, now he was desperate to get to his own mission and was simply trying to hold on.

At the sight of a grand piano and a harp, Joey and Miriam snapped to attention. Italian, Miss Brookie said her harp was, shipped from Italy while she was on a trip there. She expressed a devotion to the Italians and thought my father must know a lot of them in New York. "Don't you just love them?" she asked him.

My father didn't much want to talk about Italians; he wanted to talk about stores, and anyway he wasn't sure whether he loved Italians or not. He didn't know many, and those he knew were immigrants like himself, making their livings in their own way, in produce stores or shoe-repair shops mostly. *"Non so,"* he answered the lady, making use of two of the three Italian words he knew. It meant "I don't know," and it about covered it.

After the tour, Joey and Miriam went out to play in the yard, and my father sat on the steps of the front porch to wait for Miss

Brookie to come out.

Green things — trees, bushes — were much in evidence. The crape myrtle and rose of Sharon were in bloom, and my father had a fleeting thought that if my mother would just let herself go, she might consider them a pleasure to look at.

In various spots were plaster cherubs and, on the branches of the trees, rusted hanging baskets. The yard could be said to reach a kind of clutter climax at the side, where an arched trellis thick with indeterminate vines opened up to a clutch of furniture — a love seat, two armchairs, and a tiny table — contrived of bent willow so green all the legs had sprouted.

As my father had sensed, if anybody could point him in the right direction, it was Miss Brookie. There was something about the lady, as there had been about the boy T, that made him feel he was in good hands. Even the little one, Erv, though he did nothing but stare, stared not with suspicion but with simple curiosity.

My father's intuition had not misled him. Miss Brookie was just such a person. When my family first came to her, she was fifty-eight years old and had been a presence in the town for all those years, toiling in the Concordia vineyards to bring forth enlightenment. She had aspirations for the town. Still, little went on of even a trivial nature that she didn't know about, so chances were good that she would have a lot to say on the state of the current Concordia real estate market.

Miss Brookie came to the steps and in a whoosh of skirts sat down next to my father. Out of her "crush of kin," she told him, she ought to be able to think of somebody who could do him some good. "Lord," my father remembered her saying, "I have kin going in every front door in the county, plus a few unidentified ones who are obliged, owing to our quaint customs, to go in and out of the *back* one."

The name she came up with was a cousin, Tom Dillon. He was the town's leading property owner. And he had an empty store right on First Street.

A Jew store on the main street? It was a prospect my father had not entertained even in his sweetest dreams. What he didn't know yet was that First Street was Concordia's one and only business street, so if you had a store, it was, ipso facto, on First.

Meanwhile, Miss Brookie was making it clear that she had little influence with her cousin Tom. No, she said to my father, agreement between her and Dillon came just twice a year: In winter they "concurred" that it was cold and in summer that it was hot. Tom Dillon was very difficult — "disputatious," she called him — and, since in the past so many dry-goods stores had gone bust, he was very particular about what he would allow in his properties.

It was Miss Brookie's view that those failing stores had made the fatal error of wanting to sell the latest thing from Paris. "Rue de la Paix stuff," she said to my father.

Thinking to echo the lady, my father said, "Rudy LaPay, sure thing," and Miss Brookie looked startled again.

The important thing, my father was thinking, was that she should know that his store would be very different, that he intended to serve the workingman and the farmer. He had one other category he intended to serve but hesitated to say it, not sure of what term the lady used. He chose one and hoped for the best. "And the coloreds," he said to her.

Miss Brookie was nodding, so my father figured the word was okay. But now, now what was she doing? It was something my father had seen only flappers do, and Miss Brookie was no flapper: She was plump, not skinny; had no red spots on her cheeks; nothing dangled from her ears. But here she had reached into her pocket and brought out *a pack of cigarettes*. A woman smoking? And right out here on the front porch steps with nothing to hide her? Carrying cigarettes around and thrusting them at him?

My father said he was so startled, he took one of her Chesterfields in a sort of reflex and stuck it between his lips.

Miss Brookie stuck one between hers. She reached into her pocket again and this time came out with a wooden match, which she struck into flame on the step. Holding it under my father's nose, she lit his cigarette, then lit hers and puffed away, sending great clouds of slaty smoke over the yard.

There was a store like the one my father had in mind in a town not far away, Oliphant by name, she told him between puffs, but it too had gone bust. It seems *their* fatal flaw had been that they had too many clerks and never the right sizes.

Goyim, my father said to himself.

"I used to turn up overall sizes until my hands were literally dyed blue," Miss Brookie was saying. "Don't you know my language was even bluer?" As my father found out, the overalls were for the yardman, but what "blue" language was remained a mystery.

"Get that vision," she said to him. "A crush of clerks and one itty-bitty store."

This was not a worry for my father. All he would need was one good clerk and a little

96

help from my mother on Saturdays.

He wanted to convince the lady that she should have no doubts about him, that he knew how to do. He was impatient to tell her about being "a born sal-es-man." "My bosses all said I could take the place of two men," he told her. Whoa, too much bragging, he warned himself, and added, "Uh, maybe they meant each man had one arm in a sling."

Miss Simmons was abruptly ready for action. In my home I have a box of snapshots from those Concordia days, my share from the big box my mother kept, and among them is one of Miss Brookie standing in a half-turn at the top of her steps, looking into the sun and shielding her eyes with her hand, giving whoever is taking the picture a look that says "All right, you've got me; snap the fool thing and let me get on with what needs doing." And what needed "doing" at this moment was to telephone her cousin Tom.

Chapter 7

Xenophobia

A "misdriven nail" Miss Brookie had called Tom Dillon, and for good reason, my father was finding out. Here was a man to whom he could say nothing right.

It was immediately clear that Tom Dillon hated Yankees and hated Jews, so a Yankee-Jew, which he pronounced as one word, was no doubt as abominable a creature as he could imagine — not, I suppose, that he knew all that many. "I'm not sure our folks will want a store run by a YankeeJew," he informed my father.

Tom Dillon was a large overweight man about fifteen years younger than his cousin Brookie. Extra poundage, a grandmother, and college degrees — hers from the University of Chicago, his from the University of Tennessee — were about all the cousins shared, except for one personality trait: Both were bent on prevailing. Still, what they hoped to prevail *in* were vastly different. If

Miss Simmons struggled to bring enlightenment, Tom Dillon gave his all to maintaining the status quo. Miss Brookie, who was perhaps the only one in town who knew the word, called him a "xenophobe," which in Tom Dillon's case meant that he was suspicious of anybody who wasn't Southern, white, and Protestant. As Concordia's leading property owner and a longtime pillar of the church, he was one of the town's biggest big shots, and though Miss Brookie prevailed occasionally, his score for prevailing was probably somewhere around a hundred percent.

Dillon had an especially heavy and moist face, and as he came out with his objections one-two-three, a handkerchief gripped in his hand swiped at it. If there was indeed a Southern tradition of civility, as my father had observed there was in Savannah, Tom Dillon did not subscribe to it. He again expressed the thought, without any discernible attempt to gussy it up, that there hadn't been any Jews to speak of around Concordia and he wasn't sure the town was going to want any.

My father held up his hands as if to physically block Dillon's objections. Hoping to banter with the man, he said, "Why don't I take that worry off your hands? Why not say it's *my* worry?"

What did my father mean — *his* worry? Dillon wanted to know. *He,* Tom Dillon, was the one who stood to lose if the store failed. About the extras my father wanted, hellfire, they cost dollars, *his* dollars. Adding the upstairs my father had talked about, for instance, meant calling in "Poindexter and his bunch of idiots" to put a door in, and then after Poindexter put it in backward, he, Tom Dillon, that's who, would have to fight with him over who was to pay to turn it around. And, anyway, an upstairs in a Jew store was just "by damn, showing off," wasn't it?

Dillon's store was narrow and dark, with a single display window for natural light and a ceiling too high for electric lights to help out much. It had all the appeal of a cave. My father said to Dillon, as diplomatically as he could, that the store "ain't too big, as I'm sure you know," and outlined how he planned to put the men's suits and men's dressing rooms upstairs, away from the women's department downstairs. He also had the hope, unexpressed, to have dressing rooms that were better than the ones at Edelstein's, which were two humble cubbyholes separated from the store and each other by curtains, with pinned-on handprinted paper signs reading WHITE MEN on one and WHITE LADIES on the other.

My father's hopes did not extend to dressing rooms for Negroes, as he had learned that in the South Negroes did not try on in stores; they tried on at home. Still, unlike in better stores, where returns from Negroes were not tolerated for any reason, in Jew stores the owner would at least meet a Negro customer at the back door and arrange there for a return or exchange.

My father said that at the words "ain't too big," Dillon took an annoyed swipe at his big, sweaty face, at the overloading beads of perspiration, and, as if sincerely seeking information, said to him, "Tell me something — why in hell did you YankeeJews come here anyway?"

A *momzer*, my father thought, a real, no-doubt-about-it bastard. And was he supposed to take the bastard's question seriously? Ponder it and give an answer?

No, Dillon seemed neither to invite nor require a rejoinder. It was Brookie Simmons's business, he was saying, if she wanted YankeeJews in her house, but the town had done fine without them and he expected it would continue doing fine. My father kept trying to interrupt, but Dillon just raised his voice and continued on. He was now letting my father in on the fact that YankeeJews spoil a town. "You know that, Bronson?" he said, as if he had been doing research on the subject.

My father wondered if the bastard expected him to agree, even give a few huzzahs, to shout "You said it!" and then do him a favor and leave town. Out loud he said, "You think so?"

Dillon answered soberly that he did and gave reasons why this was so. "A YankeeJew merchant comes and turns First Street into a cutthroat place and pretty soon everybody in town is miserable," he explained. He fell silent and shook his head, as if his vision had left him completely depressed.

So where did that leave my father and the store? "About the store," my father said.

"Oh, yeah," Dillon said, coming out of his gloomy trance. "I'll think it over and let you know."

As I have understood it, my mother had come out on the porch at the very moment Miss Brookie had used the phrase "Jew store" on the telephone with Tom Dillon, before my father's meeting with Dillon. Miss Brookie had used it as shorthand for the kind of business my father had in mind, had used it with Dillon because, as an owner of business properties, he would know the expression and it would tell him that this was not to be another

102

Dalrymple-Eaton's, which was a store for the well-to-do, of which one was enough, there not being all that many well-to-do in Concordia. But all my mother knew at that moment was that Miss Brookie had said the unsayable — had said "Jew store." "How did I know?" my mother asked in later years. "How could I know she wasn't always big with the 'Jew' this and 'Jew' that?"

In my mother's mind the word *Jew* used all by itself, nakedly, as it were, was not a word but a curse. She believed it was used only by people who hated Jews. If it had its three letters — its "-ish" — on the end, ah, that made the difference. If I said that someone was a Jew, my mother would ask me, "So what is he? A no-goodnik? A gangster?" On that day, however, when she had heard "Jew store," she had not protested. She could believe she was back with the girls at the table in the factory.

Before Miss Brookie had come back from the telephone, my mother had plunked down on the step next to my father, and he had said, hoping it was true, "Like a baby you slept, Reba."

My mother could only think it would be terrible if a baby slept as she had. *Oy*, such dreams she had had — dreams of her long-dead grandmother running around with hair "wild like an animal's" and screaming that everybody and everything had gone crazy.

On the porch with my father, she had wondered if Joey and Miriam had eaten. "Don't tell me what," she had said, and my father had replied that his lips were pasted shut. And who had made their breakfast? And when my father had answered "Lizzie Maud," my mother had remembered that the lady had mentioned somebody with this name the day before.

"Miss Brookie" — my mother had heard my father call the lady this and knew that she must too — had come back from the phone and now sat down below them on the steps. After telling my father that Tom Dillon would meet with him, she had begun addressing my mother in a blue streak, her words, my mother said when she told this story, like "flies that wouldn't light." Miss Brookie had wanted my mother to go with this Lizzie Maud to some place called the U-Tote-'Em — where she could buy her own "wherewithals" and then use the kitchen.

My father had thought my mother should go, but my mother had thought no, she didn't want to go to the U-Tote-'Em. The only place she had wanted to go was back to bed.

In the end, while my father had gone to meet Tom Dillon, my mother had gone grocery shopping with Lizzie Maud.

My mother had had an unnerving morning at the U-Tote-'Em. First of all, Lizzie Maud had turned out to be a Negro. *Oy*. She had to shop with a Negro and she would have to cook next to her, too. Then, when she had looked at the meats in the grocery store icebox, just like one in a house except bigger, although she had known not to expect kosher, where was the lamb, the veal, the calves' liver? Didn't they know there was other meat in the world besides *pork?* This was not exactly a fair question, as there were certainly beef and chickens in the box, not to mention kid. But when my mother had asked the butcher — not really a butcher, just the man who ran the grocery store — for a brisket, he had looked at her as if she had brought into his store the word for the flesh from a newly evolved animal. The man had said, "Don't have no call for that, Mizriz . . . Mizriz . . . Bronson, ain't it?" "Mizriz," as my mother would find out, was for many Concordians the pronunciation of choice for "Mrs." but now sounded to her only like *misery*.

If my mother was unnerved by it all, Lizzie Maud was unnerved by none of it. Shopping at the U-Tote-'Em was something she did most every day, and, ever since Miss Brookie

105

had begun to welcome guests in her house, she had shopped with them and indeed had taken over their entire orientation. She fussed with her mistress about the extra trouble guests imposed on her, but by now it was only a habit, and in truth she had long since lost the capacity to be surprised, disturbed, or vexed by her mistress.

Her attitude toward guests was a reflection of Miss Brookie's. If Miss Brookie found the invited ones in some way disappointing — too uncommunicative, too unhygienic, too pious — and showed them the door, Lizzie Maud packed them a lunch and waved a cool good-bye.

Now thirty-one, Lizzie Maud had been with the Simmons family from the age of fourteen as "cook" — in the South a catchall title understood to mean the Negro woman who did everything. Since Miss Brookie was a total incompetent when it came to running the house — couldn't boil water without a recipe, as we might put it in Concordia — after the elder Simmonses had died, Lizzie Maud had also assumed the role of parent, though she had a family of her own, a husband, Seth, who worked for the railroad, and five children.

For Lizzie Maud there was much to be gained from working in so intimate a way with such a powerful town presence as Miss Brookie, and her personality — bossy, opinionated, unconquerable — was clearly an adaptation of her mistress's. For a black person of those times, with power so hard to come by, parenting a white woman like Miss Brookie and telling white visitors how and what to do was about as good as you could get.

So it was on the same day that my father came back from his unsatisfactory meeting with Tom Dillon that my mother came back from her unnerving shopping. When my father arrived home, my mother was already sitting on the back porch in an old rocker with a broken rush seat and staring absently into the backyard.

In the backyard was an abandoned out-house (the "privy," T called it), the gray of raw wood showing through the old white paint, the sagging door ajar, the windows broken. Farther back was a small stable, which now sheltered both Willy and Miss Brookie's horse, Harold (for Harold Lloyd), plus the buggy from which Harold had been unhitched. There was no room in the stable for our wagon, which stood outside, open to the elements.

When my father came out on the porch

with the story of his meeting with Tom Dillon, my mother immediately thought of Dillon not only as a *momzer*, as my father had, but also as a kulak, the Russian farmer-peasant, the man Jewish villagers most loved to hate. "A *momzer* Dillon was, naturally," my mother always said, "but, I ask you, wasn't he also the same like a kulak?"

It was a sentiment no one could argue with, though it was true that in certain ways kulaks had the edge. They were not just anti-Jewish, they were actively so: They worked Jews from sunup to sundown, rented them hovels to live in, and, during pogroms, when the Cossacks came swooping into town on horseback to plague Jews and maybe to kill them, they made a great show of hiding the Jews and then betraying them. Still, in basic attitudes toward Jews, kulaks and Tom Dillon were blood brothers.

Out there on the back porch, as my mother sat and rocked, these were the things she turned over and over.

Chapter 8

My Father's Fancy Footwork

No call had come through from Dillon, and my father was getting fidgety. He had thought the wait would be but a day or two, but then it was a week, and then it was a second one. All that time he could only sit on the back porch and reread the local weekly, the *Sentinel*, until it softened in his hands.

My mother was more anxious than my father. "*Oy*, what a stubborn man," she said to him after one long day of waiting. "He ain't no different than Szymanski."

My father floundered. Who was this guy Szymanski? And how did he come into it?

He came into it because he was my mother's first boss, the one who had fired her when he caught her eating matzos.

Joey, if he didn't share my parents' anxiety, has remembered sharing my mother's hostility to Dillon. Dillon, he had concluded back then, was meaner than the man in the black hat and black beard who was forever trying to outwit Tom Mix. "That Mr. Dillon's so mean," he said to my father, "he ought to live in a hollow log and drink muddy water."

To which my father said, "*Oy*, that poor man Dillon's got the curse of the Bronsons on him. I sure wouldn't take no chances if I was him."

Finally my father had read the newspaper until his eyes glazed over. How could he stand one more reading of the story of the Baileys' new baby and Louise Caldwell's wedding shower? Was Mrs. Sterling Yancey's tea for her church circle, at which the Mmes. Josiah Jones and Billy Upton staffed the table and poured ("at both ends," the paper reported), so riveting that he should read about it again and again? All right, he was somewhat interested that the north road out of town had been reoiled, but he had taken in, digested, and expelled every word about it several times. Enough was enough. He repeated to himself one of his favorite sayings — that roast chickens don't fly into your mouth — then put down the paper, rose from the chair, went into the house to get his hat and coat, and headed for First Street.

First Street was, as my father now knew, the three-block, cobblestoned street where all the stores were. Some of the stores sold things, and some provided services. The important ones were on the second block, most notably — at least from my father's point of view — the palatial Dalrymple-Eaton's Department Store. Also on this block were the First National Bank and the furniture store. The first block had, besides Tom Dillon's store, other establishments, like the barber shop, where I got my hair cut, and the Cinderella Beauty Parlor, where Miriam had her hair variously marcelled, bobbed, or shingled, depending on the fashion of the moment. The third block wound down to the picture show and the train depot. Beyond the railroad crossing was the blacksmith shop and New Bethel Baptist Church, but you couldn't see them very well from First Street.

First Street divided white Concordia on the west from black Concordia on the east, which was called, as in Savannah, "Niggertown." As far as I knew, that was its name. All the town's Negroes lived there, in the shacks, and there was a bootlegger's hut at the edge of it. The streets were dark brown dirt because, unlike the west side of town, where the dirt streets were occasionally treated to a scattering of gravel, which lightened them, Niggertown streets were never treated to anything. Niggertown did, however, have one thing the west side didn't have, and that was a "sugar ditch," where raw sewage ran.

On First Street my father walked past the bank and the drugstore and traversed the cobblestones. Between Suggs's Feed and Lovett's Hardware, he came upon a little window fronting an insurance and real estate office. He went in.

In the office he talked to Herman Tucker.

The man was built to the pattern of Tom Dillon — large, beefy, with rolls of midtorso flesh. If Dillon was combative, Tucker was all amiability. When he smiled, which was all the time, his dentures protruded so far my father figured that if the man coughed, his teeth would fly out and make a landing on him. The man was a fake, my father decided at once, all fake.

In the small, dark office, Tucker sat behind a desk. He occasionally let his smile go into eclipse while he swigged at a Coca-Cola bottle. In between being swigged at, the bottle sat on the dust and grit of the desktop. Tucker didn't seem surprised to see my father, and my father guessed that Tucker and Tom Dillon had had a little conversation about his arrival in town.

Tucker said he had a couple of "real nice places," and though my father said a wry "uh-huh" under his breath, aloud he said he was all ears. He spotted a wooden folding chair against a wall, pulled it open, sat down across the desk, and told Tucker, "You got my attention complete."

It was no surprise to my father that Tucker's first suggestion was an abandoned blacksmith shop, which Tucker described as needing only a floor to turn into a palace.

Sure, my father thought, put a floor in a blacksmith shop and it turns into a palace; and put wheels on me and I turn into a wagon. "A blacksmith shop?" he said aloud.

Tucker trained his dentures on my father and offered that "you people" — meaning Jews — were so "enterprising," they could "pure" work miracles.

In his throat my father gave another "uh-huh."

The other place used to be a "nigger" church that had been foreclosed on but already had an upstairs and only needed to have the benches taken out to make my father "mighty proud." Tucker said to him, "As I say, you Jews are so . . ."

Yes, yes, my father knew all about how Jews were so this and so that: so smart, so energetic, so whatever. This man's choice had been "enterprising." My father had finally gotten it into his head that when people said these things what they meant was that Jews were different, and he had no doubt that among themselves there was an understanding that Jews were "not like you and me." That people thought he was different didn't bother him so much. People were all different in one way or another, and if some didn't like in what way he was different, well, what could he do about it?

But for dealing with this man Tucker, he plucked an old Jewish saying from his bag of old Jewish sayings — one having to do with not spitting in the well you might have to drink from later — and kept these thoughts to himself. Out loud he wondered if those two listings were all Tucker had.

From the way Tucker shifted around, my father knew a game plan was already operating, one in which this son of a bitch with the teeth was being coached by the *momzer* with the sweaty face. For how could a man call himself a realtor (which my father pronounced "relator" like everybody else in town) and have only these preposterous listings? No, something was going on here.

My father figured it was time to counter. He told Tucker he'd think it over, that he'd come in in a few days to have another talk.

Two days later he once more meandered up and down First Street. The day was hot, without hint of breeze. Under his woollen coat, my father's armpits pooled with sweat, and wet patches showed dark along his hat-

114

band. He went into Redfearn's Drugstore and Soda Fountain and, under a ceiling fan "trying its best to quit altogether," as my father described it, bought some Camels and attempted to engage the clerk in conversation.

The clerk stood behind boxes of cough medicines stacked chest high on the counter. Above him, on a horizontal piece of bare wood resting on rickety posts, were some red rubber hot-water bottles. The clerk bent his head and, through the narrowed opening, squinted up at my father. "What's that you say?"

My father repeated that there wouldn't be many calls for hot-water bottles at that time of year. There being no rejoinder, my father said uncomfortably to the clerk, "You know . . . it being so hot, uh, and all that."

The clerk was uninterested. Summer, winter, didn't mean "diddly" to him, and, anyway, he didn't go in for doing something different "every time the weatherman farts." (Whenever a memory called for words my father judged unsuitable, he added an automatic, "Excuse me, children," and decades later he was still adding it.) The drugstore clerk, having delivered himself of this sentiment, went back to washing glasses at the fountain.

My father went out. To waste some more

time, he crossed the street and put himself on view in front of Spivey's Furniture Store, where he feigned a fascination with the window display. There was in fact no display, only haphazard heaps of furniture called "Grand Rapids," a generic term for the kind of cheap, mass-produced stuff pioneered in that Michigan city. A jungle, my father thought. It was obvious that the guy had to get rid of some trees or find a new clearing. Was it possible he had in mind a new location?

Before he knew it, he had opened the door. A bell tinkled. Then he was squeezing past overstuffed chairs to a path leading to a desk. Behind the rolltop sat a man with gold-rimmed spectacles on a nose "only a bone," as my father said.

My father held out his hand and gave his name. The man responded with neither hand nor name but with a look that my father always described as like ice forming.

My father said to the man, "I was wondering . . ." The man answered, "Ain't nothing for you to wonder about in here." The man said further that he knew why my father was in town, had known ever since he got there. (Were spies hanging from Miss Brookie's crape myrtle?) And, the man wanted to know, wasn't it true that Tom Dillon had my father under lock and key?

My father said nobody had him under lock and key.

It didn't make any difference. "Quit wasting my time," the man told him.

Another *momzer*, my father thought. Were there nothing but *momzers* in this town? The conversation going nowhere, in fact at a dead stop, my father turned and retraced his steps. The tinkling bell tinkled.

Once outside, he felt all at once something of a drop-off in spirits. Where were the people whose hearts beat faster at the thought of a Jew store coming to town? Where were the drums and the trumpets? Well, he didn't expect pounding hearts and drums exactly, but where was at least somebody agreeable to taking his money?

In fewer minutes than he would have liked, he had recrossed the street to the real estate office.

Inside he again faced Tucker. The minute he looked at him, he knew nothing good would be coming from that smile. It was a smile of which my father had grown very weary indeed. Tucker said again that all he had was the blacksmith shop and the "nigger" church.

To try to project a calm that he certainly wasn't feeling, my father walked to the calendar on the wall and pretended to scrutinize the girl on it — a puffy-cheeked girl, preternaturally pink and white, smiling brilliantly over the slogan FOR SERVICE WITH A SMILE, CALL CRUICKSHANK'S PLUMBING. "You can't be doing much business with such few listings," he said to the wall.

Tucker wanted to help "like the very dickens" and said he would give it another think. My father turned from the calendar and took a look as Tucker embarked on his "think." As the man leaned back in his chair, his head fell back, his eyes closed, his mouth sprang open, and his tongue ran under his upper dentures, as if, my father said, searching out diamonds hidden in molars. Suddenly the eyelids lifted, and there came the revelation that Tom Dillon had the store my father was looking for.

This was news? Of course it wasn't, but what could my father do? He retreated to the little wooden chair, positioned just as he had left it yesterday, and asked Tucker if he thought Dillon was ready to talk business.

Tucker answered that he never spoke for Tom Dillon.

My father gave his almost silent "uh-huh" and sat on.

Tucker suggested that my father try some other town, that there were a lot of little towns that might be in the market for a Jew store. "So why not just go on and look further?" he asked my father.

My father was suddenly undone, his confidence seriously compromised. This guy Tucker was peeing on his back and calling it rain. The man knew the shoe factory was the attraction and here he was smiling his kulak smile and telling him to go someplace else. Did he have it wrong? Had Tom Dillon *ever* taken him seriously? After all, with the shoe factory coming in, lots of merchants could be wanting a store.

My father struggled for something light — *frailech* was his word — to make the man loosen up, come around. He had some jokes, but when he ran them through his head, he realized they were about Jews, so they were out. Jewish jokes were only for other Jews' ears.

Traveling salesman jokes were out as well. My father was not a goody-goody, but he was also not a traveling salesman and didn't want to sound like one. Traveling salesmen's reputations were not of the finest.

He set himself to come up with something funny about the ride from Nashville but soon realized there was nothing funny about that ride. And if he described what had really happened, told the incidents for the horror stories they were, would this man care? Of course not. Did a boil hurt under the other fellow's armpit? This man especially would feel no hurt.

Maybe something funny about Miss Brookie? My father started talking, sure that a good story would come to him. "Say, you must know Miss Brookie Simmons," he began.

"Everybody knows Brookie Simmons." Tucker looked up, eyes brightening. He began to heave about, pleasurably, my father would always say, like an elephant wallowing in mud.

Tucker had a proposal, a bet, though it was one my father never described in much detail. My guess was that the bet had a sexual aspect and that Miss Brookie was the target.

This was not the lighthearted something my father had in mind. He told Tucker that he wasn't much of a betting man, and the wallowing stopped.

My father knew he was now supposed to get up and go. But this was proving difficult since he seemed stuck to the chair.

As he sat, feelings washed over him, all of them bad. He began to face facts: the accent that he now knew he had, his lack of an education, his size. No matter what my mother thought, he was not tall. No, he was an undersized Jew pitted against Gentile giants.

He could only think that everything was a failure, and it was his fault: He had been done in by his chutzpah, his arrogance. What had made him think that his born sal-es-man-ship would open doors? And why had he believed those Nashville big shots who were so confident that he was on well-greased wheels to success? They didn't know everything; they didn't even know there were towns that wanted no part of Jews. And now here he sat, his good luck nowhere to be seen, his hustle out of commission, unable even to get him out of the chair.

And so what if he did get up? What then? He had no place to go except to my mother, who would surely say that now they would go back to New York. And if they had to go back, he would have to wire my grandfather for the money.

It was perhaps this last galling thought that got him to his feet. And, incredible as it was even to him, he managed a smile and a thanks. Thanks for what? he asked himself. For *bupkis,* for goat shit ("Excuse me, children"), that's for what.

As he walked to the door, Tucker was yanking at desk drawers, rummaging through them, shutting them with a bang, letting my father know he had better things to do.

"You get anything, you let me know," my father said to him.

"You bet," Tucker mumbled, peering into a drawer.

In the next moment the man was on his feet, moving out from behind the desk and extending his hand. My father was thrown into severe disorientation. Could it be the *momzer* was offering a good-bye shake? He reached out to take the hand, and when he did, saw that Tucker was looking not at him but at someone just entering the office.

My father lowered his head and tried to maneuver past. He felt the newcomer's hand on his arm. The man wanted him, him, Aaron Bronson.

Tucker sat back down, his eyes deep into whatever was taking place.

The man introduced himself as Spivey, and my father recognized the man from the furniture store. A hand was out, limply hanging, and my father shook it. What was this? Had this disagreeable guy decided he could produce something resembling a friendly gesture after all? Though at this moment my father didn't question it too closely, he later figured that because Waylon Spivey and Tom Dillon were foes of long standing, Spivey had mulled it over and decided to give himself the fun of reeling my father in before Dillon did.

They crossed the street. Inside his furniture store Spivey sat down behind the rolltop desk and motioned my father to the spindle-backed chair beside it. Behind the spectacles pale eyes stared at my father.

Did my father know what was what, what he was supposed to do? "No," he always said, "all I could do was stare back."

Spivey finally spoke, and the man's words poured over my father like rain on parched corn. What the man said was that the store was for rent.

Spivey got up, turned on the lights, and the store came alive. My father knew he had found his store. Not ritzy, but what need had he for ritzy? Two floors already, and — think of it — a Number One location.

Staying unexcited was the ticket. My father composed himself, rose, and started on a leisurely walk among the jumble. As he strolled, he envisioned. Here on the first floor would be the women's and shoe departments. He climbed the stairway and saw what the second floor could be — a place just for men. He closed his eyes and allowed "Perfect" to escape his lips.

Serenely he moved back down the stairs. Back at the desk, he put his hands in his pockets, pinched a quarter hard, and asked Spivey how come he was letting such a store go. If this was all a joke, now was when Spivey would produce the punch line.

There was no punch line. The store was available because Spivey was putting in a railroad spur at the edge of town and he wanted to be near it. "Folks don't mind riding out for furniture," he said to my father.

It was okay. But not over. Now came the "how much."

His property being "a danged sight better than them fool things you been offered," Spivey thought seventy-five was about right.

My father swallowed, hard.

There was to be more hard swallowing. That figure was while he was getting started; then it would go up "accordin'," as my father always said Spivey pronounced the word. Spivey was drawing things out, having himself a good time, telling my father not to try to Jew him down, that it wasn't going to work. And oh, yes, there was a five-year lease.

A lease like that could turn out to be a sentence, but my father told himself that the man had him right by the *beytsim*, or, as my father would translate it, "right by the silver dollars." He tried to stall. He asked when he could get in, if he decided to . . . uh, if he decided to . . . take it?

Giving my father's silver dollars a squeeze,

Spivey said there was no deciding about it, that my father had to take it, had no choice. And he could get in just in time to go to market for his back-to-school trade.

Market! The St. Louis market! Back-to-school! My father felt a jolt, as if he had been dozing and a wagon wheel had rolled over a deep hole. Look here, wasn't he the one with the Jewish head, the guy with the head for dry goods? And this goy was telling him his business? In the next moment he heard himself saying that there were a couple of other things he wanted to look at but that Spivey had made him a very interesting proposition. My father saw his hustle as back on track.

He blanked his face. He understood, he told Spivey, that Oliphant could use a store like he had in mind and that he had heard that some properties there could be on the market.

"Oliphant!" Spivey spit the word out. Didn't my father know that Oliphant had already had a store like he had in mind? And that one day it just gave a loud fart and disappeared? Had my father heard that, too?

"I heard," my father answered him, remembering the store that had dyed Miss Brookie's hands blue. He started moving doorward, promising to let Spivey know in a couple of days.

And then all at once Tom Dillon was there,

125

in the store, soft-faced, smiling, walking toward my father with his hand out. "Good thing I found you, Bronson," he was saying.

In telling of this moment, my father would always say, "Children, when a *momzer* like this one gives you a big kiss, count your fillings." He took Dillon's hand and said, "That so, Mr. Dillon?"

Dillon said he had been thinking about their little talk and had about concluded it was his civic duty to assist a newcomer. "We oughtn't to turn strangers from our gates, no sir," he said, and laughed. Dillon had a laugh that went so abruptly on and off, it might have been operated by a hand-held button. "You haven't forgotten, have you?"

It seemed Dillon had decided that he could fix up the upstairs after all so that my father could have his two separate departments. "We can't have the men in the ladies' bloomers, now can we?" A huge sound suddenly roared out of his throat, the beefy body bounced, and the sweat ran. He was at the boil, my father thought, like a pot of wash in a Southern backyard.

Spivey was now a collection of paroxysms, darting to and fro around Dillon, snatching at him, elbowing him. He ordered him from the store. "Just get on out, you no-account. You dassent come in here talking business to somebody I'm already talking business to. You just move along."

Dillon moved not, only said matter-of-factly that Spivey was a goddamn thieving son of a bitch.

Spivey's turn. Dillon stank worse than a nigger outhouse. Hadn't Spivey heard Dillon had been arrested for violating the smell laws?

Spivey took hold of my father and pulled him to one side. He suddenly had another deal. The deal was that he would come down twenty-five with a three-year lease if my father signed now. "This gol-derned pussyfooting around got to stop," he said.

As my father said later, this was not his idea of "pussyfooting around"; it was his idea of full-scale combat. He told Spivey to write the lease up and he'd sign.

Dillon wasn't finished. As Spivey was walking back to his desk to fill in the particulars, Dillon was spinning my father around and yelling "Sign? Sign?" into his face. What was my father going on about? Had he forgotten their understanding?

It meant little to Dillon that they had no understanding, that there was nothing to understand *about*. He wasn't even listening when my father told him that he would never do such a foolish thing as to take a store before he knew the particulars.

127

Having dealings with a "sawed-off little Jew" was something he should have never done, Dillon now informed my father. Could you have honest dealings with a Jew? "No," he said, in answer to his own question. "Not the Lord himself could do it. Don't we all know that?"

In the doorway he turned and, handkerchief gripped tight, shook his fist while he wished to hell that the Bronsons had never come to Concordia in the first place. Finally, he charged out, sideswiping pieces of furniture as he went.

My father walked slowly back to the spindle chair. How to explain, he thought then as he thought always, why such an important man, a man with such a big reputation, should carry around so much hate? It was a moment before he could take the paper Spivey was holding out to him.

As to the signing of the lease, though I was certainly not on the scene at Spivey's, I have since that day witnessed so many such rites that I feel I can describe this one with complete confidence. First there would have been the slow reading, with my father whispering the words and occasionally looking up to consider, and then the clearing of a space on the desk to ensure that his elbows and hand, when it finally came time to affix his signature, would have enough space to dock a boat if the need arose. At last he would have unscrewed his Waterman fountain pen and scrawled out a lengthy *Aaron Bronson*, and, as this was an important document, he would have imposed an inked dot between the names and streamed a paraph under both (to thwart forgery), and then he would have sat back and read the document again.

On this day the two men shook hands, and Spivey put the lease in his pocket. My father was to get his the next day, after it had been typed up. "There's a lady at the bank uses a typewriter," Spivey told him.

My father had a store, and of course it was time for giving himself congratulations. This he did, but it was not the congratulations he had envisioned, with a "Hoorah!" and a walk on the moon. No, he wasn't moon walking. And why he wasn't was no mystery. As my father said later, he knew that when Tom Dillon charged out the door, it wasn't the end of Tom Dillon. And, of course, it wasn't. My father had made an enemy, and he knew what to expect of enemies. Still, he and my mother never had to face Tom Dillon's most hateful act against us, and that was because Miriam and I never told them of it.

Chapter 9

Bronson's Low-Priced Store

When my father came home, the story of his newly acquired store was warm inside him, ready to go. But when he saw the bedroom dark and my mother lying on the bed, a white cloth across her forehead, he decided to hold it in a bit longer.

He conformed to practice and asked my mother how her day had gone, though he could see with his own eyes that it had not only gone but slammed the door behind it. My mother said she wanted to answer with something happy, to *be* happy, to make a joke about the rag on her head. It all stuck in her throat, and out came, "I got a headache, that's how it went." She used to say that at that point in her life she was not only like a tolling bell but like a window shade with a busted spring: the slightest touch and she went flapping around.

The cloth on her forehead contained sliced white potatoes — "Irish" potatoes we called them in Concordia or, more precisely, "Arsh" potatoes, to distinguish them from sweet potatoes, just as we said "sweetmilk" to distinguish it from buttermilk. This potato contrivance was Lizzie Maud's idea of a headache cure.

My mother had been secretly feeling that *this* particular headache had come from a couple of sources: She was expecting no good news from my father, and there was a problem having to do with Lizzie Maud. My mother had noticed that Lizzie Maud's bag ("bag" to my mother, though in Concordia it was a "sack") contained only her work shoes when she came to work in the mornings, but when she went home in the evenings, there were other things in the bag. Today the bag had been full.

Could she tell my father that her headache came from Lizzie Maud stealing? And be more of a *kvetch* — a complainer — than ever? And anyway, my father would only tell her it wasn't her business. So whose business was it? Miss Brookie's? A lady who cared so little about household matters she could have been a guest herself? Still, my mother thought, it *wasn't* her business.

She had been lately trying to tell herself she should stop worrying so much, that she ought to think more on the bright side. *Should.*

Ought to. She heard these words a lot these days — from my father, who said she should stop worrying or she'd make herself sick; from Miss Brookie; and from herself. She felt the pressure of the words, their intimidation, especially since she was unable to do what they advised.

With my mother so bleak, my father decided maybe a ride out to the fount from which blessings would flow — the shoe factory, whose construction by all accounts was just about completed — would be helpful. Then, he envisioned, he would surprise her with his good news and — *poof* — her dark cloud would go someplace else. He told my mother to get up, that they were going to see how their "little gold mine" was coming along.

Gold mine? My mother did not think of the factory as a gold mine. She thought of it as a dark pit of frustration. Why should they go? To have more heartache?

My father spoke softly to her closed eyes. He didn't want her to just lie there in the dark; he wanted her to take a ride with him in the wagon. "Reba, come," he said. "Come, little Rifka. We'll take a ride. Don't that sound good?"

Another ride in the wagon? No, it didn't sound good to my mother; it sounded terrible.

132

My father was not to be put off. If the wagon was the problem, they would borrow Miss Brookie's carriage. So he got Miss Brookie's okay, hauled Miriam away from the piano, got Joey from where he was playing with the neighborhood boys, hitched Willy to Miss Brookie's carriage, and off they went.

As they drove the north road out of town, if my mother was deep into melancholy, my father was on the crest of euphoria. When he was in this state, he always brought himself up to date on all the wonderful things in his life. First of all, now that he had a store, my mother would be her old self again. She would talk and laugh and fix her hair in the New York way, when it was crowned with thick braids glistening with little blue lights.

For my mother's beautiful hair we all knew that my grandfather was responsible, for he had at some point ordered the women of his house to eschew the *sheitel,* the wig worn by ultra-orthodox married women. He liked to look at a woman's hair, my grandfather said, so why should he have to look instead at cotton strings dyed as if with black shoe polish?

Euphoria also brought my father thoughts of how Joey would surely do well in school, the start-up of which was imminent. And Miriam? Who sat like a little lamb by the piano with Miss Brookie, this child who couldn't sit still a minute and was always flying off like dandelion fluff in the breeze?

Miriam was, he thought, definitely a child with a mind of her own. And *I* had always thought that Miriam had decided not even to *look* like anyone else. Her hair was neither my mother's black nor my father's blondish but an assortment of browns; her eyes, though essentially brown, were flecked with red and yellow — my father would say "sprinkled over with paprika and mustard seed." Only in the high cheekbones did she share family traits.

In many ways they were Slavic traits. The fact was, of course, that my family's looks — my father's light coloring, his and Miriam's high cheekbones, the short features and full lips of Joey and my mother — were influenced not by the Semitic races but by the Slavs, the Cossacks who had been busy for generations in my parents' shtetls. My father would on occasion refer to this. "Can you beat it?" he would say. "Us Cossacks showing up in the U.S. of A., state of Tennessee, town of Concordia." To which my mother would say nothing, pretending ignorance.

In the carriage my brother's attention was on the roadside, his attention drawn to some identical signs sporadically appearing. My father explained they were announcements for Chautauqua. He had heard about Chautauqua, and he was pleased to see that it made a stop in Concordia. He explained that it was a traveling show. "And lots of speeches," he said.

Joey thought about a button he was carrying in his pocket. Did it come from this Chautauqua? It had been given to him by Halsey Cunningham that morning when they had been playing in Halsey's yard. Halsey had several of them, and when Joey had expressed an interest, he had given him one. Whether they had come from Chautauqua, Joey didn't know: All he knew was that they had been given out at some kind of speech, a "preaching," Halsey had said, at which somebody named Billy Sunday had "spellbinded" everybody.

My mother came slightly alert at the reference to speeches. It recalled for her one of her fondest memories — the time she had attended the inauguration speech of Mayor Mitchel in New York.

But then, Joey has remembered, he spoiled it all by pulling the button out of his pocket and showing it to my mother. That the button was big and shiny white was fine; that it said "Booster for Jesus" was not.

Booster? Booster? What was a booster, and *who* did the button say you were a booster *for?*

My mother felt at that moment that just as my father had predicted, she was going to get sick.

"Everybody wears one," Joey said, and his attention went back to the roadside, to white blocks appearing now and then in the fields. He had found out they were salt. For the cows. And he wanted everybody to know.

My mother didn't care about cows, and she didn't care about salt. She cared about buttons. Whether Joey intended to wear one, he hadn't said, but my mother assumed the worst. "Joey! Joey, look at Mama!" she cried. "You can't mean it!"

My brother could tease, too, just like my father, and he remembers saying to my mother, "Sure I do. Cows need salt just like human beings."

He kept it up. "It's a good thing cows have long tails. Otherwise only stubby cows could flick the flies off."

The only one Joey had entertained was my father. Miriam wasn't listening, and my mother had no intention of being amused. The, um, *Jesus* thing had started already. And what could she do about it? Her answer was that Joey should know his own religion. And what was she doing about *that?* Nothing, that's what.

Well, to be fair, on their first Friday in Concordia, my mother had already initiated "Friday nights," and that was something. For this special night — what my parents called *Shabbos bei nacht* — my mother had worked out a routine that followed custom: In the morning she had salted a chicken in the kosher way to make the blood run out; in the afternoon, as no cooking was allowed on the Sabbath, she had cooked the *cholent* (the food for the Sabbath); and on Friday night she had spread a tablecloth on the kitchen table and brought out the candlesticks that had come with them from New York, fitted out with candles from Nashville. And with her head covered by a shawl, she had murmured over the bread the prayer she had learned from her mother.

As if Lizzie Maud hadn't been astonished enough by all this, when my mother had baked her own challah, she was totally nonplussed by the braids on top of the bread, and she had emitted one of her "shoot-dog"s when my mother pulled the fat from a chicken and rendered it. "You tell me you gwine put that mess in *mash taters?*" she asked my mother.

And when into the icebox had gone the Mason jar of chicken fat cheek by jowl with Lizzie Maud's can of bacon grease, Lizzie Maud had said, "It be in there, and it can stay in there, all I care." But Miriam has remembered the day Lizzie Maud saw her eating the crisp bits of fat left from the rendering, tried some, and became a convert. "Ain't a whole lot different than my bacon rinds, Miz Reva," she had said, my mother "Reva," as always, to Lizzie Maud. "Both just oozing good-tasting grease."

My mother actually had it over New York Jews (those who cared about it, at any rate) in one way: Lizzie Maud's wood-and-coal stove stayed banked and glowing at all hours on all days, and my mother would therefore need no "*Shabbos* goy," the Gentile boy who for a penny did the work of lighting the stove so that food could be warmed up on Saturday.

Well, so what? she thought now as they rode out to the factory. All what she did for *Shabbos* might help Miriam to become a *balabusteh*, an expert housewife (though she had so far detected little enthusiasm emanating from Miriam), but did it help Joey for bar mitzvah? No, she thought sadly, of course not.

The woods finally cleared, and there at last in the center of a large field was the factory, all three stories of it, every inch of the three stories red brick. It was a building softened by neither tree nor bush. Of natural growth there was only a stubble of grass, as if the land had been shaved hurriedly by a giant straight-edged razor.

My father, Joey on his heels, dropped down from the buggy. The rows of windows were in place, the glass in them painted blue, a sure sign that the factory was near completion. My father stood gazing, feeling the building's purpose.

In front was the sign, and my father read the words out loud, directing his voice toward the buggy: "GRAND OPENING/ON SUNDAY, AUGUST 21, AT 11 A.M./THE REVEREND CHARLES BOOMER JONES OFFICIATING/COME ONE, COME ALL." At the bottom it said, THE PINDER SHOE COMPANY/TO EMPLOY 175 PERSONS.

In the late afternoon as they drove back, my mother began thinking of supper, of the potted chicken that just needed to be warmed up.

My father halted the buggy on First Street. "*Sha,*" he said to the family. At such a moment, he wanted no talking. He got down from the buggy and, while the family watched, walked across the street to Dalrymple-Eaton's Department Store. He counted its five display windows and, for his trouble, got a painful poke in the chest.

He knew it was foolishness, this envy. His Jew store and this plush palace were *supposed* to be worlds apart. Still, he had to say that

139

when a goy turned on the ritz — like these guys Dalrymple and Eaton — only a big merchant Jew like a Cohen in Nashville could match, even if he in turn was overmatched by a Bergdorf in New York.

Through the windows he could see the mahogany counters gleaming richly in the store's night lights. All right, he'd have only tables, even if they were just lengths of wood laid over sawhorses, but they'd hold plenty. As for how customers would pay, so okay, Dalrymple-Eaton's had this fancy overhead pulley system, but he could make do easy with a secondhand register — if he was lucky enough to find one — or a cigar box, if he wasn't. Still, he had to blink away the image of my mother standing dignified behind a shiny register, chatting with the customers as she made change.

The windows also offered sightlines into the shoe department, an island to itself, and set about with upholstered chairs of such luxury that every customer would feel like a king. Of course, like all shoe departments in the South, it was for white trade only. Negroes tried on shoes from atop a crate in the back alley and tested them on a strip of rug laid down there.

In Dalrymple's windows he found on display only a pair of shoes with a beaded vamp

140

and spike heels. A tchotchke, a lady's pretty. Well, *his* windows would be jammed full of shoes to show the entire range — tough ones for the fields, fancies for church. If, as was printed on the scalloped awning in front, Dalrymple's had everything for the discriminating, my father joked that his would say, EVERYTHING FOR EVERYBODY, EVEN IF YOU'RE NOBODY.

It was finally time to let the family in on it. In front of the furniture store, he pointed, and a meaningful point it must have been. "Okay," he said to the family, "everybody take a look at our store."

He even had the name and how it would be displayed: gold lettering, and, very important, on both windows. And the name?

BRONSON'S LOW PRICED STORE

Chapter 10

Green Eyeshades

With a store safely his — "*my* store" or "*our* store," my father called it from the moment the lease was in his hands — he made up his mind to go to market right away. With Mr. Cohen's letter of credit in his pocket and Miriam at his side, who had begged to go, he set off for St. Louis.

My mother thought Miriam at five was too young to go but decided not to argue. It seemed to her that every time she opened her mouth lately, she spit out stones. "Be a warm stone in your husband's pocket," her mother had said, and by no stretch of the imagination had she meant these hard, hurtful little things. No, she had meant a nice smooth stone heated up by two warm hands, something to comfort a man who might need comforting but was maybe not showing it.

As my mother and my brother waved the travelers good-bye, my mother felt a kinship with the shtetl women who stood at their

142

doors watching the men set off for the city to find work. Still, in the old country when the men were gone, the women had one another. And who did she have? A lady who talked an incomprehensible language and a Negro she didn't quite trust.

They had walked to the depot, and now there was the walk back. It suddenly seemed to my mother that Miss Brookie's house was a very long way off.

On the front porch she sank onto the swing. How could she be always so tired, so *lazy*, when she had almost nothing to do? A few meals, two beds to make, a flick here and there with the dust rag, and she was finished. That wasn't housework, that was *noodling*. She didn't even have washing and ironing: A Negro woman came around every Friday, picked up the week's laundry, and brought it back on Tuesday, the clothes so starched they could not only stand up but maybe even walk around, and everything ironed. Miss Brookie had recommended it. "The best thirty cents you'll ever spend," she had said. My mother was too embarrassed to say she would rather do the laundry herself and put the thirty cents toward the family's debts.

She felt herself slipping into the role of "poor soul." All her life she had heard about "poor souls," those upon whom life had inflicted crushing sorrows. How often had she heard "Molka, poor soul, since her Peretz passed away (*olov hasholem* — may he rest in peace), she don't have nobody"? Or "Fageh, poor soul, she don't have two pennies to rub together"? Wasn't there some sort of measure by which she would qualify as a poor soul?

At this moment she had to get Joey something to eat, but she could not summon the will to do it. Her body was heavy, suffused with a kind of lethargy. And her eyes kept wanting to close.

Miss Brookie appeared behind the screen door. Then she had pushed the door with her hip and was bearing down on my mother with two glasses of iced tea. "All sugared and lemoned," Miss Brookie announced as she handed one over. She sat down on one of the wooden rocking chairs, held her own glass up to the light, and said to the air, "In the South this is truly the elixir of life. . . . Though up in the hills they set store by more intriguing refreshment." She laughed.

Always with the talking and the laughing, my mother thought. She glanced down at the glass in her hand. *Oy*. No mistake. Ice again. Whoever heard. In a glass of tea. She put the glass down on the little table beside her.

"Did the travelers get off all right?" Miss Brookie sipped and smiled at my mother.

144

My mother didn't sip or smile; she blinked.

Miss Brookie seemed undeterred and began, as my mother always said, talking a blue streak. My mother could not "do" Miss Brookie talking a blue streak and would turn it over to Miriam, who could. As Miriam told it, what Miss Brookie was saying to my mother out there on the porch was "You know, Reba — and by the way, it occurs to me that I'm old enough to be your mama and therefore ought to have the privilege of callin' you by your first name . . . unless, of course, you plan to have a fit on the floor over it — in the old days I used to go to St. Louis right much. . . . Oh, Lord, here I go plungin' headfirst into nostalgia. . . . Well, the fact is Mama and Daddy and I used to go to the opera there. And mercy, that heavenly music and those beautiful ladies in those glorious gowns. And the men in their boiled shirts. Just dead attractive."

On the porch my mother blinked some more. It was her turn to say something, she knew that; but what could she contribute about "heavenly music" and "dead attractive" men in "*balled* shirts"? Maybe she could start a new something, maybe about how nice that Miriam was learning to play the piano. She opened her mouth. No words came. Her mouth was as dry as an ancient riverbed.

She pawed at her throat, pinching the flesh between her thumb and forefinger. Miss Brookie was staring at her, waiting. My mother knew that if she didn't speak when she was supposed to, Miss Brookie would rush to rescue the silence, in the way that she did, with that profusion of words, "like the ceiling was falling down on my head," as my mother described it.

My mother didn't want the silence to be rescued. And she didn't want Miss Brookie thinking she needed to be cooed over, as if she was one of her "precious lambs." No, she didn't want that at all.

So she got up and went into the house and into bed and didn't get out of it for three days. When Miss Brookie came in to see her, my mother couldn't say what was wrong, nor was she surprised that she couldn't. It was the old saying of her mother's come to life: The deeper the sorrow, the less tongue it has.

Miss Brookie and Lizzie Maud saw to Joey, and Lizzie Maud brought soft-boiled eggs, which my mother didn't eat, having no appetite whatsoever. The two of them acted as if my mother had the flu, but my mother knew that it wasn't anything like that. What it was was what my father had predicted: She had made herself sick, so sick that she couldn't get out of bed.

Lying there, she tried hard to think of nothing. She had a little trick to help her do this: She pretended to have green shades over her eyeballs, and when an unwelcome thought hove into view, bang! down went the shades, blocking it out.

There were a few images she permitted. These had to do with her Bronx family and were for tears. She had discovered that after she cried, she could sleep.

With the High Holidays — Rosh Hashanah (the Jewish New Year) and Yom Kippur (the Day of Atonement, the day of fasting) — approaching, on the third day she lay in bed fashioning reveries about the holiday dinner that would be taking place in her parents' apartment. She saw her family at the massive dining-room table, the place for all social occasions, for there was always a sure serving of tea and honeycake, or, at the very least, a piece of fruit.

But on this day, in my mother's fantasy the table was in use for the post–Yom Kippur feast, after the long hours in shul, but she soon realized she had blundered: She had allowed herself to think of her family being together without her. The thought made her not sad and sentimental but anxious. It had reminded her of how her life had changed. If she waited for tears, she waited in vain. She could expect no wet cheeks, no drifting off to sleep; she had remembered that there would be no mother and father, no Sadie, no Meyer, no Hannah, no Philip, and no shul in this place. There was only one thing to do: She lowered her green shades.

At the end of this day Miss Brookie came into the room and stood at the foot of the bed. She clearly thought enough was enough. She told my mother to get out of bed.

My mother didn't move.

Miss Brookie said everybody knew about being homesick (though perhaps not *everybody*, as most Concordians had not gone much further than Pottsboro, fifty or so miles down the road). She said, "Rise up, Reba. Rise up and make contact with the world again." Where this contact would be made was on the porch.

At the mercy of a truly commanding voice that wasn't going to go away, my mother could resist no longer. She got up, put on the first skirt and blouse her hand touched, and walked stiffly out onto the porch. There was, however, an added complication: She had gotten it into her head that if she was walking oddly, it was because she was encased in a wooden box. There was a hole in the box, to see out of. Through the hole, she observed an unknown woman sitting with Miss Brookie.

Miss Brookie introduced her as her around-the-corner neighbor, Mrs. MacAllister. In Concordia, along with "Mizriz," "Mrs." was also pronounced "Miz," and this was the way Miss Brookie pronounced it.

Some words or another — she didn't know what — fell out of my mother's mouth.

She looked at the woman through her hole: pale skin, and black hair so densely marcelled it had taken on the corrugated look of a clay road washed over by many rains.

When the woman spoke, it was in a hearty voice that my mother's box muffled only slightly. "I like to have a fit to meet you," my mother heard. The woman smiled broadly, and oversized teeth were put on view. "It sure is nice to meet Joey and Miriam's mama."

This new talker pressed on. She was glad there was going to be a Jew store, glad they no longer had to depend on a Jew peddler coming to town just every once in a while. "If you can believe it," she said to my mother, "the last Jew peddler we had, well, him and Agnes Kimball . . ."

Miss Brookie sprang into action. "Lord, Carrie," she said, "I doubt Miz Bronson has the slightest interest in Agnes Kimball."

Mrs. MacAllister changed the subject. She was now "tickled" that we didn't rent Tom Dillon's store, because Tom Dillon was "such a mess," there was no telling how much trouble he'd cause. And why was he "such a mess"? According to Mrs. MacAllister, it was because his wife, Martha, stayed "poorly" so much. "Now don't stop me, Brookie," she said. "You know good as I do that Martha don't do nothing but stay in bed, and it's gotten so that . . ."

Carrie MacAllister was full of stories. Miss Brookie said that if the *Sentinel* was our weekly paper, Carrie was our daily one. Harsh description though it was, Carrie MacAllister herself laughed at it, knowing it was true.

At this moment, Miss Brookie refused to accommodate Carrie MacAllister's need to divulge. Though she knew, and the whole town knew, that Martha Dillon was always in bed — and what the whole town also knew was that she was in bed with a jar of white lightning — Miss Brookie no doubt feared that Carrie was going to frighten my mother right back into bed. She said that if Carrie was determined to tell my mother something, she should tell her about her baby, Billy.

Mrs. MacAllister tilted her head toward the end of the porch, and my mother looked through her hole at a fat, open-faced, blond-haired boy of about a year — Billy Sunday MacAllister — sitting squarely on his bottom, chirping and trilling at a toy on wheels. He

150

was, his mother said, going to be as good a talker as the man he was named after. And why was the baby named for Billy Sunday? "Because," Carrie MacAllister said, "that man was sent straight from the Lord to help us poor sinners." She closed her eyes, and her body trembled and shook.

My mother was truly frightened. What was this, this shivering, this quivering? *Oy*, this was something beyond the usual Gentile strangeness. At this moment it looked to her like craziness, though in later years my father tried to get her to see it in a more evenhanded, more realistic way. "So you never seen Jewish people rocking back and forth when they pray?" he would ask her, and she would think about it for a moment and say, "Maybe it's the same." It was the best she could do.

At any rate, in another moment Carrie MacAllister's eyelids flew open. She had another story my mother needed to hear. It was from a couple of years earlier, when Billy Sunday had come to town, at a time when Mayor Bailey's daughter had gotten into trouble and Mayor Bailey had cut off her hair. My mother told this story often, and as faithfully as she could: "Lord," she would say, trying to imitate Carrie MacAllister, "here come Miss Floy Inez Bailey into the tent, and she's near bald as a egg."

151

Miss Brookie had then interrupted to say, "Looks like we're in for talking some trash."

Carrie, not having been told definitely by Miss Brookie to *stop*, simply went on with her story. She was now reporting Floy's hair as *"plumb gone."* It was gone, apparently, because Floy's father had got Floy from where she was staying with the traveling salesman and cut it off.

When Floy had announced she wanted to declare, "Law," Carrie said, "the fight was on. For the soul of Miss Floy Inez Bailey, don't you know." It was a night, Carrie was pleased to say, when Billy Sunday "took to preaching only hellfire and damnation," to the point that the whole tent got down with Floy. "Chalk one up for God," Carrie said.

Perhaps sensing that Miss Brookie was about to call her to a halt, she leaped up and, all bones and sinew, marched down the porch and grabbed up her child. Settled back in the rocker, she flung open the buttons of her dress, grabbed a breast, and pushed it at the baby in her lap. He sucked hard, and a fist pounded the air. Then his eyeballs rolled up, and he considered the ceiling.

Mrs. MacAllister spoke over the head engaged at her nipple and expressed the wish that big Billy could be there for little Billy's baptizing. "Crawley's where we do our baptizings," she said in my mother's direction. "They got a river over there lends itself real good for dipping." She did an unsure grin, and after a moment, she said in a tone suddenly shy, "Do y'all . . . um . . . do y'all have any water in the Jewish faith?"

Jewish *faith!* Jewish *faith!* My mother always said the words tore through her box and ripped it to shreds. "Jewish faith" was not an expression she was unfamiliar with. Her co-workers had used it on those rare occasions when they'd determined for reasons unknown that politeness was required. It was as if calling it a "faith" somehow took the curse off. Well, she thought now, is that what everybody thinks? That the Jewish religion is a *curse?*

My mother was suddenly hearing another voice, and it was angry, no doubt about it, "Ain't ours a *religion* like everybody else's?" it was saying. She was amazed that this furious voice sounded so much like hers. And even more amazed when she realized it *was* hers. "You ain't going to get nothing from me to laugh at," she exploded at the women. "You only want to know about our religion so you can call us *loony* or whatever word you use in your language."

Mrs. MacAllister sat Billy up. Mother and child fastened china blue eyes on my mother.

153

My mother remembered it all, how she was not to be put off, how the more she thought about everything, the more she shouted. "Did you ever think how *loony* I might think it is that you dunk that little baby in a river?" Oh, she was screaming, no doubt about it, screaming loud. "Or that you cut off a girl's hair when she done wrong?" She paused for only a second. "No, you can't believe your *religion* could do anything *loony*."

She now took all her courage in her hands and turned on Miss Brookie. "And you, you and your high-toned ways and how you talk and all what you know." Though she knew her English wasn't coming out properly, with the words tumbling over each other, she couldn't make herself care. "So how come you don't look down your nose at this lady when she brings out her breast in front of a stranger? Ain't it because she's Christian?" She stomped on the shreds around her feet. "Well," she went on, "I may be just a *Jew*, but that's one thing we don't know from. Only time I seen that is with the Russian peasants. For shame, for shame."

When words began to slow, she knew it was time to quit. "I'm going in now," she said more quietly, "and I'll leave you two to talk about me. You'll talk plenty, you're so good at saying things."

She said later that she was shaking, shaking hard, and not from religious fervor but from having been so mad. Her legs were going wobbly, not holding her. When she got to the screen door, she put out her hands and clung to it. And all at once Lizzie Maud had hold of her. From out of nowhere she was at the door. "You best take it slow, Miz Reva," she said. "You gwine be just fine. All it was was you was just full fit to bust. Don't we all know how that is?"

Just fine? My mother would have taken any bet that so terrible was this thing she had done, so much trouble had she stirred up, she would never be "just fine" again. She let her body sag toward Lizzie Maud's. It would have been wonderful to remain in Lizzie Maud's embrace forever.

In her room she closed the door. She thought she would sink instantly onto the bed and quick, quick pull down her green shades. Instead she found herself in front of the mirror studying herself, looking hard at her forehead, as if to burrow through to the place where would arise the headaches she had just set into motion. "Fit to bust," Lizzie Maud had said.

She stood there, looking, waiting. So where were they, those headaches, those squeezes like from a too-tight hat? Where were the moans and the groans, and the weeping that came not from memories but from misery? By now she should have been awash in tears, sinking in water like a leaky ship. Instead, there was, incredibly, a buoyancy, a sympathetic tug, and the feeling of being towed into a safe harbor.

What she also felt was *cleaner*. As if she had taken a ritual bath, a *mikveh*. Was a *mikveh* anything like a *baptizing?* With the question came a sound in her throat. It was a sound she had not heard from herself in a long time, a hint of a laugh.

Several minutes went by. She pulled the pins from the bun, and her hair plunged into a full fall. She brushed it and, after plaiting it into a braid, arranged it on top of her head.

She went back to the screen door and looked out onto the porch. Miss Brookie and Mrs. MacAllister were gazing anywhere but at each other. They were in a world of dead silence.

It took the reappearance of my mother to bring things back to life. As if she had been gone for days, the other women opened their eyes wide and flung greetings. Mrs. MacAllister grinned hugely, as if my mother's coming was only slightly less welcome than that other one yet to be.

Chapter 11

No Picnic

Miriam has always remembered that she had a wonderful time in St. Louis with my father. Although they stayed, and ate, in the home of one of the wholesale men, she and my father went to *two* restaurants. My father introduced her to the wholesale men as his "bookkeeper," and, not knowing yet how to write, she nevertheless scribbled some things down. The men made a big fuss over her, and she came home with dresses so beguiling that they were perhaps what made her fashion-conscious for the rest of her life.

My father too had success in St. Louis. The men accepted Mr. Cohen's letter and treated him, if not like Diamond Jim Brady, then at least, as my father used to say, like a man with money to spend. This was the first of my father's annual buying trips to St. Louis, though he also ordered occasionally from the houses' traveling salesmen.

When my father and Miriam came back,

nobody much mentioned my mother's collapse, and though my father was surprised to find her in such improved spirits, he didn't go on about it. The shoe factory was about to open, and there was little room for other than thoughts of business.

Miss Brookie had advised that the family go to the picnic to celebrate the opening. "Let them see that you share their species," she said.

Despite that the thing on my mother's chest had lightened since what she called her *mikveh* day, and though the day of the picnic dawned sunny and clear, my mother herself was not very sunny and definitely not clear.

What she was not clear about was the food she should take. She could certainly not partake of Lizzie Maud's chicken, fried as it always was in bacon grease the volume of a small pond.

She had decided at last on hard-boiled eggs. That morning, however, when she had gone about boiling them, she had gotten the message from Lizzie Maud that eggs were too lowly for a picnic. Lizzie Maud had said you "dassent" go to a picnic without fried chicken, "no, *ma'am*." As with my father's "God," Lizzie Maud's "ma'am" was just a word. She didn't "ma'am" or "sir" every white person in sight, as if to honor them for just being white, though she did with older persons. Not that everybody in Concordia didn't "ma'am" and "sir" older people, but Lizzie Maud awarded the honorific to both older whites and older Negroes.

When my mother had said she didn't know how to make fried chicken, Lizzie Maud had said that first of all, my mother should understand that you didn't *make* fried chicken. "You don't make things you eat," Lizzie Maud had said. "You fixes them." In this case it didn't matter: Where she was from, my mother had told Lizzie Maud, they didn't even *eat* fried chicken.

"Then where you from don't know nothing," Lizzie Maud had answered. There was, she had said, nothing to it, that even her "knee baby" knew how. She had muttered a "shoot-dog," had herself gone to the icebox, taken out some pieces of chicken, contemplated the can of bacon drippings for a moment but, since she had already been informed of the rudiments of "kosher," withdrew the Crisco.

She had run through the fundamentals, about the coating of the pieces in flour and the hot, hot grease and the pan lid being off and on and off again — to bring back its "ship-snap" — and "how you dassent leave no smidge of pink," and had then said to my mother, "See can you do it."

In the end the chicken was "fixed" by Lizzie Maud.

As my mother sat now in the buggy on the way to the ceremonies, clutched in her hand was a paper sack containing her fried chicken and a cucumber stand-in for the still suspect potato salad. For Miss Brookie and the rest of the family, along with the basket of Lizzie Maud's chicken and accoutrements, there were her lemon meringue pies for "sharing time," when, Miss Brookie said, "everybody puts out the word out on everybody else's cooking."

It was one of those late summer mornings when the sun was everywhere and the air was like new. With my father holding the reins, Harold Lloyd clip-clopped briskly, as if happy to at last be on a mission worthy of his talents.

My father, with his own opening day nearing, was most decidedly, as my mother would say, "flying with the birdies." Indeed so elevated was he, he had taken to declaiming. The day, for example, was "a day for princes, for kings!" He thought to compare it to a day in New York, and New York suffered in the comparison. In New York where was the sun? Hidden by the apartment houses, that's where; or, if it managed to squeeze between

160

those brick fortresses, it fell on the streets in odd, sharp-edged wedges like hunks of cheese. And trees? *Oy*, what a schlep to Central Park or to the north Bronx if you wanted trees. And here? Here was a countryside full of trees. And a smell from the pine needles and good earth like perfume. And the air? Nowhere so soft, so clean.

To show appreciation of air of such high quality, my father put on a show of deep breathing, holding the reins with one hand and pounding his chest with the other. He gestured to Joey and Miriam to follow.

Miss Brookie told them to save the oxygen for my mother. "Since it's all kosher," she said, "she can partake of it without guilt."

Every time Miss Brookie said something like this, slipped in some Jewish something, my parents were surprised until they learned that Miss Brookie knew about "Jewish somethings" because she had known Jews. Specifically, she had known them in college, at the University of Chicago, where she had roomed with a Jewish girl — Dora Landau by name — and had spent a summer with Dora and her brother, Jack, and their parents. When she first told about that summer, she said that it had been nothing less than "momentous" and that it had changed her a lot. It was only much later that we learned just how "momentous" that visit had been.

German Jews the Landaus were, my father thought at Miss Brookie's first telling of this story. Who but German Jews would send a *daughter* to college?

Therefore when Miss Brookie said, "They were German Jews," my father said to himself, So was I wrong?

As they rode along in the carriage toward the picnic, my mother was aware that she had laughed with the others at Miss Brookie's joke about kosher oxygen. Since her *mikveh* day she had discovered that a laugh wasn't always for somebody else.

They arrived at the factory grounds at about eleven o'clock. A crowd had already gathered. Joey spotted T fooling around with some other children, and he ran over, Miriam chasing behind. Miss Brookie put her hand on a picnic table, thereby claiming it, and my father deposited the baskets.

My mother opened up one of the folding chairs and sat down.

Miss Brookie, after observing the scene for a moment, thought my father should do some "mixing." She herself wanted a talk with Roscoe Pinder, the factory owner. She asked my mother if she wanted to come along. "It's a chance to meet the movers and shakers," she told her.

By this time my mother had learned to separate the wheat from the chaff in whatever Miss Brookie said, or, as she put it, "the barley from the soup," so she knew not to bother with "movers and shakers" and just answered, "Maybe later."

After Miss Brookie and my father left to go "mixing," my mother put on a pleasant expression and looked into the crowd.

Out on the picnic grounds everybody was all dressed up. The adults were in their Sunday best, the little girls in longish, densely smocked dresses, the boys in fedora hats and vested suits and celluoid collars from which stiff ties hung. The boys in the Bronx wore similar clothes to shul but these boys seemed to look different, like little imitation men. And their faces were small, too small, as if they had shriveled from the long summers of farmwork with the sun beating down every which way. Of course, as my mother sat thinking about little boys, and especially Bronx boys in shul, it made her think of her little boy *not* in shul, and here came a pang.

There were things to laugh at here, too, especially the tall, skinny older boys — long noodles, strands of *lockshen,* as my mother called them — with their bony hands and wrists sticking out from outgrown jackets like new shoots on a bean stalk, and she wished for my Uncle Philip, the one in the family she always laughed with.

The music at the picnic was a puzzlement. On the platform a band of musicians was jingle-jangling away on violins. Such a long warming up, she thought. Only when one of them stepped forward and delivered himself of some unintelligible words did she realize the performance was under way. And what strange music it was. She certainly hadn't expected Jewish tunes, but why not songs that everybody knew, like "Valencia" or "Janine, I Dream of Lilac Time"?

At the fringes of the field Joey and T were in a game with a baseball and Miriam was playing Drop the Handkerchief. My mother spotted my father standing near the platform with a group of men dressed in suits and hats but whether he was doing any talking she could not determine. She finally located Miss Brookie: She was talking to Roscoe Pinder and looking as if she had been set upon by bees.

And then all at once Miss Brookie had broken off and was marching back. Then she had dragged a chair over, plopped herself down, and delivered herself of a "double dog damn."

My mother waited.

"We've got us a very bent hairpin here," Miss Brookie said, and my mother knew she must wait some more. Finally Miss Brookie said plainly that Roscoe Pinder was most certainly going to hire children. "And work them long hours, too." She stared darkly out across the field. "If that don't blister it, I don't know what does."

Children? Working? In Concordia? Though it seemed incredible to her later, my mother said she had never until that moment entertained the thought that behind those blind blue windows children would be working.

"Everybody knows it's a vile practice and that it's wrong," Miss Brookie said to my mother, "but there's no *law*, nothing to sic on the man."

My mother suddenly began to see that it was not so different from how it was in the factories in New York. She confessed to Miss Brookie, though she was reluctant to do it, it not being anything she liked to talk about, that as a girl, as a *child*, she had worked in factories. And then, after the day's work, there were the bundles.

Bundles were items from the factory brought home to work on. In my mother's case the bundles were from the ladies' dress factory where Aunt Sadie worked before she was married. Aunt Sadie brought home bundles of belts and buttons, and at night the women of the family turned the belts and sewed on the buttons, for which they were paid fifteen cents a bundle. "We made a little money that way," my mother told Miss Brookie.

"*Very* little, I'd be inclined to say," Miss Brookie answered her. "Slave labor was all in the world it was." Next question. And how old was my mother when she did this?

Not quite eleven she had been. What had a young child been doing in a factory? my mother suddenly asked herself. A *child* in those awful places? Those crowded, airless, roaring lofts? Those places with the smells from unwashed bodies, from the same clothes worn day after day, from the foul toilets? My mother would say that out there on the picnic grounds, she had to give her head a good shake, to rid her ears of the noises and her nose of the smells.

In later years my mother often spoke of how she survived those days. It was because, first of all, all the children were doing it, not just her; then with the bundles, her family was around her; and when she got older, she was working with flowers, or at least what she saw as flowers. Or maybe, she said, it was that she had seen worse in the old country. In Russia children would have been glad to work, "to have what to eat," she explained. "But it was not right, none of it," she would say. "Children should have *naches* all day long, not *tsores*." Joy, not trouble.

My father was approaching the picnic table. Like the other men, he was dressed in a black serge suit and vest and a black fedora hat, but somehow he looked, well, softer around the edges. The others — their hats, pants, even their faces — seemed sharply creased, as if, my mother said, they had stretched out on ironing boards and been ironed.

The speeches were about to start, and Roscoe Pinder had already mounted the bunting-draped platform. As the crowd gathered, he declared himself grateful for the turnout, for the show of support, for the good wishes of friends and neighbors. He introduced Brother Jones, the minister of the First Congregational Church — a new church name for my mother.

She wondered to Miss Brookie if, being a minister, Brother Jones might speak out against hiring children.

"If you believe that, you believe the Easter bunny lays candy eggs with pink and green dots," Miss Brookie answered her.

My mother's eyes were on the ground all through what Brother Jones had to say, as he called upon God to bestow His blessings on the new factory and asked Him to do the same for the owner and the men. ("Why just men?" Miss Brookie was hissing. "Why leave out the *children?*")

Brother Jones had words about the goodness of honest toil ("And long hours?" Miss Brookie asked him sotto voce) and got all wrapped up in the joyous farmer with his plow and the happy carpenter with his saw, the latter "in the way of our Lord Himself," he said. When he arrived at "Let us bow our heads in prayer," my mother just kept her head down. He finally said, "In Jesus's name," and when everybody looked up, she did, too.

The preacher moved to the back of the platform, and from the grounds some kind of group all in white moved toward it. A play? my mother wondered. But what kind of play was this, with everybody in the same costumes and pointy hats down over their faces with just a couple of eyeholes? She nudged Miss Brookie.

"That bunch?" Miss Brookie expelled a "Foot!" — a word whose spelling is unknown to me but for expressing vexation, a favorite of Miss Brookie's and of all Concordians — and shot them a glance that would curdle milk, as Miss Brookie herself would have said. "The bedsheet brigade," she muttered to my mother.

There were about thirty bedsheets in all.

My father knew exactly who they were. They were the Ku Klux Klan. He had heard about them in Nashville, where there was talk that these Negro-hating, Jew-hating, Catholic-hating groups were coming back to life after a long period of dormancy. When my father had heard the talk, he had taken only a little notice, vaguely picturing them as operating in some faraway place, somewhere way out in the country. Uh oh, he suddenly thought. Wasn't he now in that faraway place, *in* that somewhere way out in the country?

He studied this curious bunch. Why the disguises? Even the Cossacks didn't wear disguises.

Ku Kluxers, in order to inspire fear, had to operate differently from Cossacks. Cossacks had only to be Cossacks to intimidate: They were tough soldiers who lived in barracks; Kluxers, being the guys next door, had to don sheets with eyeholes to transform the little man who delivered your milk into something that could scare somebody.

Miss Brookie scoffed at the disguises. She wondered how "old Vermin — excuse me, *Vernon* — Prendergast" expected to be anonymous. "Lord, that lumbago of his makes him walk like an anteater," she said.

One of the white-sheeted figures detached itself from the group and climbed the platform stairs. After a moment, a high voice filtered out through the sheet and greeted the crowd with "My white Christian brothers and sisters." It was a salutation that chilled my parents to the bone.

The voice then imparted how grateful was the community for the new facility, how thankful for "a place in which white Christians can labor and prosper." It concluded with the thought that "the Klan accepts proudly the responsibility for the factory staying forever free of foreign agitators who might want to upset our traditional ways." All was said "for God and the glory of His Kingdom and in the name of our Lord, Jesus Christ."

At last the figure reached a hand out from the sheet, touched the cone hat in a salute, lifted the skirts, and moved down the stairs.

My father first had to know what "white Christians" laboring and prospering meant. Why limit the hoped-for prosperity to whites? Did it perhaps mean there were to be no jobs for Negroes? If so, this would mean a Jew store without solid Negro trade, and this was impossible. The jitters starting, my father asked Miss Brookie, "No jobs for Negroes?"

No "white men's" jobs, Miss Brookie explained. There would still be Negro ones. "Toting crates and like that," she said.

And the salutation to "Christians"? "We sure ain't Christians," my father said. His elatedness of earlier was declining fast. And what about the dark reference to "foreigners"? "Ain't we foreigners?" he asked Miss Brookie. He had a small hope that by some formula the Bronsons would fall outside that description.

Miss Brookie was of some comfort. "Foreign agitators," Miss Brookie explained, was just a phrase the Klan had picked up from the pamphlets the organization sent around. "Truth is they wouldn't know a foreign agitator if one bit 'em on the rear while they were hymn-singing in church."

But all things considered, it seemed to my father that the Klan could take a very hard line on trading with him. "Ain't I got that correct?" he asked Miss Brookie.

This time all Miss Brookie said was, "We'll have to wait and see."

There was reason for her unwillingness to make a prediction. The opinion about Jews, not just among the Klan but among the town's general population, was very unsettled. On the one hand there was "this doggone international conspiracy," as people said, among Jewish bankers to control the world and those "infernal orders" Jews were under to kill all Christian babies. And of course there was the worst charge of all — that Jews had killed their Lord.

On the other hand there were the mitigating factors: the fact that their Lord was born Jewish and the fact that their Old Testament told them that Jews were God's chosen people. All this back and forthing, as Miss Brookie would have said, put their britches in a pretty serious knot.

Miss Brookie told my father that the local Kluxers *might* just carry out their Klan duty by exhorting folks to stay vigilant. "That's the going word — *vigilant*," she said. Her advice to him was to hope they forgot all about him, since they all knew they really needed a Jew store.

In the middle of all the conjecturing, picnickers were beginning to come around to get some of Miss Brookie's pie. "We always like to see what Brookie's whomped up," one woman said to my mother. "Her lemon meringue's a town treasure . . . like Minnie Horner's six-toed cat." The woman did a guffaw and winked at my mother.

My mother's eyelid defied a return wink. The best she could do was pull her lips up.

Still, she did think it strange that the pie

was talked of as Miss Brookie's when she knew for a fact that Lizzie Maud had made it — *fixed* it. She had watched Lizzie Maud at work, even saw the lard going into the crust. I had early on appointed myself the Lizzie Maud mimic, and what I imagined she had said in a severe teacher's tone on this occasion was, "Don't you be sassin' my lard, Miz Reva. You gots to have lard. With lard your crust don't stay in your mouth long enough to say 'How do.' "

Miss Brookie handed out slices of the pie — doing it slowly to ensure that the towering white meringue not come loose from its pale yellow moorings — while having a word with each seeker. "How you doing, Otis?" she would say. "Your new barn up yet?"

Meanwhile, my father was mulling things over. The Klan didn't like Catholics either. Could it be that the Klan would concentrate on Catholics and leave him alone? Not that he wished this bunch on anybody, but he certainly didn't wish it on *him*. Anyway, it was a foolish thought, as there were no Catholics in Concordia, had never been any, and perhaps never would be. Still, this didn't stop Concordians from believing Catholics to be a threat, and so Christians — Catholics were not considered Christians — must be constantly on guard.

The day had gone to twilight too quickly. What was my father to think about what had happened? It was different here in Concordia, he was finding out, different from Savannah and Nashville.

On the way home he stared silently at the road, feeling no desire now to offer encomiums to the beauties of the countryside. The others were quiet as well, and Harold Lloyd was back to desultory plodding, paying little attention to any light flicks my father might send his way.

My father could finally stand the gloom no longer. He put on a cheerful face and invited Miss Brookie to supper. He tempted her with gefilte fish. "How long's it been since you've had some?" he asked her.

"Too long," Miss Brookie answered him. And she would "adore" to come.

My father told my mother she had customers. As he found out, he had said the wrong thing.

My mother said yes, she had customers, but, feeling as cheerless as the darkening landscape, added, "Now let's hope you get some, too." But because this sounded too much like one of those little cold stones that she had hoped would never fall from her mouth again, she lifted up the corners of her mouth and said, "It will be all right, Aaron." But in her head she was saying, And if it ain't, then "tem-po-rary" will be sooner than later.

Chapter 12

Opening Day

According to Joey, he got up an hour early every day during the week before the store was to open and went out by himself in the wagon to pass out the handbills announcing the opening day. He says he studied the handbills beforehand, memorizing exactly what they said so that he could inform those unable to read. He did not want people just to accept one and then put it in the outhouse for further use.

It took him a long time. The houses in town were easy, and the factory was a snap — just a ride out to it. He left a pile there with Roscoe Pinder, who didn't exactly say he'd see that the men got them but didn't exactly say he wouldn't. Anyway, most of the men lived out in the country, and Joey was delivering out there as well. He also distributed the handbills to the churches and left some at the picture show.

On the farms, locating someone to hand

the handbills to took a bit of doing. Sometimes the ladies of the house were not in the
house but hanging out wash, or hoeing the
garden, or slopping the pigs; the men might
be out in the back forty behind a plow. Still,
whether they read the handbill for themselves
or had Joey read it to them, they were interested, though it could have been, Joey
thought, that what interested them the most
was the note at the bottom of the handbill,
which said FREE SOUVENIRS, or, to be accu-
rate, FREE SOUVENIERS.

At any rate, by the time Saturday rolled
around, Joey was sure that everyone in Concordia and surroundings had been put on notice that Bronson's Low-Priced Store would
be open for business from 8:30 A.M. sharp until 11:30 P.M.

My mother had selected the souvenirs. For
the men there were paper roses for the lapels
of their Sunday suits; for the women, floral
handkerchiefs; for the children celluloid pinwheels roughly resembling oversized, bicolored
chrysanthemums.

On the target Saturday — the Saturday after the factory had opened on Monday — the
long days of hauling and shelving and fixing
were over, and the store stood ready.

All the furnishings had come from the store
in Oliphant that had gone bust. Miss Brookie

177

had taken my father to the place where the bank was selling at rock-bottom prices the foreclosed furnishings, and in the pile of stuff, he had unearthed a lot of useful things, even a cash register. It was an impressive thing, with elaborate silvery scrollwork along the sides, and two wide drawers, one of which was for checks. This particular drawer would have to be assigned to other duty, as there would be no checks at Bronson's. The pay of the factory hands would be in cash, and they would pay Bronson's the same way. Farmers dealt in cash as well. Still, my father said, even then he was contemplating a future day when he might institute a charge system. Whenever he had this thought, he always added, "if the store goes" so as not to jinx anything, and knocked on wood (as if he were superstitious, which he was not, but "could it hurt?")

He set up the register on a tall table against a side wall. It overlooked the floor, which was crowded with counters and tables loaded high with pants and bolts of fabric and other soft goods. Even the ceiling was pressed into service: Bunches of handkerchiefs dangled down from it on strings.

Men's suits were upstairs in a cupboard behind tarlatan curtains that my mother had hemmed. She had done this by hand, sitting night after night enveloped in the dark gray stuff, like a small boat holding on in stormy seas, as my father described it. Upstairs also was a single dressing room, with a door, and by the window a three-way mirror with a narrow strip of rubber matting on the floor in front of it.

The rest of the upstairs floor, like the downstairs one, was carpetless, rugless, linoleumless, just its dark wood self. The downstairs was dominated by the women's department, which had the two dressing rooms my father had dreamed of — wood-partitioned ones made extraprivate with doors. Spivey had given in to my father's requests, though each concession was punctuated by a yelp of outrage. "You're just set on driving me to the poorhouse, ain't you, Bronson?" he would say.

Like the floors, the stairs were bare. Still, the mahogany banister had been sanded and varnished so that what had been pocked and pimply was now almost smooth.

Under the steps my father had managed something resembling a shoe department. In Oliphant he had come upon another find — a bench with shared arms, which he positioned as an area definer. It sat now in a welcoming mode, stools for clerks squatting at either side, and wooden foot-measurers hanging from the shelves above it.

The store's crowning glory was, of course, on the two front windows; each had BRONSON'S LOW-PRICED STORE spelled out in big gold letters. The name could be seen up and down the street, and on this opening day, in the sunny weather, the letters shone brightly. And, as my father had seen when he had gone to the store night after night before the opening, the gold letters gave off glints in the dark.

To wait on trade besides my father, there was my mother, Mrs. MacAllister (Billy Sunday with her), and Vedra Broome.

Vedra Broome was a former saleswoman of Spivey's. Spivey had recommended her, mainly because her husband worked at the plant. "She'll give you a one-two punch," he said to my father.

My father agreed, silently hoping he wouldn't also need a three-four.

My mother and Mrs. MacAllister were to take turns holding Billy Sunday, and if both got busy — when they said this, they exchanged something that passed for a smile — Billy Sunday would go into the feather-pillow bin.

On opening day my brother was to respond speedily to a summons from anyone; my sister, if she could be induced to take leave of the three-way mirror, was to hand out the souvenirs.

My father walked the store doing last-minute checking, moving from place to place, inspecting, tidying — picking up a flannel shirt here, a woman's hat there. He looked to see that price tags were correct, and readable.

Not everything had a price tag. The more expensive items, like suits and better dresses, would depend for prices on the clerk's knowledge of the markup and on his ability to hold his own in the early bargaining. In Jew stores, if the negotiations got hot, the owner would be called in: "Say, boss, Mr. Callcott here 'clares this suit is just what he had in mind, but he don't care too much for the price. I done told him the price is to the bone as 'tis. He says anythin' more you can do for him would surely be appreciated."

Everything my father had ordered had come, plus a few things he hadn't. Spanish combs, for example, had been sent by the wholesaler with a note scrawled on a magazine picture of a girl crowned with the long-toothed, elaborately crested ornament. "Latest craze, hot seller," the note said. "Try them on your yokels." St. Louis people always felt St. Louis served as the sophistication capital for several states, and maybe it did.

My mother was anxiously running language samples through her head. *Pin* and *pen* were pronounced the same, she already knew that. And *kindly?* Oh, yes. It meant not "considerately" but "sort of," so that a dress that was "kindly long" was not designed to hide leg defects but was "sort of" long; in other words, it needed shortening.

As eight-thirty came closer, the salespeople began to move about the floor. Conversation ceased; silence, tense silence, was all there was.

Suddenly there was a clatter at the back, and T burst in. Beside Erv there was with him a tall, skinny youth with the remnants of the telltale farmer's sunburn around his neck and forehead.

My father took his watch out of his vest pocket. Ten minutes. He walked over to the boys.

T introduced the boy with him. He was another "cudden," one named Nathan, who was "near nineteen years old" and who, according to T, had "never seen a Jew person in all his life" and, despite T's insistence to the contrary, was convinced that Jews had horns.

My father stood very still, hands at his sides, feet planted, and offered himself up. "Here I am, sonny. Here's your Jew," he said to Nathan.

Nathan stared. In a moment anguish surfaced. "But by golly, Mr. Bronson," he cried out, "you won't do atall!" Jews were *supposed*

182

to have horns. The Bible said so.

Hadn't Nathan noticed that Jew peddlers didn't have horns?

But Nathan had never seen a Jew peddler either. Every time a Jew peddler came to town, he said in a very aggrieved voice, by the time the news came out to where he lived way out in the country, the Jew peddler was on his way out again.

My father took out his watch, saw that there were seven minutes to go. In spite of it all, he was still able to banter. "I sure am sorry about the horns," he said to Nathan. "I got to tell you them kind of Jews have gone out of style. None of the new kind have horns."

My father thought to make it up to Nathan by giving the boys a little gift. Socks? What kind of treat was that for boys who wore shoes only when strictly necessary? As he mulled over possibilities, he told himself to be grateful for these little boys and this little problem, for this one moment of respite.

He reached behind a table, from a box pulled out three polka-dotted bow ties on elastic strings, and handed them around.

T took one, placed it around his neck, snapped it together, stretched it out with a forefinger, and let it pop back. Erv and Nathan did the same.

T said it "sure beats the fool" out of any tie

183

he'd ever seen; Nathan said, "I reckon you could pure slap the tar out of your neck if you put your mind to it." Erv said his usual nothing, just left with the boys, all of them pop-popping away.

At the register Carrie MacAllister, whose white skin was growing whiter by the minute, made a stiff little speech about when to expect the factory trade. "Not till after six," she said. "The whistle don't blow till six." She turned to Vedra Broome for confirmation. "Ain't that a fact, Miz Broome?"

Vedra Broome was just entering the circle around the register. "Mercy, I have no idea," she said, touching her headful of curls. It could not be missed that no matter how Vedra Broome moved, her headful of curls remained stationary. Closely resembling sausages confined in a sausage box, they were called — what could be more expected? — sausage curls.

Vedra Broome had never before worked in dry goods. All her experience had been in furniture. "But I do know one thing," she said to the group, repinning the fake camellia on the jacket of her dress, "and that is, don't look for quality trade. They wouldn't want anyone to see them over here."

When Vedra Broome said this, my mother understood Vedra felt she had gone down in

184

the world. Clerking in furniture was superior to clerking in dry goods, because divans — as sofas were called in Concordia — were a more prestigious item than, say, work pants.

"So who does that leave?" my mother asked of anyone who might answer. "Will somebody please tell me that?"

My father picked up the pinwheel lying next to the register. He blew hard on it, making it whirl madly. "That leaves plenty," he said, and since everyone was staring at him, he produced a smile. "We wasn't counting too much on the *quality* people anyways."

"So who's left?" my mother persisted, anxiety turning her voice up a notch or two.

My father said who was left were the farmers and the coloreds. "They'll keep us plenty busy till the shoe people come in." My father turned to the others. "Don't everybody agree?"

Only Mrs. MacAllister answered, and all she said was, "Let's hope so."

The conversation tapered off. It died altogether. And then my father's watch said eight-thirty. He gave a last glance at the counters and moved to the front door.

When he lifted the shade over the glass, he had a moment of doubt as to what he was seeing. Then there they clearly were — a crowd of people, a blur of faces, some

185

pressed against the glass.

He unlocked the door. In no time the crowd was swarming all over the store. My mother left the cash register. Mrs. Mac-Allister put Billy Sunday into the pillow bin. Everyone was rushing toward a customer.

My mother approached someone — a man. She pushed out the unfamiliar words "Can I help you?" The man shook his head and said he was just looking. When she turned to find another customer, she saw only children. Everywhere children — children running up and down the aisles, hiding under the counters, playing peekaboo in the dressing rooms.

In God's name what did it mean? The farmers were supposed to be there, so where were they? And everyone had said the coloreds would come, so where were *they?* There were not even any dark *children* in the store. The smiling faces next to the fluttering pinwheels were pale and freckled, and their smiles seemed to my mother to hold a secret.

She looked for my father and the others. They too were surrounded only by children.

My father called to Joey. He wanted him to go outside to see where everyone was. Maybe by some careless reckoning, no one had realized today was a holiday. "Go. Go now," he said to him. "See if there are people in town."

In a few moments Joey came running back. The town was full of people, he reported. "Even Dalrymple-Eaton's!"

Close to panic, my mother rushed up, to question Joey, to *challenge* him. She always said it was like her life depended on what Joey answered. She asked, as if angry with *him*, "So? So? And what did you see there? A few rich ladies? So tell me. You saw a few rich ladies?"

"Yes, Mama, yes! A few rich ladies!" The rich ladies had been in the coat department.

"Buying coats?"

Joey tried his best. "I didn't say buying, Mama! Maybe they weren't buying! Maybe they were just trying on!"

My mother's eyes gripped my brother's, willing him. "The other stores don't have no customers? Like ours?"

"No, no, you don't understand!" Joey has remembered being near to tears. How could everything have gone so wrong? But he knew he had to tell my mother the truth, and the truth was there were plenty of customers everywhere — everywhere but in our store.

My mother looked frantically around to find something comforting, something to tell her all was not lost. Everything only mocked her. As she said later, everything was telling her they had been fools. The tables so carefully laid out, the sizes meticulously in order so that no one would waste time, not the customer, not the clerk — why had they taken so many pains? The register with the beautiful silver sides — who needed anything so fancy? The handkerchiefs that my father insisted be fresh and white and arranged on their strings just so — who was there to notice them?

She walked to the front door and looked out. The register did not need her.

And then T was back in the store, come to see if Joey and Miriam could go with them to the picture show.

My mother had no patience for him. A reasoned decision was beyond her. It was easier to say, "No, T, no. We need them."

"Yes, ma'm," T said to her. And then his eyes flicked up in the way they did when you knew, my mother said, that he "couldn't believe nothing what you were saying." "You need them *now?*" he asked her.

Mrs. MacAllister came forward. She reported that the children were finally leaving. "Maybe now we can have some peace and quiet," she said.

According to my father, if there was one thing they didn't need at that moment, it was peace and quiet.

Joey asked T if he couldn't stay and then go to the next show. T said he couldn't and tried to explain the Saturday picture-show routine. How it worked, he said, was "you kindly eases yourself in" and see the serial while the others were out buying with their folks. "The others see it first," he said, "and it takes the fire pure out of it."

Mrs. MacAllister, listening to T, suddenly knew why the farmers hadn't been in. The answer was that they were out buying their important stuff — their feed, seed, "their living, other words," she said. And they did their "personal shopping" in the afternoons.

"I ain't sure I'm on the same page as you, Mrs. Mac," said my father, "but I sure hope you're reading the words right."

A few people trickled in. My father took out his watch: four minutes to twelve. And here came Miss Brookie, a basket lifted high and saying, "I brought some lunch, but I wouldn't complain a speck if y'all were too busy to eat it."

My father said customers weren't exactly knocking them down. He took a chicken leg and napkin and asked if Carrie MacAllister had it right, and Miss Brookie agreed. After the farmers bought their "necessities," they'd eat their dinners in the courthouse park, and then, she said, "You might look for them to come in."

Might. My father took notice of the word.

My mother came over and refused a deviled egg. "On such a day, how can I eat?" she asked of nobody in particular. Among her worries were the "coloreds." None had been in.

Easy to explain, Miss Brookie said. They were waiting on the Klan, hanging around on First Street to see what the Klan was up to. If a Kluxer walked into Bronson's with his family, the Negroes would take this as the sign that they could do the same.

This consoled my mother not at all. She used to say she rubbed her hands so much on this day, she thought both skin and bones would disappear. *"Oyoyoy,"* she said to Miss Brookie. "So much worry before somebody comes in to buy something."

"But what if the Klan don't put its okay?" My father's nervousness had turned the word into the long-discarded "hokay."

Miss Brookie said that "without the *hokay*," the Klan would take action long about suppertime. "Just drape themselves in muslin and march," she said.

"March?" My mother, in her innocence, was slightly buoyed by the idea of a march. In 1909 she and her family had attended a parade to commemorate Henry Hudson's discovery of the Hudson River, and it had been through the years one of her proudest memories. How glorious the celebrated Goldman band had been, with sunlight glinting off tubas, and white uniforms sparkling as the men stepped smartly down Fifth Avenue, playing with gusto, aware they were thrilling the crowd. "There'll be a parade?" she asked Miss Brookie.

Miss Brookie, as if reading my mother's mind, said this was not going to be like any parade my mother might have seen. No, this one would be men in grubby sheets shuffling down First Street. And for music, only whoops and hollers from the crowd.

Where they would march *to* was to our store. My father always said that at these words he could feel his face go pale, and when Miss Brookie said they'd want to paint a cross on the store's window, since they wouldn't want to *burn* one on First Street, he felt his whole body go pale. And here was this lady, this Miss Brookie, being so unexcited, so calm, so . . . goyish.

My father wondered if there wasn't something they could do, somebody they could talk to, and Miss Brookie, in her unruffled way, said no, there wasn't, and that my father should "disabuse" himself of the idea that they would listen to *her*, whom they trusted, she said, "about as much as a goat in the gladiolas."

As predicted, the farmers came in. They came in a surge; everyone had work to do. The farmers were eager to buy. The children needed shoes, the women needed yard goods, the men needed work pants and shirts. They needed, they needed; and since times were good, they bought. Joey was moving quickly to replenish, and Miriam was busy with her souvenirs.

It was clear the farmers were delighted to have such a store to trade in. One man, eyes squinting as if he were still in the field under a glaring sun, told my father, "Lord help us if Miz Turnpaugh ain't been as excited as a pup. I reckoned if you didn't open up soon, I'd have to ice her down."

My father's banter was unflagging: "You the one with that nice-looking farm out on the south road?" he might say. "With that fine stand of cotton? And the cows everybody says give such good milk? Well, you'll want some shirts I got in mind. You don't want those cows to be handsomer than you. Right over here, sir." The customers, perhaps reserved at first, ended up laughing, joking back, buying.

Miss Brookie was taking it all in, but my father knew she was thinking that yes, it was nice to see all the farmers, but if the Klan turned thumbs down, they wouldn't be seeing them for long. As for the factory workers, they wouldn't even *appear* until the Klan said it was okay.

So as he turned from one customer to the other, my father would say he had one eye fixed on First Street, and once or twice he thought he saw sheeted figures on the cobblestones.

The day wore on, the farmer families came in fewer numbers. Tom Dillon came in, Miss Brookie gave him a word, and he gave a word back. After a sweeping look, he walked out again.

Did Miss Brookie have any ideas on Dillon? "I notice he didn't drop any money on us," my father told her.

Miss Brookie thought Dillon was probably just looking to see who was there. And hoping to find the store empty. And it was a kind of shame that it wasn't because if nobody was there, he might decide it wasn't worth the trouble.

Trouble? My father felt a renewed paleness.

The trouble it took to start up the Klan, Miss Brookie said.

This was new information: Tom Dillon was a Kluxer? "Him?"

"Sure, him. He's a leading light. When he gives the word, sheets start flapping." Apparently there wasn't a "white soul in town" who didn't "run with" the Klan — farmers, factory workers, the lot. Miss Brookie had the ultimate example: the Baptist minister who had been the Klan chaplain. There was a story that went with this — the man had eloped with the choir soloist, leaving behind a wife and four children. It was a story that, had it come from Carrie MacAllister, Miss Brookie would have called gossip, but since it came from her, she called an illustration of the town's sociology.

Six o'clock neared. If anything was going to happen, it would happen pretty soon. My father thought Joey and Miriam would be better off in the picture show, but what if they got busy (was it possible they would get busy?) and needed them?

They waited, Miss Brookie in the shoe department holding Billy Sunday in her lap; Mrs. MacAllister having an exchange with a customer; Vedra Broome upstairs eating; my mother sitting rigidly on her register stool; and my father, whenever free, positioning himself at the front door.

He was there when the door pushed open and a stranger in a blue shirt and dark pants came in, trailed immediately by a wife and several children.

Miss Brookie, Billy Sunday held in front of her like an offering, darted forward. From her lips came an impassioned cry. "Wister! Wister

Rankin! Why bless your heart!"

Wister Rankin, though clearly puzzled by this ardent welcome, got out a big-toothed grin that opened up most of his face.

Mrs. Rankin grinned also. The children glued their eyes to Miss Brookie, plainly hoping she would do something else outrageous.

Miss Brookie's greeting was endless. "It's just so *good* to see you!" She grabbed Miriam's box. "Here, take some pretties."

"Already got some," Mrs. Rankin said.

"Then take some more."

Wister offered that they had been looking forward to the opening like to Christmas. "Yes, ma'am," he said, "And I'll probably spend my last dime here, too." He laughed.

Miss Brookie laughed with him, heartily, as if he had made the funniest possible joke. "That's really so funny," she said, and laughed harder still.

What Miss Brookie was laughing at, my father, standing beside her and listening, had no clue. What did this wild laughter mean? Could it be that Miss Brookie was going to pieces? Had she at last, as she had always predicted, been pushed over the edge by the people she had to deal with, people who had the imagination of that concrete orb in her yard, as she would say?

Wister was expressing a desire to meet "the

195

man"; and Miss Brookie swallowed hard and at last got her laughter under control. She reached out and pulled my father into the group.

When she did the introductions, she also *mentioned* — nailing my father, he later said, with a look about as delicate as "a *klop* to the chops" — that Wister worked at the shoe factory. So the Klan had come to their decision, and it had been to do nothing. It was then that my father was able to fathom Miss Brookie's hitherto unfathomable laughter. It had been the laughter of relief.

My father's hand went forward and he said to Wister, "A real pleasure. . . . What can I show you?"

Miss Brookie asked Wister to excuse them and pulled my father into the shoe department, where she stood looking at him. They exchanged victory smiles. "You did it, Aaron, you did it," she said.

That night there were plenty of sales for all. Nobody, of course, had more than my father. As the evening wore on, he took off his coat, and in his shirtsleeves with the rubber band on the sleeves to hold the cuffs up and keep them clean, he was here, there, everywhere. It was nothing for him to outfit the whole family from father to baby, then to go outside to the family wagon, pull out Grandma and Grandpa, and outfit them as well. He was a sal-es-man doing what a sal-es-man did best.

In the kitchen that night, Miss Brookie had one more instructional tale. As she passed around Lizzie Maud's pineapple upside-down cake, she told everybody she had "divined" the reason the Klan hadn't marched, that it had to do with the competition between Dillon and Spivey. "Thing's this," she said. "In the Klan Spivey's got muscles about as big as Tom's." And since Dillon and Spivey got along "like spinach and peach preserves in the same jar," if Dillon wanted the Klan to march, Spivey would be hell-bent to see that they didn't.

It sounded plausible, but my father had another theory. His had to do with the "accordin' thing" that Spivey had tacked on to the lease. With the "accordin' thing" operating, if my father did well, Spivey did well. It was as simple as that. Anyway, he told Miss Brookie, whatever was the reason, it was a good night.

To which Miss Brookie laughed and said, no, it was not a good night *entirely*.

So why not an entirely good night?

Because, Miss Brookie said, my father now had to pay her four dollars a week rent. "Into each life some rain must fall," she said, and gave my father a wink.

My father used to say there wasn't much Miss Brookie could tell him about rain falling that he didn't already know, but on this night, with all the money that was in the register and all the customers who had left happy, he didn't point this out, just winked back, and said, "My pleasure."

And when my father went to bed that night and thought it all over, what he really wanted to believe was that the Klan hadn't marched because Concordia truly needed a Jew store.

Chapter 13

In Christ's Name, Amen

I've been told that in the days following the store's opening, business stayed up and anxieties went down, though of course my mother always had a little stock of anxieties she could turn to, and she now turned to Joey's school. In Tennessee, children started school at seven, Joey was seven, and the first day of school was approaching. The opening date, however, was later than in New York, as in Tennessee harvest time was taken into account.

She was anxious about all manner of things: first of all, whether the teachers would like Joey, though, as she said to her invisible third person while giving Joey's cheek a forceful pinch, "What could there be about my Joey not to like except he's Jewish?" — at the same time trying to ignore my father's look. She fretted about who Joey would play with, knowing the answer — Gentiles, of course; and about what, in this little town, the children wore to school. In New York pupils wore uniforms — navy blue knickers, white shirts, and ties blue or red; girls wore navy blue skirts, white middie blouses, and also red or blue ties. But here? Did they dress as if for church? Or was it farm clothes? In which case were shoes considered an urban affectation?

T arrived on the first morning of school, to see to things. Though himself in starched and sharply ironed overalls and high-topped, thick-soled shoes, he pronounced Joey's corduroy knickers and high-topped, *thin*-soled shoes "fitting." Erv was dressed the same as T. Though not a pupil in the technical sense, Erv was allowed to be in school and share T's seat. He wouldn't go "for real" until next year.

My mother spotted another opportunity for worry: T was carrying a book satchel. When my mother looked stricken, Miss Brookie rushed around and found a satchel in her attic. Its leather was dry, its color like bread mold, its buckles rusted. My mother gave it a quick scrub job, scouring it with Old Dutch Cleanser, then finishing off with neat's-foot oil from an old bottle Lizzie Maud had found.

My brother has always said he was of two minds about the satchel: It was pitiful looking, he remembers — and Miriam has backed him up on this — but he knew my mother was eager that he have what the others had. Maybe it *was* true, as my mother thought for as long as she lived, that Joey had a special way of feeling her feelings, as they say now; it was obvious to all of us that even if he didn't exactly share her feelings, he always took them into account. Perhaps the fact that he looked like my mother — he had her freckly fair skin and short features — carried with it this responsibility. So he said yes, Mama, he would carry the satchel.

"And it's clean enough they won't call you 'dirty Jew,' " she said, out of anybody's hearing, specifically out of my father's.

My mother was going along to school to register Joey. She had wanted my father to do this, but he was busy at the store and anyway would have said that she should "take every opportunity" to meet people.

The school, called Westerly, was three blocks away. My mother and the boys walked to it as a little band, T in front with Joey, Erv a pace behind, my mother trailing.

The school was a stubby building of red brick, set on about two acres of land. The principal, a large woman with dark hair tucked over an encircling "rat" and with a shirtfront stiffly protruding, met the little band at the door. "Mattie Barksdale," she said to my mother. "How do."

My mother said "How do" back.

Miss Mattie, as she was called even in my day — though in the intervening years she had married and was no longer "Miss" at all — took my mother and Joey into her office while T and Erv went on. When my mother told Miss Mattie that Joey had been born in New York, Miss Mattie said to her, "Mercy, such a lot he'll have to tell the others."

And they'll have such a lot to tell *him,* my mother thought. "Yes, maybe," she said to Miss Mattie.

The very next question was about church. Miss Mattie said she "understood" that Joey was Jewish. "Too bad we have no church for him here in Concordia," she said to my mother.

She laughed then and said that Concordia had every church "known to man" except a Jewish one. This was not quite true, as there was no Catholic Church in Concordia, but if she meant every *Protestant* church, she was on firmer ground, though there was no Episcopal one. "He'll just have to wait till a Jewish church gets built, I reckon," Miss Mattie said to my mother.

That eventuality, in my mother's view, was so unlikely as to be nothing to talk about. She knew, and she knew this lady knew, there was not going to be any Jewish "church." And it was at that moment, my mother always suggested, that she understood with piercing clarity that among the great ships in the religious Concordia mainstream, the Bronsons didn't even have a rowboat.

After the registration my mother left, and Joey followed Miss Mattie out into the square hall. Four rooms — for grades one through four — came off it. Miss Mattie led him into the first-grade room and handed him over to Miss Nannie Temple — the same Miss Nannie Temple who would later preside over my first grade — and she motioned for him to sit in an empty seat at the back.

After Miss Nannie had added Joey's name to her roll, the class went out to recess, which was a period in the morning when the pupils were let out to play in the yard. It had been arranged that T, who was in the second grade, was going to "spring" Joey at this time.

Joey went out with the others, aware that they were whispering and shooting him looks. After what seemed to him a very long time, Miss Mattie climbed up the school's back stairs. On the landing she clapped her hands, and everyone gathered. She had several announcements, the first being that Friday was to be a field day that would take them to the firehouse and the icehouse. The pupils were to pack lunches, though not sliced tomatoes.

If any of their mothers still had tomatoes, Miss Mattie said, they were not to slice them, since sliced tomatoes "squish bad."

The next announcement was that there was a lost-and-found something. Miss Mattie held it up, and Joey saw a chain on which dangled a small object. In the bright morning light, he made out the small object to be a cross.

Miss Mattie asked, "Who lost this pretty thing?" and a hand went up. As the cross and chain were passed along to a reunion with their owner, Joey, who was always pleased to have a chance to check out anything animal, vegetable, or mineral, held it for a moment. This was interesting, he thought — his first hands-on experience with a cross. After he had gleaned whatever information the cross had to offer him, he set it to swinging on its chain and passed it on. A simple thing, he thought; just two rods, one horizontal, one vertical, in this case stamped out of a nice piece of silver.

There were a couple of other announcements, the most important being that Chautauqua was coming to town, the signs for which Joey had already seen on that first trip out to the shoe factory. Chautauqua continued on in my time. It was where we heard classical music and saw plays that weren't acted by locals, and heard about such things as the latest in Egyptian tomb finds. This year, according to Miss Mattie, there was to be a talk on the principle of radio waves, and she thought everybody ought to make a "special effort," though everybody always went to Chautauqua, with or without Miss Mattie's reminder.

Up on the landing Miss Mattie motioned for T to join her, and he bounded up the stairs. Even if everybody already knew Joseph Bronson was in school, T said, there was still a surprise. He pointed to Joey, told him to hold up his hand, and proclaimed, according to Joey, "Doggone if you ain't lookin' at a Jewboy!"

All heads turned. Joey has always said his arm went up, but then, as if it had a mind of its own, went right back down. After a bit, heads turned back to T, but instead of the cheers that T had clearly expected, there were only murmurs.

If T was elated to include a "Jewboy" on the school's rolls, it was a feeling directly attributable to the mentoring of Miss Brookie, though T had perhaps missed the lecture that cautioned against saying "Jewboy." By this point in his life T was convinced that everything his "cudden" Brookie did or thought was exactly how to do or think, as if it were not a man's world but Cudden Brookie's. She said "Nigra" instead of "nigger"? He was already working up to "Nigra," with "darky" as a transition. She had gone to college? He aspired to the same. She liked strangers? Well, so did he.

James Lovelace, on the other hand, had not been mentored by Miss Brookie but by his farmer father, Ollie Lovelace, who would have said that the school was not so much lucky to have a "Jewboy" as doomed. Standing among the pupils, the son was now delivering this thought, along with a gratuitous blast at T. "You don't have no more upstairs than a field nigger, T Medlin," he was saying. And then came his main message: "Don't you know all them Jews is *Catholics?*"

At this murmurs went up — some of agreement, some no doubt of bewilderment — and James Lovelace continued on. "And everybody knows a Catholic takes his orders from Rome," he said. "From the Pope. Just ask my daddy."

Miss Mattie pushed past T and, perhaps seeking to drive as small a wedge as possible between James and his father but also seeking to shed some light, said gently that Jews were Jews and Catholics were Catholics, and, furthermore, not everybody went to the churches they went to. "There's lots of other religions in this world," she said to the pupils. Joey wondered at the time if she would make some sort of judgment about this, as my mother might have thought, but the principal said nothing more.

Mary Cantey Dalrymple raised her hand. The talk was about religion, and, as everybody knew, Mary Cantey had a special problem in this area, her family being Episcopalians in a town where there was no Episcopal church, and they were therefore forced to go to the Methodist one. "We could be anything we want," Joey has recalled Mary Cantey saying, "but Mama says the Episcopal Church is where we belong. . . . You know, us being so rich and all."

Miss Mattie then bowed her head and called upon the others to do the same. When she began, "We beseech you, O Lord . . . ," Joey moved to the fringes of the crowd, and he heard her say, "We ask this in Christ's name, amen," just as the bell clanged, ending recess.

According to Miriam, on the day Joey registered for school, Miss Brookie had rescued her from a fate worse than death — having no one to play with. As the others had struck out for Westerly, Miriam has remembered being left sitting on the platform swing feeling "utterly forsaken" — an expression she learned from Miss Brookie and has never let go of.

Miriam had been thinking that maybe girls were not allowed to go to school in Concordia, but Miss Brookie assured her that they were, even if, she said, some folks had "grievous misgivings."

She had a suggestion: Miriam would become a "Sunshine Girl." "Honey," she said, "we're going to have us a high old time. Just you let these old boys go their way."

The Sunshine Girls turned out to be an important part of Miriam's life and, later, of mine. It was where Miriam met the girls she played with, the same girls who matured into the crowd she "ran with." It was where I played with my friends as well, though I never "ran with" any of them, as I left Concordia before I got old enough to be said to "run with" anybody.

Sunshine Girls was a kind of club for girls who were too young for school. It gathered every weekday morning for arts and crafts, which consisted sometimes of pasting pieces of wallpaper to jars, outlining the pieces in India ink, and calling the result a vase; and sometimes of winding and gluing straw or yarn around and around until we claimed it had turned into something.

At any rate, on this first day of Joey's school, when Miss Brookie said, "Let's go, precious," Miriam jumped off the swing, took Miss Brookie's hand, and headed with her for the Sunshine Girls.

They walked quickly through several streets before stopping in front of a tall white building with a long thin pole rising into the sky.

"First Presbyterian Church," Miss Brookie announced.

They descended into the basement and into a large room where ten or twelve little girls were sitting in a circle on the floor. As Miriam and Miss Brookie entered, the girls lifted their heads and stared. The room was murky, as if a fog had entered and never left, and Miss Brookie declared it a "mighty curious setting" for Sunshine Girls.

She introduced Miriam to the lady sitting in the chair — Miss Clara — then waved to Miriam, and went out.

Miss Clara asked Miriam to tell about herself — her last name, what she liked to do, what church she was in, and "like that."

A lot of questions for a five-year-old, but Miriam tried. "Bronson," she said in answer to the first item on Miss Clara's list and set herself to thinking what the next one had been. Oh, yes. "And I like to play," she said. Now for the last one, about the church. In the event Miss Clara was testing how smart she was, Miriam tried to remember what Miss Brookie had told her and answered, "I'm in the First Presbit."

This is a joke the family always enjoyed: Miriam would say to us, "Well, wasn't I *in* the First 'Presbit' Church?" and we would all agree that she had been.

Of course, Miss Clara wasn't asking about what church Miriam was presently *sheltered* in but what church she *attended*. And when she asked if Miriam was a Presbyterian, Miriam reports herself as having been "totally nonplussed."

The girls were no help. They were just staring at her, waiting for her answer. "Not this one?" she asked Miss Clara.

"If you do, you're a Presbyterian."

Miriam thought that didn't sound right.

"Then what are you? A Baptist? A Methodist? An Episcopalian?"

None of those sounded right either.

"You're not Jewish by any chance?"

Finally! "Yes," Miriam cried. "Jewish!"

"Then you can't go to this church," Miss Clara said to her. "You have to go to the Jewish church. Once you're Jewish, you're always Jewish, and that's the church you have to go to."

Miriam felt her heart falling. "Then I can't play here?"

She held her breath until Miss Clara answered, until Miss Clara said, "Course you can."

"Here, here!" yelled one little girl in the circle of girls — who turned out to be Vadah Fay Pridgen, one of the enduring members of Miriam's crowd — and she patted the spot next to her.

When Miriam got home, according to how she has told it through the years, she went straightaway to Miss Brookie and told her what Miss Clara had said, that since she was Jewish, she would stay that way. She had been turning the thought over, that something was *forever*. Was it like my mother's freckles, Miriam wondered, which no creams rubbed off and my mother saying that she guessed she'd die with them?

Miss Brookie worked hard at clearing up for Miriam what Miss Clara had told her. Though Miriam has always claimed to be able to remember *exactly* what Miss Brookie said, she will, when challenged, say that it was what Miss Brookie "most assuredly *would* have said." At any rate, what Miss Brookie was said to have said was that Protestants could change religions but Jews weren't allowed that privilege. As Miriam has told it, Miss Brookie said, "Protestants can join and

211

unjoin churches like they're samplin' preserves at the fair, but if a Jew becomes a Hottentot and takes to stammerin', folks will say he's still a Jew and always will be." If Miss Brookie didn't say exactly this, we all agreed that she *might* have.

Chapter 14

A Gleam in My Mother's Eye

My mother always said that I was born because Lizzie Maud said I should be. Where Lizzie Maud had said this was on the porch, on which my mother had taken to sitting for lack of anything to occupy her since Joey and Miriam were in school, and since, though the store was thriving in the year since it had opened, she was needed there only on Saturdays and rush days. She had spoken to my father about this wish for something to do, and was he any help? No, he had said she had a job — to be happy.

Miss Brookie was not much help either. With an "I'm gone," she was out of the house and on one of her missions. On the day of Lizzie Maud's suggestion she was down at the depot picking up her three-times-a-year order of books, and then going on to deposit them in the library — actually a one-room house near the courthouse. She herself had established the library and hired Miss Wilma as librarian, though she was not entirely satisfied with Miss Wilma: Miss Wilma refused to reject the religious tracts and treatises people kept dropping off ("The library looks for all the world like the waiting room for God's own office," Miss Brookie would say), and Miss Wilma's view of a book's suitability did not always coincide with hers. As to the latter, Miss Brookie made a habit of dropping by the library *unexpectedly* to make sure the books she had placed on the shelves were still on them.

Spending her time visiting was not a viable choice for my mother. Though she greeted the neighbors when she saw them in the yard, there was no visiting with them. Miz Earp, who lived to the south, was a very old lady whose only companion was a dog. She spoke warmly to her dog but, as far as my mother could judge, had social exchange with no other living thing, unless it was the Spanish bayonet plants in her front yard, which she carefully tended, doubtless because under them were the remains of two previous pet dogs. She spoke not a word to my mother in response to her greeting, just gave a quick jerk of her head. Later, there would be no welcome for my playmates and me either, even though, when we cut across her yard, we never went near the bayonet plant area and indeed wouldn't have gone near it with a pole, as we would have said. No, there was no visiting with Miz Earp.

Miz Ezell lived behind. My mother was even less drawn to Miz Ezell, chiefly because her Southern accent was so thick that whatever she said gave my mother a pounding headache, and my mother gave up quickly on Miz Ezell.

As to the Gaskins across the street, it had been Lizzie Maud who had discouraged a visit over there. They were not for visiting; they were, Lizzie Maud had informed my mother one day, white trash.

My mother had not met the Gaskins. She had observed that there were a lot of them, what she took to be parents and children, grown and not grown.

Still, from what she had heard about white trash, the Gaskins didn't seem to fit. She had it in her head that white trash were poor people living on the other side of the railroad tracks, whose "menfolks" sometimes turned up for work and sometimes didn't, who sat on back porches all day Saturday and drank "moonshine," whose yards were full of cast-off mechanical items and old iceboxes. None of this figured in the Gaskin way of life. So, my mother had wondered, in what way were they white trash?

They were white trash, Lizzie Maud had said, because of the most recent Gaskin baby. Hadn't my mother noticed that Miz Gaskin was past her time to have babies?

My mother had put together a picture of Miz Gaskin, of a wrinkly woman with gray hair caught in a tiny fist of a bun. Yes, the lady was definitely past her time for babies.

There had been no way for my mother to prepare for what she had then heard. The baby, Lizzie Maud had said, her voice dropping low, wasn't "Mr. and Miz Gaskin's atall," but Mr. Gaskin's and Miss Evelyn's.

My mother's brain had gone reeling. Miss Evelyn, my mother knew, was a Gaskin daughter. A father having a baby with his daughter? "That can't be!" she had cried, thinking, hoping, it was just something somebody had only "suspicioned."

Lizzie Maud had given a grunt of scorn. Had somebody made up Miss Evelyn "all the time" sitting on her daddy's lap? And Miss Evelyn going round with "a belly big as a peach basket?"

My mother had been struck dumb. Was it possible? Where was she? In Sodom? In Gomorrah? No, she was in this . . . this . . . *Concordia.* She didn't care that my father said these things went on everywhere; she was convinced that Concordia had more than its share. And, maybe, isolated and insular as it was, it did.

On the day of the "suggestion," Lizzie Maud came out on the porch, an empty pot in one hand, an apronful of snap beans gathered up in the other, and settled across from my mother on the porch swing.

Lizzie Maud wanted to know why my mother was "sitting up but not taking no notice." She said, "If you don't move once in a while, you gwine seize up."

My mother was glad to have Lizzie Maud join her. She had gotten so she understood most of what Lizzie Maud said, and she could talk to Lizzie Maud about children and household matters. Of course, when the subject got around to household matters, a vision of Lizzie Maud's sack immediately made its appearance. *Oy,* that sack. A "torn" in her side. And what should she do? Start something she didn't know how it would end? No, she kept telling herself, it was not her business.

"Stop this foolishment, sitting here being lonesome," Lizzie Maud said to my mother. She dropped a handful of beans into my mother's lap and said, "Here. Help me snap these," her "help" being "hep." My mother snapped, tossing the snapped beans into

Lizzie Maud's pot. Lizzie Maud, according to my mother, sat, snapped, and looked pensive. In another moment came the proposal: "Whyn't you have you another baby?" she said. "You know, to get you to feeling you got a place for yourself."

My mother decided immediately to talk it over with my father. I was finally to be a topic for discussion.

The moment to talk about it came when my mother was helping out in the store on the first day of the Easter rush. The day started like any Monday morning, with my father going to the bank before the bank was open, knocking on the door, and being admitted by the head teller, Mr. Hedgepeth. Mr. Hedgepeth would then offer, "Morning, Mr. Bronson. Looks like our calendar ain't lying. You're here so must be Monday all right," and my father would reply, "Yes, sir, time to deposit the Bronson millions."

Once in the bank, my father would walk across the brown wooden floor to the tellers' windows in the back and plop down a small cloth bag containing Saturday's receipts. Afterward, back in the store, he would pull out his checkbook and write a check for five dollars to my grandfather.

My mother, watching on this particular Monday, felt a sudden rush. So stirred was she by my father's writing of the check to her father, so joyful, she blurted it out. She told my father that she wanted to have another baby. My father took it in stride. If my mother wanted another child, with business so good, why should he object? That's what you want?" he said to my mother. "So that's what you'll have."

My mother knew she was pregnant when the smell of Lizzie Maud's breakfast bacon gave her true nausea rather than just the usual queasiness. On the other hand, my mother's own breakfast did not go down well with Lizzie Maud. She would shower my mother with cautions and admonitions. "I swan, Miz Reva, you is the color of whitewash," she might say. "You best eat some of this here breakfast meat before you scare the chickens."

Though for church Lizzie Maud's hair was ironed and straight, at work it was either caught up in the rag snippets my family had seen on that first day or braided into short and numerous pigtails that stuck out like twigs on a newly plowed field. Holding a piece of "breakfast meat" in front of my mother, she would say, "Do you a sight more good than that mess you eat." My mother's "mess" would be either soda crackers crushed in milk

— which Lizzie Maud predicted would turn my mother into a "lick of chalk" — or the crappies that neighborhood fishermen were always bringing by — which, if too many of *them* were eaten, would turn my mother into a "puny slippy thing with fins going every whichaway."

It was a little later in the pregnancy that my mother had a caution of her own. She had come fully awake during the middle of one night with the realization that they had made no plans for a boy baby. A boy! A boy had to be circumcised! *Oy!*

"Aaron! Aaron! Listen to me!" my mother cried out on that night to my father, shaking him hard. "We can't have no baby!" "What are you talking?" My father was finally awake and looking at my mother, my mother used to say, as if pregnancy had made her lose her mind. "We're having it. How can we not?"

The possibility of having a baby with a penis was the problem. A *bris* — the ceremony at which the snipping of the foreskin of the penis is . . . is the word here *celebrated?* — would have to be held. "But what if it has a *putzel?*" my mother shouted, leaping out of bed and charging about the room. "We got to *do* something!"

My father told her to stop galloping, that

everybody would think they had Willy in the room.

Actually, in Nashville there was a *mohel* — a religious functionary whose job it was to perform circumcisions according to the rites and regulations — who made a practice of going to little towns when his services were required.

So Joey, my father said, would write to the rabbi, to alert him, and when the time came, a long-distance call would be made. Everything settled, my father told my mother to come back to bed.

My mother had started to climb back in when another alarm went off. How could they have a circumcision without a minyan, the ten men needed for the ceremony?

My father said so there wouldn't be ten men, there'd be just him: "The *mohel* will forgive us."

But what about the *bris?* What would people say about a *party* for cutting off a piece of a penis? "Like savages they'll say the Bronsons are," my mother said to my father.

The next morning, before school, Joey wrote to the rabbi. When the letter was finished, my father, handwriting being a big thing to my parents, took time to approve eight-year-old Joey's. Joey's penmanship followed the Palmer method being taught in

221

school, which allowed a couple of curls here and there but in the main was neat and precise, with all the letters leaning to the right like trees bending to the wind. My father much admired Joey's handwriting, since his own had remained unruly despite the efforts of the Savannah girls to teach him Palmer. But it remained for Miriam's to capture my father's highest praise. When it came her turn to learn, she too was taught Palmer, but she soon developed a style of her own, one so abounding in frills and furbelows, the words danced off the page. It was perhaps what a graphologist would have described as Spencerian revisited. She cared not at all that this brought her a D in penmanship, and neither did my father. He loved her exuberant style, and, perhaps in homage, his paraph — "that wavy thing when you sign your name," my mother called it — grew ever more baroque.

When the doctor came on a cold early morning in February of 1922, all the planning went pretty much out the window. With my father and Miss Brookie and Lizzie Maud standing by, my mother delivered not a someone sporting a little *putzel,* but an unadorned baby girl. I was finally on the scene. And with me came those semi-obligatory Cossack features.

My naming followed the Jewish custom of honoring deceased relatives, and so it was that my first name, Stella, came from my father's grandmother, Sprintza, which my parents took upon themselves to Americanize, and my middle name came from my mother's Aunt Raizel, Americanized into Ruth. And, following Miss Brookie's dictate ("The itty bit of sugar is a Southerner, don't you know"), everybody called me Stella Ruth.

Chapter 15

Two Social Calls

Of course I don't have much of a grip on the first couple of years of my existence, and what little I do remember may well not be actual memory at all but family lore, so often told. I know that my father's store was prospering and that whatever my mother's continued grievances, he at least was well satisfied with existence in a town in northwestern Tennessee. As for my brother and sister, they were happy with the town, their playmates, and just about everything else in their young lives.

We lived in Miss Brookie's house for several years after I was born. As I progressed from a bassinet (once Billy Sunday's) in my parents' room to a crib (likewise previously owned by Billy Sunday) in the other bedroom, Joey was put on the "Victorian affliction" divan (buttressed by pillows and quilts) in the front room, where every morning he woke the house by plunking on the harp, thereby producing what Miss Brookie called "a little twelve-tone number from Schoenberg."

The harp was in the corner of the front room behind the grand piano. It was golden and much admired, though Lizzie Maud had given up dusting it — "all them teeny tweeny places" — and there was now, as she would grumble to anyone in hearing distance, dust on it so thick "you could plant 'gemiums.'" She would say, "That thing don't belong in our front room nohow." Where it belonged, according to Lizzie Maud, was in the funeral parlor.

Miss Brookie didn't play on the harp anymore. Required too much muscle, she said, so she indulged her musical yearnings on the piano. She played whenever she had a moment and in a transported way, throwing her head back and closing her eyes, oblivious to the fact that her sheet music had slipped to the floor.

If Joey was trying to compete as a harpist with Miriam as a pianist, he had a long way to go. Miriam's daily afternoon piano lessons from Miss Brookie had convinced Miss Brookie that she had talent. Miss Brookie "vowed and declared" that Miriam was truly gifted. "And so *devoted*," she would say. "Bless my soul if she doesn't practice on her own *volition,* if you can feature such a thing."

On occasional evenings we had a recital — what Miss Brookie called a "soiree" — when Miriam played her pieces for an hour or so. Never mind Miriam's talent: My mother and father were surprised to find themselves the parents of a piano-playing daughter at all. In the Bronx it was only the offspring of the affluent who played the piano, and my parents knew no one who did. The custom among Bronx Jews was for sons, and occasionally for daughters, to play the violin, as had been traditional in the old country, where, the joke went, violins had been the instrument of choice because when the Cossacks were chasing you out of town, you couldn't run with a piano under your arm. At any rate, my parents were grateful for the presence of a piano in Miss Brookie's house and for her willingness to teach Miriam. It was a serendipitous circumstance, what they called *mazel.*

Still, my mother had to confess that as she sat and watched Miriam's fingers run over the keys and her long brown hair toss and her shoulders rise and fall, her thoughts would fly northward, to her family. *Oy,* how she wished for them to see. She longed for Miriam not to be just a rose blooming in the wilderness. But, my mother would always say later, that was what she thought *then,* before she grew up.

★ ★ ★

In the immediate years after I was born, my mother and I were together during the week, but come Saturday she was off to the store, taking my brother and sister with her. At the store, as I have understood it, Joey did his usual stock chores, and Miriam wrote things down in the big black-and-white-splattered ledger. Unlike the first visit to St. Louis, she may at this point have been doing actual bookkeeping, so simple was it. All that was required was to put down the figures as my father gave them to her — daily "paid outs" on the left page and "receipts" on the right.

My father was full of compliments for Joey and Miriam: Joey was "Johnny-on-the-spot," Miriam's work was "aces." My father said she must be "taking in good" the arithmetic they were teaching her in school.

Joey, wanting as always to keep the record straight, said then — and he hasn't changed his mind since — that she was good at arithmetic from playing so much casino with him on Sundays.

Miriam and Joey played cards on Sunday because Miriam had nothing else to do. Her friends were all in church or having their Sunday dinners afterward; and though Joey could have found other diversions, to Miriam a day without friends was no day at all. She would go around the house yelling, "I *hate* Sundays! There's not a bless-ed thing to do!" until Joey would agree to play casino with her.

Casino was a favorite card game in the Bronx, along with pinochle, and my brother and sister had learned it from my parents. It was the only card game my mother ever played, because it was the only one she knew how to play. My father preferred pinochle, but though my mother had seen pinochle played all her life (a game was in progress virtually around the clock at my grandparents' apartment on the weekends), it remained to her a man's game and a mystery.

On Saturdays, with the whole family off at the store, I was left home with Lizzie Maud. I made no protest, I've been told, probably because Lizzie Maud always had something for us to do. Right after she had put the greens or the snap beans to simmer (without fatback) on the back of the stove, we were out of the house, if only to go strolling past the uptown stores or around the courthouse park.

Miss Brookie sometimes strolled with us, and according to how Miss Brookie later described these strolls to me, Lizzie Maud would smile hugely at passersby, to encourage them to ask whose baby she was minding. As the questions came, she would pick me up and say, "This here my Jew baby," then turn me slowly around to display my head. "See, ain't no horns on this child. Ain't no way to tell she Jerrish" — her way of pronouncing "Jewish" — "unless you knows the family."

My father needed my mother on Saturdays. Mrs. MacAllister, pregnant now, was in semiretirement, and Vedra Broome was the only one working full-time.

Vedra Broome's husband, Gaither, always came to pick her up after work. As a man from strictly farming people, Gaither was proud of his wife for being a store clerk and of himself for being a worker in a factory; and he liked to talk things over with my father when he came to get his wife. When my father wasn't busy, he was glad to listen, especially when the talk was about the factory. It was true that Gaither actually knew very little, being only a worker behind a machine, but his chatter allowed my father to make some educated guesses.

All this listening my father was doing perhaps made Gaither feel close and comradely, because one day — possibly, as my father always said, before he knew what he was saying — he had invited us out to his parents' place for Sunday afternoon lemonade and cake.

When we went out on this visit to the

Broomes, I was coming up on three years old, old enough to begin having my own memories.

Though we had often gone out into the country, to buy farm produce and such, this would be my first visit out there to somebody's house. I have a recollection of my mother trying to resist going and wanting my father to take us and leave her home, protesting that she wouldn't have anything to say to them, "no more than a stick."

My father paid no attention, borrowed Miss Simmons's buggy, and out we went, my mother too. We were in our best clothes. As befitting my post-toddler status, I was in a lawn dress on whose dropped waist my mother had added tiny ribbon rosebuds, thus carrying out her own dictum that if there was a place for a flower, you put one there. She herself was in a new dress with ruching around the collar. She said she was all dressed up to get hanged. Hoping for the best was not an option; she only expected the worst.

The house we were going to was shared by Vedra and Gaither and his parents. My mother's apprehension was not eased by the long ride out to it nor by the sight of it. It was a narrow, tall, white frame two-story, attenuated by an assortment of lightning rods on the roof.

The Broome parents greeted us from the front porch, rising from their rockers like the handles of butter churns. Their smiles were wintry, though whether from age or disapproval, as my father would always say, who could tell? Rising also were Gaither and Vedra, and Vedra's twin sister, Vyvid.

With gaits stiff and slow, the elder Broomes led us through the front door and into the parlor, where they took their places on the horsehair sofa and sat gazing, as if their part in the afternoon had been concluded according to plan.

My parents sat on horsehair chairs and Joey and Miriam on small ladderback ones, in front of the mahogany secretary whose writing surface displayed some porcelain ladies and gentlemen dancing around a gold-rimmed clock while a tiny lady in a vast quilted skirt looked on.

I plopped down on the floor, on the braided rug near my mother's legs.

Vedra and Vyvid half-sat on the sills of the two tall windows, from which hung stiff, dark cretonne draperies. Between the windows was a tall three-branched plant stand holding spiky sansevierias and a trailing pothos, probably the only species able to survive in this sunless room.

Any signs of life from the parent Broomes

came from two sources: heads turning in tandem to seek out whoever was speaking and Mrs. Broome spitting tobacco juice into her glass. They neither asked a question nor answered one, only sat as if ready for the show — perhaps a ritual Jewish jig — to get under way.

After a few moments Vedra and Vyvid left the room and returned carrying a tray of glasses of lemonade with red cherries floating and plates of thick slices of chocolate-iced dark, dark chocolate cake, along with tiny napkins edged with tatting.

Certain of the presence of fat in the cake, my mother pushed her slice around until she had a chance to shove it into her handbag. Then, to cover her deed, she asked for the recipe, and whereupon she learned that in Concordia "spec-i-al-i-ty" recipes were not to be shared. At my mother's question everyone just went on eating. "Like what I said went in one ear and right out the door," my mother used to say, in one of her famously mixed metaphors.

I finished my cake, plunged my fingers into the lemonade, brought out the cherry, and chewed on it. The cherry being truly nasty, I spit it into the tiny napkin edged with tatting.

This was the most excitement for a while. The conversation spluttered. It died altogether. The clock ticked loudly. Conversation was revived now and then by Vedra offering more cake or lemonade. Everyone said, "No, no, thank you."

Gaither told things that had happened at the factory. Everyone had heard it all before. My father's anecdotes about the store did not bring smiles.

I contemplated Vyvid, focusing on her speech patterns, which featured synchronization. When Vedra started to speak, as when she said, "Can I fetch you some more lemonade, Mizriz Bronson?", Vyvid's lips would tremble, and she would come into sync with Vedra on the last syllables. I waited for it, for the sisters to say as one, "-ade, Mizriz Bronson?"

When the novelty of this wore off, I sought attractions elsewhere. I eyed the little lady with the big skirt on the secretary, at her skirt stuck through with pearl-headed pins. I fixed a look on Miz Broome. Her orangey-brown spit had just about filled up the glass. Miriam was now sitting with her legs curled around her chair, as if in this way to keep from collapsing in a heap on the floor; Joey had revived slightly and was counting cracks in the ceiling.

I got up and went outside. I ran into the clean-swept yard and dashed over to the old rubber tire that hung from the large elm in the front yard. I climbed into it and tried to swing by pushing with my feet. This being harder than it looked, I jumped off and ran for the fields in the back.

Behind the house, I chased aimlessly through some corn stalks before I made for the fields beyond. I skirted the tomato plants and plunged through the squash rows, making an attempt to avoid the squashes and noticing in passing that since they hadn't been picked when Lizzie Maud would have said they should have been, they were now as big as watermelons. I dashed on, trying not to step on anything important, heading for some trees in the distance. And then suddenly I found myself not on dirt, not on tilled soil, but on a small expanse of wooden planks. Now *this* was something.

I looked down and tried to figure out what I had happened on. Whatever it was, it was lying flat on the ground and had a handle with a rope attached.

By tugging on the rope with all my might, I finally managed to pull the thing open. I had opened a door to a flight of stairs going into the earth. Down below was a roomful of home-canned things.

I wandered, I touched. I stood for a long moment in front of the toe-dancing pigs' feet.

Only when the light grew dim did I think of going out.

I picked my way up the stairs. At the opening I drew back: While I had been playing underground, thunder and lightning had overtaken the outdoors. I was all at once unable to take another step. The only thing I could do was to go back down the stairs. But when I looked into the darkness, it was no longer friendly.

It was a long moment before I heard a voice. "Come on, Stella Ruth," it said. "Come with me." Joey. Come to save me.

I said nothing, just took his hand.

He walked me back through the dying rain. An occasional disapproving drop, cold as lake water, fell on my skin. We trudged on through the fields, the earth muddy and clinging to our shoes, until the house at last came into view.

My voice came back when we were in the buggy and my head was in my mother's lap. I dug my face into her skirt, into the still-present mustiness of the Broomes' parlor furniture. "It was scary," I said into it.

My mother thought a big hole in the ground was "ridikalus."

My father tried to explain that it was a storm cellar, a place to go for safety during big storms. "In case of tornadoes," he said.

My mother had no wish to have things explained. "Talk about storms! It's like God is punishing! I never seen such storms!"

My father said yes, she *had* seen such storms, in Kiev *and* the Bronx, but my mother wasn't listening. She was saying "My poor Stella Ruth" over and over, smoothing my hair impatiently, and mad that we had visited the Broomes in the first place. "What were we doing out there anyways?" she asked my father. Why had we been all dressed up? After all, it was *their* Sunday and *they* were the ones who had just come from church.

Did we have anything in the world to talk to them about? No. Had we sat there like bumps on a log? Yes. *Oy,* my mother said, what she wouldn't give to see some Jewish people.

It was obvious even to my father that the Broomes wouldn't do, and although he wasn't sure that only Jewish people *would,* he agreed with my mother that they needed friends. It was a thing that needed working on. Seeking help, he sent out a rush call for his good luck.

His luck showed up some months later, this time to provide us with a visiting opportunity more to my mother's liking. On one of his sporadic visits to Concordia, Sammy Levine, the young traveling salesman who carried my father's underwear line, brought with him the news of a Jewish family named Rastow who had opened a store in Sidalia, a town in Kentucky not too far away.

My mother fell on this news as if a sudden shower had coursed over her after many days in the desert. "Sammy says there's *Yehudim?* And not too far?" she asked my father.

Excited as my mother was, she had to first understand how it was that Sammy Levine had been in Concordia and had not come for a visit as he always did.

My father explained that Sammy was in a hurry and had no time. My mother was puzzled. No time to come to us and speak the old language, as Sammy loved to do? And then the deeper puzzlement. "No time to eat my pot roast?"

My father, knowing, as he always said, that his explanation "would sit with Mama like a bad piece of fish," told her that Sammy was taking a girl out.

A Jewish boy taking out a Concordia girl? My father was right: My mother had tasted the fish and it was truly bad. She wanted to know who — "So who on earth?" — he was taking out.

It was Laverne Bascombe, and when my mother heard this, she said it wasn't right that he should be taking out "a little shiksa." "A

Jewish boy and a shiksa," she said to my father. "You can't make me believe that it's right."

My father protested that Sammy Levine was lonely, that it was a hard life being a traveling salesman. "So what do you want him to do?" he asked my mother.

To which my mother answered, "Not that. I sure don't want him to do that."

So *nu,* so anyway, she said, she wanted to talk about something better, their trip to Sidalia.

Fine, my father said, delighted to be off the subject of Sammy Levine and his shiksa girlfriend. He now had another surprise: We would go in our own buggy. Business was thriving; indeed Bronson's was attracting customers countywide. So why not a buggy of our own? It would be light and comfortable, with two seats and a hood, a change from the wagon, which we still used whenever my father thought we had been borrowing Miss Brookie's buggy too often. "We can afford it, so why not?" my father asked my mother.

"So why yes?" my mother asked him right back, making a quick stab for "tem-po-rary." "We can't drive it back to New York."

My father dropped on my mother one of his looks and said, "Did I say we could?"

The next day my father sat Joey down to

write a letter to St. Louis, and inside of a week, a buggy was delivered.

In case Willy might require an explanation, my father and I brought him to the side yard, where the buggy sat under the trees, the old tarpaulin over it.

"Ain't you proud, old horse?" my father asked. "Now you can go high-stepping around in front of a buggy."

Willy stared for a moment, moved his head in a dignified way, and made a stately return to the backyard, as if accustomed by now to my father's leaps into the new.

Sidalia was just across the border from Tennessee, a ride of some twenty-five miles. My mother made sure we all looked our best. She had no plan to notify the Rastows of our impending visit. She reasoned that since they were Jewish people they didn't expect other Jewish people to "stand up on ceremonies."

We piled into the new buggy and, with Willy on the job, took the north road out of Concordia, out of Tennessee, into Kentucky. In about three hours we pulled up to a two-story brick house. It was a solemn house. No exuberant greenery here, just typically trimmed ornamentals.

The Rastows were Irving and Gladys and their two children — Delores, about Miriam's age, and Sheldon, a year or two older than I. There was also a bachelor older brother of Irving's, Manny, who, it turned out, was the real owner of their store.

Mrs. Rastow said they were "delighted," as she opened the little front door to let us file into the front room. "We knew you were in Concordia — by the grapevine, you know. I'm so glad you didn't wait for an invitation," she said, in a way that my father always said let us know we should have waited.

My mother chose not to notice. Nor to dwell on the meaning of "the grapevine." How could she bother with such things when she had all at once been transported to a world she had thought lost, a world with Jewish people in it? She explained that we had heard about the Rastows from Sammy Levine.

"Yes, Sammy Levine," Gladys Rastow said, as if she didn't know Sammy Levine all that well, probably because Sammy Levine carried a cheap line and, as we found out, if Rastow's carried cheap lines, and they did, Gladys Rastow wasn't keen on getting too friendly with the persons who sold them.

My mother said, "Anyways, that's how we knew."

Mrs. Rastow said, "Delightful."

My mother had been pleased to see there

was a son. Now maybe she could have a serious discussion with *someone* about bar mitzvahs. My father was never any help. Even I had noticed that he didn't so much as discuss as go "hmm."

After a moment, my mother found herself taken aback by Gladys Rastow. Gladys's hair, thick, dark, and wiry, was bobbed; Gladys was busy, involved, *modren,* as my mother pronounced it. She seemed to belong to every women's club in Sidalia, maybe in the county, maybe in the *country.* When Gladys said to my mother, "I must say the Sidalia ladies keep me on the move," my mother always said she thought of herself at that moment as not only not on the move, but stuck tight, like a spindled bill.

Unnerved by Gladys or not, my mother let it all out. "Like a fire hydrant I was," my mother said in later years, "and to this lady who acted like I was just off the boat."

She had gone on about all the things that were lacking — a shul, a rabbi, a Hebrew school. She finally got to her main point: that since there was no shul in Sidalia either, what was Mrs. Rastow going to do about Sheldon's bar mitzvah?

Apparently Mrs. Rastow wasn't going to do anything. "Do? What's to do?" she said to my mother. If my mother cared so much, why not

241

just send Joey to Nashville?

Nashville? If the sofa had not been of mohair, which was very grabby, my mother would have slid right to the floor. *Send Joey to Nashville? Her Joey?* To who in Nashville? To Mrs. Moskowitz, who would have him make his own meals out of the little inch she would give him in her icebox? To the rabbi's wife, who was so busy being the rabbi's wife, she would *maybe* have five minutes for Joey in between being the rabbi's wife?

My mother said no, she didn't think so. After which Mrs. Rastow suggested *commuting.* "You know," Mrs. Rastow said, "go back and forth by train."

Miriam has always said that if it had been about her, my mother would have given her two bananas — one for going, one for coming back — put her on the train and waved goodbye. But then Miriam has always thought Joey was my mother's favorite, and Joey, though he has always laughed at this, has also never denied it. In any case, my mother felt that *commuting* — or whatever it was Gladys had said — was no answer at all: It was a heavy foot planted right on her body. Her Joey so much on the train?

That was the end of the bar mitzvah discussion, such as it was, though my mother was not out of things to talk about. She wanted to

242

know what Gladys thought of the food. "Like on the moon, no?" my mother asked her.

She surged on. She talked about the people, about how my father said they were not strange, as she herself thought, just different. She kept waiting for Gladys to "chime in."

Mrs. Rastow did not "chime in." And why? Because she had a different view of things. And it was different because Gladys Rastow had been born in America.

Yes, Gladys had been born in America. She was born in the Bronx, and grew up in Yonkers, in tony Westchester County, just over the northern border of the city, to which her family had moved when she was very young. Unlike my mother, she had not grown up in a big apartment house surrounded by Jews, but in a place that, when she lived there, was populated almost exclusively by Gentiles. In Yonkers her father operated a humble enterprise called a candy store. This was a slight misnomer in that this kind of store carried not only sweets but also tobacco products and newpapers and accommodated soda fountains (which served up "two-cents plains" — a shot of seltzer that cost two cents and that at some point I understood to be New York's elixir of life, as Miss Brookie had said iced tea was the South's).

Gladys helped out in the store, before and

after she finished high school. My mother would occasionally say, "What kind of job was that for a girl not only born in America, but a finisher in high school?" To my mother, if you had finished high school, you had at least a job in an office, like her younger sister, Hannah.

Gladys was hard for my mother, but my mother tried through the years to be charitable and attributed Gladys's personality difficulties to never having gotten sufficient respect for being born in America and being a high school graduate. Still, she would usually add, "Just because I'm taking up for Gladys don't mean I was crazy about her."

At this first meeting the worst was to come. Mrs. Rastow had two suggestions for my mother: First, she should bob her hair, and second, she should call her by her first name. Braids and calling people by their last names were "out of the Dark Ages," Gladys said, and it was clear that "out of the Dark Ages" was the last thing Gladys wanted to be. Born in America to a T, my mother thought.

In the dining room the men were having a good time. They were talking about business. My father's business was continuing to grow, Manny Rastow's showed promise, and, since Manny's store was the main thing in his life and my father's was second only to his family, the two had every reason to be cheerful. Irving, who was quiet (his wife had opinions for two, my father would say), mostly listened, but he was the sort who was happy to be in happy company. My father immediately liked Manny and Irving Rastow.

Manny had gone from New York to Alabama as a peddler's helper and after a year had gotten his own wagon. He had peddled on his own in West Virginia and Kentucky, saved his money, and, after a few years, had had enough of the nomadic life. When a store came available in Sidalia, he'd bought it and sent for his his brother and family to join him. He himself had no wife, something of which my mother took serious notice.

In the back of the house we heard Manny's call to come into the parlor, and when we gathered, Manny gave a speech of welcome. "What it is is a great occasion," he said, as if he were giving a formal speech in a great hall, "and I want you should know how welcome you are in our house. If I didn't say *shalom aleichem* before, I say it now. I say welcome, and peace. You should know how good it is to have Jewish people here."

He said that Irving had "a big surprise to pull, in honor" and that he would pull it in the kitchen. In the center of the kitchen table was a wooden barrel as squat and round as an oak tree stump.

Irving picked up a metal pry lying next to the barrel and proceeded to work off the lid, which responded with groans and squeaks. His reticence was gone. He was in full command. "Now!" he ordered. "Close eyes! Smell hard!"

Eyes closed. Noses inhaled, noisily.

My father cried, "Herring!" My mother cried, "Pastrami!"

Irving lifted items out one by one and gave each an honored place on the table: pink oiled-paper packets of corned beef and pastrami tied with string; ones of thin, thin slices of lox; tiny mustard-filled paper cornucopias; a whole tongue; a fat smoked whitefish; pickled onions, cucumbers, and tomatoes in white cardboard cartons with tiny metal handles astride; and, down in the bottom, rye bread, bagels, and nut-and-fruit pastries.

Miriam felt a tug. She turned and there was Delores, hissing at her. "See?" Delores said. "It's just Jew food!" So what that it was "Jew food"? All we knew was that Mr. Rastow had performed mouth-watering magic.

For Miriam, Delores was a "burden" (Concordia's word for anything calling for patience). To this day she will say, "Delores was the most *irritating* young 'un I've ever known."

"Am I seeing what I'm seeing?" my mother was asking. She too called it magic.

Irving said indeed it was magic — magic sent from a St. Louis delicatessen, with which he had placed an order for a weekly barrel. Then every Sunday morning there was, as Irving said, "a magic at the front door, courtesy Railway Express."

In her ecstasy at having "real" food, my mother told about a a recent encounter with some store-bought pickles. "Feh! So sweet they were, I should have given them for dessert. Whoever heard from sweet pickles?

"And the bread! Before you can chew it, it's gone — like some kind of trick! And no taste! When I'm eating a sandwich, if I didn't have something between, I wouldn't know I was eating nothing!" My mother speared a slice of rye bread with her fork and held it high. "Now, this is *bread*. It looks like something, it tastes like something!"

After the Broomes, this was the second visit in a row that hadn't been a great success, but my mother took comfort in the fact that the Rastows were Jewish. As if asking for confirmation, she said to my father on the ride going home, "That's the important part."

My father answered noncommittally. At this moment it seemed best to leave well enough alone.

My mother persisted. The *most* important thing, she said, was that Miriam and I would have Jewish friends.

This inspired a Miriam explosion. "For pity's sake, Mama!" she cried out from the buggy's back seat. "So what if Delores is Jewish? She's about as much fun as a dead cat!" Furthermore, she couldn't understand why my mother wanted us to be friends with somebody who was so clearly hostile to anything Jewish. What about Delores saying "Jew" this and "Jew" that? "Just the way you hate it, Mama," Miriam said.

"Did I hear anything like that?" my mother asked her invisible person. "No, I didn't hear nothing like that."

"I know you didn't," Miriam responded crossly. "It's *pathetic* the way you hear some things and not others."

My mother waved a hand toward the back. "She's just a little girl talking. She don't know what she's saying."

"Delores is a bent hairpin," I contributed. "And Sheldon is a . . ." I was stuck.

My brother whispered something in my ear, and I said, "A snaggle-toothed comb."

"Hush, Stella Ruth," my mother said. "And, Joey, you quit telling her things to say. . . . Anyways, you'll make the best of it. They'll be your friends."

Miriam argued that we had plenty of friends, plenty right in Concordia, so why did we need more?

My mother said we didn't have any *Jewish* friends, that was why. "I only wish Joey had some Jewish boys," she said.

"You and your Jewish!" my sister said. "Honestly, Mama!"

My mother closed it out. "You're a Jewish girl, Miriam. Are you forgetting that?"

Was Miriam forgetting? As far as I could tell, it wasn't so much forgetting as never thinking about it. "It's just that it's so gol-derned silly!" Miriam yelled. Then she yelled, "Gol-derned silly" to the great outdoors until she got tired of saying it.

My mother already had other things on her mind, specifically that Manny Rastow was a nice man and a bachelor and that her sister Hannah was a lovely girl and likewise unmarried. Plans for my Aunt Hannah were beginning to percolate.

The very next day my father placed an order for the St. Louis magic. So eager was he, he made a long-distance call, the kind of telephoning usually reserved for wholesale houses when an order, perhaps for superfrilly, superflouncy dresses needed for an Easter Sunday only two weeks away, had not yet arrived. But my father figured that my mother had been so joyful about the barrel, he should do whatever it took to keep her light shining.

My mother had told Miss Brookie all about the visit to the Rastows, especially — it was important to my mother to call attention to admirable things about Jewish people — how *modren* Gladys Rastow was. "She makes me feel like a sure enough greenie," she had said to Miss Brookie.

Miss Brookie hadn't thought that *modren* was all that much. "When it boils down to the low gravy," she had said to my mother, "it takes more than being *modren* to be a mensch."

A woman could be or not be a mensch? My mother had been a bit flustered, having never before heard this term applied to a woman. Was it right? she had wondered out loud, and Miss Brookie had said, Foot, all it meant was a *person,* a person who could be counted on.

Chapter 16

A House and Neighbors

What with Bronson's Low-Priced Store fast becoming a fixture in Concordia — and what with the Rastows having a house — all at once my father was agitating for a house of our own. He put it to my mother. "We ain't poor, so why should we live like we are?"

My mother sent up a wail. "Leave Miss Brookie?"

One thing my mother kept hold of: There was to be no *buying*, only *renting*. "It ain't as if we're here forever," she said to my father.

Places to rent in Concordia were scarce. Houses in the "good" section of town were passed down through families, or, if not, were bought, not rented.

Carrie MacAllister took my mother to see a house that was on the rental market. It had been built six years earlier by two men who had come from Memphis to open an antiques shop. Before they moved into it, they had lived at Miss Brookie's. Miss Brookie had enjoyed them and admired their artistic bent. When the men gave up their shop and left Concordia after about two years, the house had stayed empty.

The house was more than unusual. It was one story (the men had no doubt been caught up in that period's craze for bungalows) and had yellow stucco exterior walls. Over an open, concrete-floored porch were several brown wooden beams, one of which supported a chain-hung swing. In Mexico it would have fit right in, but not in Concordia.

Mrs. MacAllister was keen to share what she knew about the house. First of all, the men were not "interesting," as Miss Brookie would have said, but "plain *peculiar*." Though they were friendly to one and all, they never dated any of the local girls. Carrie summed them up as "the flat-out oddest people you'd ever meet."

Like the Bronsons, my mother thought. Still, she agreed with my father that we should take the house.

When my father came home from the lease signing, I was sitting on the front porch swing, across from Miss Brookie. She wanted to know how it went.

"There wasn't nothing to it," my father told us. "Herman Tucker directed his teeth at me, said 'But, but' a few times, not too loud, and that was that." He eased into the seat next to me and looked across at her. "Seems those teeth of his are chewing on butter and honey with me lately. Must think I'm making money."

The late-afternoon sun was in Miss Brookie's eyes, and she shielded them with her hand to look at my father, exactly as she did in that snapshot of mine. "No doubt," she said to him.

"So it's all set."

Miss Brookie said, "I sure hate it that y'all are going. Still, I know you got to."

"That's right, we do."

Miss Brookie thought my mother needed to make some friends other than "an old maid and a Nigra servant and the *Daily Clarion*," meaning Carrie MacAllister. "Anyway," she said to my father, "y'all aren't going to Mars."

I knew we weren't going to Mars, we were going two blocks away. And Miriam would still be taking piano lessons. "But," Miss Brookie wanted to know, "who's going to wake me up mornings with sounds of mortal combat with the harp?"

The house had *almost* enough room for us. My sister and I were still together in one bedroom, but my brother had his own — one that stuck out from ours like a wart on a finger.

253

What was supposed to be the dining room, behind French doors opening into the front room, became my parents' bedroom.

The furnishings my mother chose for the bedrooms were simple and utilitarian. She hung straight marquisette curtains at all the windows, though in the matter of color, Lizzie Maud had prevailed. "You got to get you some color on them," she said to my mother. "These look like stuff you lays out the dead in."

My mother, having spent long hours hemming the curtains by hand, went into full protest. "Enough's enough with the curtains," she said, and hoped it was the last word.

In the end Lizzie Maud tea-dipped them, giving them a color that was "kindly red and kindly got some sun in it, too." As she hung them back up, she said to my mother, "The thing is, if y'all got to leave us, we wants to be proud of y'all, don't you know."

All the furniture in the minuscule front room was newly purchased. A gray mohair sofa and two matching easy chairs sat cheek by jowl in front of the red-brick fireplace. With their identical curving backs and rotund arms, they had the look of a well-fed family having a cozy chat. An iron floor lamp was behind the couch, and, at the side of each chair, a smoking stand.

In the space next to the fireplace sat a cabinet with a windup phonograph, which had been liberated from storage in Miss Brookie's basement. On the long wall were two windows facing the street, both curtained with lengths of white lace, with which Lizzie Maud had no quarrel.

Positioned squarely in the middle of the fireplace mantel, in a blackish-brown tortoiseshell frame, was the portrait of my mother's family — a studio photograph flanked by a vase of wax lilies of the valley and the nine-branched menorah for Hanukkah, which had come with the family all the way from New York.

There was one other chair in the front room: a way-too-big bentwood rocker Miss Brookie had brought down from her attic and sent around. There was only one remaining space — the doorway of the little square central hall, which housed the formidable presence that was the space heater — and a route had to be planned for going around it. But since Miss Brookie had sent the chair, we planned it.

Joey's room was very private, perhaps because of the way it related to the house or perhaps because of its modest dimensions, which allowed accommodations for only a narrow bed and a skinny chest of drawers. We had taken out the floor-to-ceiling shelves. Since, according to Carrie MacAllister, the men had gardened and put things up, we'd assumed the room had been used as a pantry. At any rate, its ceiling was so low that T, who was undergoing a growth spurt, could barely stand up. Still, Joey's erector and chess sets fit nicely under the bed, and the books sent by Uncle Philip were in reach on the slim shelf above.

With the dining room in service as my parents' bedroom, it fell to the breakfast nook — a table and benches tucked into a little alcove in the kitchen (a sure sign of modernity, according to my mother) — to serve for eating.

The kitchen was remarkable only because the sink had not a pump but a spigot. Otherwise, it was the usual: a dominating coal stove; two tables, both wooden — one on tall legs next to the sink and the other an all-purpose one in the middle of the room; and an icebox on the minute screened back porch.

My mother's most favored thing in the kitchen may have been the coal scuttle, a black metal open-spouted pail for bringing in coal from the shed attached to the back of the house. It spoke to my mother of America's wonders. In Russia, coal, treasured like gem-stones, had been brought in piece by piece, in hands. And here my mother had coal in great heaps, could fill the scuttle to overflowing, use it as extravagantly as she chose. Not that she ever *would,* but the choice was there.

The neighbors immediately came to call. They came in all manner of attire, some in gingham "wash dresses" with gardening sun-bonnets still in place, some gotten up as if for church. Each came bearing a gift — a pie or baked apples or a few jars of home-put-up something from their gardens. (In Concordia things weren't "canned," they were "put up.") One, a young bride from across the street, placed into my mother's hands a slice of country ham wrapped in newspaper.

My mother thanked each one and tried to say more, knowing they all wanted to chat, but words stuck in her throat. The talk went quickly strained and soon trailed off. In just moments there were formal, self-conscious good-byes.

My mother put aside for Lizzie Maud not just the ham but the jars of vegetables as well. *"Seasoning meats,"* she said to Lizzie Maud. "These ladies never heard of vegetables without no *fatback.*"

To which Lizzie Maud said, "And you

think that be worse than chopped-up livers with *chicken grease?*"

There came the day when the young bride — Miz Reeves — perhaps having learned of her folly in bringing us a housewarming gift of ham, dropped off a cutting of her "big inch" plant. This my mother accepted gladly. When the other neighbors brought cuttings, she accepted them gladly as well.

With the offering of plant cuttings, my mother found she could speak. She asked instructions, she listened, and as soon as the ladies left, she did as told.

It wasn't long before she stood before her own plants and snipped off cuttings for the neighbors. In short order there were visits where the conversation revolved not only around plants but around children, and school, and even cooking.

It was the neighbors who had urged my mother to take the step of planting a garden. They said it was easy, nothing to it. They recited a poem: "Just seed it and weed it, wet it and get it."

So out from under the sycamores and elms, on land where the sun shone most of the morning, my mother made a plot for spring bulbs and one for summer flowers, the latter, in the fall, to become a patch for chrysanthemums. Another one was set aside for vegetables.

Almost every day she did something in the garden. She planted, she pulled out weeds, she dug the earth around the bulbs. And almost every afternoon Miss Brookie stopped in and offered encouragement. "Your four o'clocks are going to bloom fit to kill," she'd say, and she often ended her visit with, "You do have a way with plants, Reba, indeed you do." No matter how often my mother heard this, she never tired of it, never tired of any compliment from Miss Brookie. As my mother would say, "It was more music to my ears than music."

My mother was so well acquainted with every square inch of her garden that when she came across a growth a couple of inches high that she had never seen before, she was truly surprised. How was it possible that it had gotten so big behind her back?

She asked herself if it was going to be *tsores* or *naches*. Trouble or joy.

At first she decided it didn't belong, that it was a weed to be pulled out. But when she looked more closely, she was unsure. It was dense with leaves — small, deep green, sturdy leaves, not weedlike in the slightest. She hesitated. She knew she had not planted it, but it clearly had more menschness, more substance, than some errant growth. She withheld action until Miss

Brookie had been consulted.

When Miss Brookie appeared, the two women strolled to the backyard and brought the little green shoot into their sights. On hands and knees, skirts trailing in the dirt, they peered from all angles at the tiny growth.

Miss Brookie finally rose back up, clapped her hands to dislodge the soil, and issued one of her "vows and declares." After entering a disclaimer — "If I'm not a demented old lady" — she vowed and declared that in my mother's garden an azalea had volunteered.

It came to my mother that she had heard something about Tennessee being the Volunteer State. "You mean it only grows here in Tennessee?" she asked Miss Brookie.

Miss Brookie explained that no, a volunteer plant meant a plant that wasn't planted, wasn't invited, and appeared entirely of its own accord.

My mother's decision was made. It could stay in there with the bulbs. "It's been growing so hard, it would be a shame to do anything bad to it," she said to Miss Brookie.

Miss Brookie took off her glasses, pulled her handkerchief from her pocket, and gave them a wipe. Message time. Volunteers, according to Miss Brookie, had ideas of their own: If they'd a mind to come up, up they'd come; but once they were up, they had to be well cared for. "Then they can be as pleasing as anything in your garden," she said. She had a caution: Sometimes, for what would seem no reason at all, they would just "turn up their toes." She said to my mother, "Volunteers are always a teensy bit different from cultivated plants. Or so it seems. Anyway, that's what makes them so fascinating, don't you know."

My mother decided she'd just wait. "I can always pull it out later if I have to," she said to Miss Brookie.

As time went on, the relationship between us and the neighbors grew closer and closer. They lent and borrowed, we lent and borrowed. We exchanged little gifts. If we sent around items from the St. Louis magic, they sent us pies and cakes (carefully unlarded in deference to my mother's sensibilities). My mother crocheted soakers for new babies; the neighbors sent around aprons and tea towels, which they had "run up" on their sewing machines. And they were Bronson customers to the core.

I was a creature of the neighborhood. Betty May Nipper and Ouida Kimball went with me to the Sunshine Girls, and when we got to be school age, we walked together to Westerly, where we were in the same class. I scooted on the scooter of Chloe Campbell,

261

who was a year older, until I got one of my own. It was her brother who provided me with my first glimpse of male embellishment, when we peeked through the bathroom keyhole while he was in the bathtub. Since there were no riding academies or even riding stables in Concordia (it not being that kind of town), if you wanted to ride, you went to somebody's backyard, and I went to Lois Stanback's and rode her Peaches (our Willy didn't understand about somebody on his back). At the house of Rosemary Buffaloe on the corner, she and I climbed her crab-apple tree and threw crab apples at squirrels.

Miz Reeves across the street finally had a baby, and I visited him every afternoon. I felt I was indispensable since Miz Reeves depended on me around the baby's bath time, to fetch talcum powder and such.

One day I found in the house across the street Miz Reeves's niece Dorissey, from Jackson. Miz Reeves explained that as her niece, Dorissey was the baby's cousin. Dorissey was my age and a cousin to somebody real! I knew I had some cousins, but they were in New York and might as well have been on a page in a book.

Dorissey said she had something to show me and led me to a bedroom closet, from which, standing on a chair, she withdrew a dress of bright yellow organdy, circled by a sash so white it shimmered. She laid it on the bed, went over to the dresser, and opened a drawer. From it she extracted a tiny reticule of ivory satin gathered together with a silky cord — a miniature of the accessory that accompanied ladies to elegant occasions. She put it beside the dress on the bed.

In what breath I had left, I managed to ask whose they were.

"Whose do you think? Mine, of course," Dorissey said,

I stared. "What are they for?"

Dorissey played with the ends of the sash. "I'm fixing to wear them this Sunday."

"Where you going this Sunday?" I asked her, not wanting to hear the answer.

I heard it anyway. Dorissey slid open the reticule drawstring and drew forth a dainty mirror. She looked into it and, crinkling her eyes and pursing her lips, said, "To church."

"Everybody around here goes to church," I said to Dorissey.

"You don't," Dorissey answered.

My voice declined to a mumble. "It ain't so much anyway."

"It is when you go for something special."

"What something special?"

Dorissey tossed her head, and her straight, dark blond hair leapt about. "We're sprinkling the baby this Sunday."

Sprinkling the baby? Was he, like my mother's garden, in need of regular watering? "I know it," I lied.

"You don't know nothing of the sort." Dorissey's blue eyes appraised me. "Why's he getting sprinkled if you know so much?"

I didn't know so much. "Why?" I asked miserably.

"To make him into a Methodist, that's why."

My chin trembled, my lips quivered against each other. I let out a loud wail, and Miz Reeves came running in.

She took in the scene in one glance. "Run, Stella Ruth," she said. "Run ask your mama can you come with us."

I ran. "Mama! Mama! Miz Reeves wants to know can I go help sprinkle the baby!"

" 'Sprinkle'? What means 'sprinkle'?"

"It's something they do in church!"

"Oh. Church." My mother began to turn away.

I grew frantic. "But it's for *babies*, Mama! And little children are supposed to be there!"

This seemed to make an impression. "Oh, it must be Sunday school," my mother said.

"Yes! It must be Sunday school!" Was this a lie or, hopefully, just a fib?

My mother might have thought about Miz

Reeves and the plant cuttings and the sweet baby and the fact that the Reeves family traded at Bronson's, but whatever the reason, in the end she said I could go. "But only to Sunday school," she cautioned me.

I went with the Reeveses in a pink organdy dress with a green sash. On my arm hung a pink sateen purse.

The Reeves kin were at the church. Miz Reeves's granny was there — a small, wrinkly lady with veins on her hands like tree roots raising up in the ground. "My, what a nice little girl," she said to me. "Are you a Methodist, too?"

I could see Miz Reeves, standing to one side of me, frantically shaking her head. "No, Granny," she managed to say, "she's the little girl from across the street."

"The Jew child? Oh Lord Jesus have mercy," her granny said.

The preacher threw drops of water over the baby's head, repeated his name several times — Loomis Joyner Reeves — and held him while he said a Jesus prayer.

I came home. I waited for my mother's questions.

"Did the baby enjoy it?"

"Guess not. He screamed his head off."

This seemed to be all the questioning there would be.

I went to Sunday school the following Sunday with Dorissey. After Dorissey left, I made Sunday school rounds with a selection of Baptists and Presbyterians as well as Methodists.

How do I explain my mother's acquiescence in this? My mother, who winced at the word *Jesus*? Who quailed at the sight of a cross? There's no ready answer other than that she had it in her head that Sunday school had nothing to do with religion or perhaps that my being born Jewish automatically immunized me against untoward influences. I think, however, it was chiefly that in the matter of religion for the children, my mother stressed only Joey's need to have a bar mitzvah.

Well, what *was* Sunday school? It was hearing a lot of Old and New Testament Bible stories and coloring a lot of pictures of Jesus and Mary (which I was careful to leave behind in church). Maybe I *was* vaccinated at birth, but these Sundays schools meant to me only more ways to play. Given my mother's focus on Joey and my father's disregard of religion, I didn't give a whole lot of thought to the subject. Still, like most early experiences, these Sunday mornings have no doubt turned up in one form or another (perhaps through the poet's "wandering vegetative dreams"), sometimes to bite me and sometimes to give me a nice little nuzzle.

So Joey was my mother's target, and religion for him meant religious *training*. She said so often that Joey needed to go to Hebrew school, that all of us, not just Joey, were tired of hearing it.

Joey always protested that he knew a lot of Hebrew. On one particular day, as my mother sat on a chair crocheting, he was doing his protesting from the floor, where he was playing with his erector set. In his hand was one of the perforated metal pieces for an elevator he was planning, one that would actually go up and down by means of the string and wheel provided in the set. "The whole alphabet," he said to her.

This did not impress her. Joey should be learning lessons. Exactly what he should be learning my mother wasn't clear about, but whatever it was, it had to be learned in the Hebrew school. "You need to go to cheder," she said to him, her crochet needle going in and out furiously.

My father interrupted. "So what do you want the boy should do? You act as if something could be done about it." He rattled his newspaper, a sure sign that irritation had set in.

Maybe, my mother thought, she had been

too quick to dismiss Gladys's Nashville suggestion. She put it to my father.

The paper rattled wildly in my father's hands. "What? If that ain't the limit! You might as well say New York!" No, he needed his "stockroom boy." What would he do without his right hand on Saturday mornings?

He went back to the *Sentinel*, turning the page to find the Bronson ad. Lately he had been doing this with some want of confidence: Three weeks earlier the paper had left out the r in the ad banner that was supposed to read BIG SHIRT SALE. "So you'll stop already, Reba, yes?" he asked my mother.

My mother rose, and leaving her needle and crocheting in the chair, motioned Joey into the kitchen, to get away from my father's rattling paper. She slid into the breakfast nook and Joey slid in across from her.

Joey tried to say that everything he needed to know was in history books. He tried to impress my mother with all the learning that was in the books Uncle Philip had been sending — not just general history, but Jewish history as well, and the philosophy of Jewish scholars through time. But though my mother accepted without argument that the books were full of important information, learning from books was not the point.

She tried to make the point. "You can read

till your eyes fall out, it won't do you no good for bar mitzvah," she said to Joey. The point was her dream, her dream of the bar mitzvah ceremony, where my brother would stand with a lustrous white satin yarmulkeh on his head and a magnificently embroidered prayer shawl on his shoulders and read from the Torah in exquisitely enunciated Hebrew.

She suddenly began to see that there was really only one way out: Joey must go to New York. What my father had intended as a joke was taking hold in her head.

Taking hold also was one of her headaches, and she slid out from the bench and went to lie down. As she lay on the bed, she was thinking that soon she would have to talk to my father. And when she did? His blue eyes would go dark as if in sorrow for her wrongheadness. She closed her eyes, but there was no relief. In a few minutes she went into the kitchen and filled a napkin with sliced raw potatoes.

Chapter 17

My Mother's Dilemma

We had a new residence, and business being what it was — that is to say, very good — my father bought a new automobile to go with it. It had been Joey's idea. He had convinced my father that automobiles were no longer a joke, that they could now be started with a key instead of a crank. "And they don't bounce all over the road," he informed my father.

When my father could resist no longer, he and Joey went to St. Louis and bought one. Given two driving lessons by the salesman, twelve-year-old Joey drove the car home.

The car was a Studebaker. It was long and it was dark green and was called a "touring car," a type of car that featured roll-up isinglass windows and a roll-down fabric top.

If not the first car in town, it was the longest, and as such was the object of much curiosity. Parked in front of the store, it drew a crowd. One man said, as my father told it, "I swan, Mr. Bronson, if Concordia 'twas on the Mississip, you could sail this thing clear down to Orleans."

We were keeping the carriage. My father had decided — crank or no crank, bounce or no bounce — not to learn to drive.

So, at the wheel, as we said then, was Joey.

Miss Brookie came to see the car, but she really wanted to have a talk with my mother, and not about cars. It was about children working at the shoe factory. "What are we," she asked, meaning my mother and she, "going to do about it?"

Do? My mother was startled.

Miss Brookie thought they should go out to the factory and have a talk with Roscoe Pinder. She knew with not "one iota" of doubt the factory management was working children for twelve and fourteen hours a day. Furthermore, they weren't hiring Negroes anymore, since they could get the children to do the work more cheaply.

My mother was of two minds about going with Miss Brookie: "To the bottom of my feet," as she would say, she wanted to go, but the bottom of her feet were also warning her that we were in business, and how could she go and tell the boss of the factory, the factory that meant everything to the business, that he wasn't doing right? Miss Brookie might not care if the boss got mad, but my mother had to.

My mother was right about one thing: Miss Brookie didn't care if the boss was mad, glad, or perched on a poker. When she was expressing one of her "truths," if people chose to respond with what she called "weeping and wailing and gnashing of teeth," so be it.

My mother being so reluctant, Miss Brookie finally gave her an option: She could just be along for the ride and would not have to say a single word. "All right?" she asked.

Though my mother could resist no longer, it was not "all right." And when she told my father about it, it wasn't all right with him either. If Miss Brookie "starts up," he said, my mother was to stay out of it. "Remember," my father told her, "you don't never spit into the wind, you're liable to get it back in your face."

On Wednesday afternoon Miss Brookie picked me and my mother up in her buggy, and we trotted off behind Harold Lloyd on the north road to the shoe factory. Miss Brookie had called Roscoe Pinder, and he had invited us to come on out for tea.

"We're in for a right social occasion," she said to us.

"A *what?*" my mother asked in alarm.

Miss Brookie told my mother not to come

272

"all unglued." She wasn't, she said, going to wrestle Roscoe Pinder to the ground.

I saw the two of them on the floor, Miss Brookie on top, pummeling a hapless Mr. Pinder into submission.

I was exceedingly pleased to be going to the factory, the place that figured so prominently in our lives and seemed to me to be so glamorous. Miss Brookie, on the other hand, thought a factory was dangerous and that I should have been left at home.

Of course, there was nobody to leave me with, and this brought up the subject of "help." It seemed to be on everybody's minds that my mother had no help.

Miss Brookie was trying to understand why my mother was so "disinclined" to have help. And it was probably true, as she said, that Concordia was abounding in Negro women who'd "bless their stars" to work for us.

The picture came promptly to my mother: Negro women carrying home their sacks. To avoid opening up a whole can of worms, she told Miss Brookie she didn't want somebody — a stranger — around all the time.

If my mother hoped this would get Miss Brookie off the subject, she hoped in vain. Miss Brookie gave a fixed stare to the road, as if an answer might turn up in the next hollow. And there it was, she saw it: She would "spare" Lizzie Maud in the afternoons. "Lord knows, she's no *stranger*."

My mother was hard put to explain why Lizzie Maud wouldn't do either. "I ain't like you," she said, hoping to convey that Miss Brookie's mind was a more elevated one and occupied with loftier thoughts. "I notice more little things."

Miss Brookie instantly challenged. "What 'little things'?"

My mother went wobbly. "Nothing," she said to Miss Brookie. "No little things."

After a long moment of silence, Miss Brookie said, in a plainly exasperated tone, "Look, Reba, do you want Lizzie Maud or not?"

My mother had no fight left. "Yes, I guess," she answered.

The factory owner, Roscoe Pinder, was a tall man, and skinny. He was standing at the top of the factory steps, one hand holding his hat and the other out for a handshake.

In his office he took some wooden folding chairs from against a wall and opened them up. My mother sat down and quickly pulled me onto her lap. Was she giving the impression of innocent bystander? She fervently hoped so.

I looked around for some sights. There

wasn't much, just a desk, a shelf holding cardboard boxes, a metal cabinet, and a couple of windows with their panes painted blue.

Pinder said it was nice to see "you ladies" and wanted to know if we should have tea now or later.

Miss Brookie suggested having it now and said we'd see the plant afterward.

"Fine," Roscoe Pinder said, and went to the office door. Holding it open, he let out a bellow. "Horace! Oh, Horace!"

In a few seconds a red-haired boy about as old as Joey came scooting in. He pulled up in front of Pinder, peered into his face, received his orders, and scooted out.

"So here you are, Brookie," Pinder said. "Been a while since you been out here sticking your —" He caught himself. "Well, looking us over."

If Miss Brookie took offense, there was no way to tell.

In a few minutes the red-haired boy was back, carrying a tin tray on which were glasses of iced tea and a box of cookies. Where to put it seemed a problem. When nothing offered, he darted here and there, a small fish testing watery spaces.

My mother shoved me off her lap, then herself got up, making a place. "Here, sonny, here," she said.

The boy dashed to put the tray on the vacated chair and shot out of the room.

Pinder made a clearing on his desk, picked up the tray, and brought it back. "You'll have to excuse the boy, Miz Bronson. Truth is these boys don't really have much sense." He gave a laugh that seemed heartier than his spare body should have been able to produce. "I declare I thought he was going to hold on to that tray till hell froze over." He looked a little stricken. "Beg your pardon, ladies. . . . But what I'm trying to say is . . . well, take your Joseph for comparison, Miz Bronson. I reckon he would have found a better place for this tray than your chair." He said something about Joey being the smartest boy in school "of course," and winked a little wink at my mother and me.

What did "of course" mean? And why the wink? Did it mean Pinder was sharing with us an "understanding" that because Joey was Jewish, he was automatically "the smartest boy in school"? My mother longed to think of Joey as making good grades because he *was* extrasmart, but my father kept trying to tell her that Joey worked hard. It was because, he said, Joey had a motivation to learn, which was, he also said, "nothing to sneeze at either." He tried to explain this thing some Jews possessed — what we would now call a strong work ethic — by historical reasoning, but he couldn't quite do it, his learning in history being informal and his grasp of it tenuous. But even I found myself puzzled by the "Jews are born smart" thing. If this was true, and Jews had only to be Jews in order to make good grades, how come Miriam didn't get in on it? Her grades by anybody's standard were merely average. My father would have said that if it was a gene thing, Miriam, being Miriam, had genes that made her social.

That day, in deference to my father, even if my mother had been a winker, she would not have winked back at Pinder. She just returned to her chair and pulled me once more onto her lap. Fooling around with my collar, she answered the factory owner with, "Boys just ain't very good with trays, Mr. Pinder."

Pinder put a thumbnail in the seam of the cookie box, slit it open, and tendered it, along with glasses of tea. Miss Brookie plucked a sugar cookie from the box, poked it into her mouth, and sipped quickly at her tea. She was clearly in the grip of a terrible impatience.

In another moment, she had stood up and, with all of us to the rear, had marched out to the factory floor.

Walking opposite to the direction from which we had come, we found ourself abruptly on the floor, where we were greeted by the sound of powerful machines operating all out. The roar was so intense, it seemed a physical force that had to be struggled against. I understood immediately why Miss Brookie had thought it was dangerous for me to be there, and even as I understood this, I was seeing a dozen or more children racing around the floor and running to and from the machines.

My mother was gripping my hand tightly as we went from place to place, and I was gripping back. Miss Brookie was striding ahead. After about ten minutes she stuck into the air an authoritative forefinger, which directed us back to the office.

"Well, how you doing, Roscoe?" she asked. "Lord, by now you ought to be sitting on a pile as big as the state capitol."

It didn't seem that Roscoe *was* — sitting on a pile, that is; as he explained, the factory was only "doing best as we can." Pinder said it was that "gol-derned" competition from up north. This was plainly a bewilderment. Didn't the fact that he had newer machinery than theirs count for something? "It's a crying shame," Pinder said.

If he thought that Miss Brookie was going to let him play victim, he was in for a rude awakening. She said she didn't give a hoot or a holler about who was "beating out who."

What she did give a hoot about, she said, was that that North and South alike were hiring altogether too many children. "And altogether too young," she told Pinder.

"Yes, ma'am," Roscoe Pinder said.

Miss Brookie blew air, forcefully, which I recognized as an opening salvo. "You don't think it's disgraceful?"

Pinder took it well. "Truth to tell," he answered, "the little ones don't do much but pick up scraps."

To which Miss Brookie retorted that of course they didn't "do much but." "They certainly don't go to school, if that's what you mean."

From behind his desk, Pinder gave my mother another of his winks. This one was no doubt directed to her in her role as the wife of a businessman. Surely she could understand his position, would know "how 'tis." "We know how 'tis when you're trying to scratch out a living, don't we, Miz Bronson?" he asked her. "You do your best to keep expenses down. That's how 'tis, ain't it?"

My mother abruptly resumed smoothing my dress collar. I knew for a fact that Jimmie Mae over in Niggertown always dealt faultlessly with our laundry — even my mother said so — so what about my collar needed *doing?*

Actually, as my mother smoothed, she was reminding herself on the one hand what my father had said about keeping out of it and on the other that Miss Brookie wanted her to get in it. She was, as she often said, being stretched, pulled, and slapped like biscuit dough — Miss Brookie on one end, my father on the other, Pinder in the middle. "Something like that," she said into my neck, hoping to sound neutral.

In Miss Brookie's view, however, there was no such thing as neutral. Lack of support for her meant support for the enemy. She grew testier. Had she arrived at the point, I wondered, where she would wrestle Pinder to the ground? "Now you listen to me, Roscoe Pinder," she was saying, clearly having given up thoughts of a calm discussion. "I know all about making a living. You think my daddy came out of the womb in a sack of green-backs?"

Miss Brookie wanted to know why Pinder couldn't hire Negroes instead of children, and Pinder answered that he didn't hire Negroes because he'd have to pay them more. And the Negroes weren't as dependable as the boys. It seemed the boys showed up no matter what act of God descended on them. If the boys didn't turn up, he just let their "daddies" know, and they would be there the next morning without fail. "Niggers always have some excuse not to come to work, and they don't do much when they do. Y'all know that well as I do."

Did we all know that? I thought of Lizzie Maud, the "nigger" I knew best. She came to work every day without fail and did a lot. Miss Brookie didn't have to so much as put a dishrag to a teacup, as we said in Concordia.

Miss Brookie planted a look on my mother. In the heat of battle, her promise that my mother would just be along for the ride was forgotten. "Tell him, Reba, tell him," she ordered. "Tell him how you'd like it if Joey was in this place from early morning to late night. And no schooling. Just cooped up in this airless place with the netherworld's own din to keep him company. Tell him how you'd like it, Reba."

She wouldn't like it at all, of course. Her Joey to work the way these boys did, the way she had? She should speak out and say it was awful, a punishment, a curse.

She didn't say any of it. All at once I was being stood up and pushed forward in quick thrusts. "Hurry, Stella Ruth, move!" my mother was saying. To Miss Brookie she said, "Please, Miss Brookie, let's go!"

Miss Brookie got up, though with a last word for Roscoe Pinder, a wish that she had a

281

law to "sic" on him. Since she didn't, she said, she'd just thank him for the tea. She sailed out ahead of us, and my mother and I rushed to catch up.

Pinder maneuvered to hold open the factory door. "Thank you for coming, ladies," he said. He lifted my hand up. "You, too, little lady," he added, and it made me feel that my presence had for sure brightened his day. It was Southern charm, no doubt about it. As Miss Brookie would have been quick to point out, yes, it was a delightful custom, and it would have been "truly transcendental" had it been colorblind.

Leaving Pinder at the factory door, we hurried down the steps and ran to catch up with Miss Brookie. My mother kept calling out excuses to the starched white blouse ahead of us. "I couldn't speak," she said to it. "It all stuck in my throat."

Miss Brookie kept walking, *marching,* to the carriage. "You were about as much help as a one-legged clothespin," she threw out over her shoulder. "You of all people. You who could write the book on child labor, and you sit there like the cat had your tongue in a vise."

My mother was struggling for a way to excuse herself, to find a difference between the way these boys worked and the way she had.

What about that these boys didn't work on Sundays, that they didn't take bundles home? But the minute these things were out of her mouth, she knew they were "ridikalus." Children working was children working.

Standing beside Harold Lloyd, Miss Brookie let my mother have both barrels. Was it my mother's belief that the boys slept late on Sundays and got breakfast in bed? "If so," she said to her, "let me take the time to disabuse you of that notion."

My mother, she said, should understand how went a factory child's Sunday. According to Miss Brookie, the first thing the child did on a Sunday morning was to get dressed in a stiff little suit — "like as not with a patch here and there because it's in its third or forth incarnation" — and go off to church, where he sat for two or three hours listening to a preacher threaten him with eternal damnation. Then he came home, had some dinner, changed his clothes, and did chores until dark. "Even without bundles, don't you think that's a pretty hard day?" She thwacked Harold Lloyd on the rump. Poor Harold Lloyd. His mistress was angry — at Pinder, at my mother, at laws that should have been passed but hadn't been — and taking it out on him.

Miss Brookie had more: the figures. There

were, she said, thousands of children spending their childhoods in mills and factories. And as many of them under twelve as over. And not just boys, but girls as well. "Girls of six and seven working thirteen hours a day," she said to my mother. "Doesn't that give you some inclination to speak?"

She climbed into the buggy and grabbed up the reins. My mother and I had to scramble to get in before Harold Lloyd took off. "Don't think we're finished yet," she announced to the road. "You can never tell what kind of dance they'll do once the fiddling gets to going." She flicked the reins, hard. "Giddy-yup, Harold."

The minute we got home my father knew something had gone wrong. My mother's face had *vai is mir* — woe is me — written all over it.

I thought it was because Miss Brookie had gotten mad at her. She had called my mother a "one-legged clothespin," and from what I knew, nothing was as useless as a one-legged clothespin. So it stood to reason that Miss Brookie was seriously mad.

Still, this was not my father's primary concern. No, it was that Pinder and Miss Brookie had had a fight, and my mother could have been seen as her accomplice.

Chapter 18

Seth's New Job

That day at the factory brought about some changes. A definite coolness set in between my mother and Miss Brookie, and she no longer put in appearances at our house. But Miriam still went to her house for piano lessons, and Lizzie Maud was coming to us on Saturdays and for two hours every afternoon.

When Lizzie Maud first began to come on a daily basis, her paper sack loomed large, so large that whenever Lizzie Maud was in the house, my mother used to say the sack was "a corn always between my toes."

One day, still feeling the stress of the factory incident, she could stand the tension no longer. Her terror at bringing the subject up was finally overwhelmed by her need to know, and at the end of one particular day she did it — she asked Lizzie Maud what was in her "bag." This was a give-and-take with Lizzie Maud my mother would always say she was imparting to us *exactly*.

According to my mother, Lizzie Maud stopped at the back door, held out her sack, and took the time to make a vocabulary correction. "You mean this here *sack?*"

My mother, her heart in her mouth, nodded.

"Nothin' but stuff be in here," Lizzie Maud said.

"What kind of stuff?"

"You know. Totin' stuff."

As my mother had no clue as to what "totin' stuff" was, there was only one thing left to do: look in the bag. She steeled herself. "Let me have a look," she said to Lizzie Maud.

Lizzie Maud didn't move. My mother said that for the first time she was seeing honest-to-goodness anger in Lizzie Maud's eyes. "You think I be thievin'?" she asked my mother.

Her hands trembling, my mother took the sack from Lizzie Maud and looked inside.

What she saw were three pieces of bread showing mold, a jar with some jelly under the lip, a chicken drumstick that smelled, as my mother said later, like it had died a long time ago, and a cooking pot with a cracked side, unsuitable even for a plant.

"You be satisfied?" Lizzie Maud asked, and my mother said she wanted to hide where no one could find her for the foreseeable future. She rattled away. "Nobody told me. I didn't know. . . . If I had known . . ."

Lizzie Maud let my mother go on making a fool of herself. When she finally relented, it was with a look that said that someone so ignorant should have a keeper.

This was the day of my mother's introduction to the time-honored practice of "totin' privileges." "Don't you know I has totin' privileges?" Lizzie Maud asked her.

It seemed all the "cooks" did. As Lizzie Maud put it, "You gots to have your totin' privileges." That way, she said, "You gets to tote home dabs of leftover or wore-out somethin's."

Lizzie Maud had no trouble reading my mother's mind. "I know what you be thinking," she said. "You be thinking totin' privileges be a way for colored peoples to steal."

Well, she said, maybe they did. If somebody had to eat off some old dented pie tin and drink out of a chipped jelly jar and was paid three dollars a week "for the honor," while having all "them hungry mouths" at home, she'd be "blessed" if that person — meaning my mother — wouldn't do some stealing, too.

And this, my mother always acknowledged, somehow managed to be the important lesson

— more important than totin' privileges, or how to "fix" fried chicken or tea-dye curtains.

Finally, finally, Lizzie Maud asked her, "Have I done said enough?"

And my mother said yes, yes, she had said enough.

The paper sack matter finally settled, attitudes relaxed. So when Lizzie Maud came in one afternoon and said, "Has you heard?" my mother prepared herself for the latest in gossip. But no, Lizzie Maud had a personal problem: Her husband, Seth, had been laid off from his job at the railroad. A train had backed into him. He now needed a job, and though Miss Brookie had offered to let him work at this and that, he wanted more than make-do work.

My mother said she couldn't understand why he would be fired when it wasn't his fault, and Lizzie Maud gave her that you-need-looking-after look. His fault or not, she explained, he was unable to work the way a Negro was supposed to, and when folks caught sight of his limp, they thought he didn't have his strength anymore. As she put it, "What man gwine find nigger work where he don't have to be like Samson?"

My mother had to accept this. She thought, What's true is true — trouble comes to people like rust to iron (she had old shtetl sayings, too), and she decided to speak to my father.

My father went right out to Niggertown, to Lizzie Maud's house, to find Seth. I tagged along. Since Lizzie Maud always shooed me away when I tried to follow her home after work, this was my chance. Niggertown was also the site of Lizzie Maud's church: Ebenezer Baptist (which turned out to be a small, patchy white structure with no steeple at all), about which I heard a lot. It was where Lizzie Maud and her family went without fail every Sunday, Lizzie Maud and her daughters not only dressed up but with their hair ironed, and where the congregation sang the songs Lizzie Maud sang around the house. I often wondered if Miss Brookie would speak to Lizzie Maud about her strict churchgoing, but to my knowledge she never did, perhaps understanding that because she herself stayed home on Sundays, her thoughts on religion were considered irrelevant by everybody in town, including Lizzie Maud. Or perhaps she did not want to cast doubt on one of Lizzie Maud's greatest joys.

At any rate, when Seth wasn't at home — wasn't in the tiny house with the four tiny rooms — my father knew where to go: to the bootlegger's shack, an unkempt, rundown hut where the Negro men hung out on

Sunday afternoons, if they were working — or all the time, if they weren't.

My father had been to the shack many times. Ever since he had instituted a charge system, he had to go out there when payments hadn't been forthcoming for a while. Sometimes he went at their wives' requests, when they would say, "See can you do something with that man of mine, Mr. Bronson," explaining that instead of paying bills, he was just "th'owin' " his money away.

Sometimes lack of money came from buying moonshine, after which the men got drunk and skipped work. Sometimes it was the illegal numbers game — a flourishing Niggertown racket, which conventional wisdom held was run by the Negroes themselves but in reality was controlled by a couple of white men with reputations as pillars of the community. And sometimes it was that the men couldn't resist the Jewish peddlers who came through on their wagons on Sundays with tray after tray of jewelry.

My father spoke to the men with some lack of conviction. He knew the kinds of jobs they had: terrible ones that made them long to get lost in something, whether drink or adornments, or to make a grab at the only hope in their lives, a numbers hit.

So we went into the bootlegger's shack. It

was dark, the only light coming from the cracks between the siding. There were Negro men sitting at a couple of unpainted wooden tables, and they got up when we entered. Did I come in like a little white girl in a spotless dress of lawn dotted about with rosebuds and wearing shiny Mary Janes? Maybe I did.

Anyway, Seth was there. My father spoke to him, offered him the job of handyman in the store, and Seth accepted.

Seth's job was to get the furnace going, take the wagon to the depot, dust and polish, and in general stay handy. "You'll be my third arm," my father said to him, "and leg, too."

Seth said my father was not to worry, that he could tend to it all. Actually, according to my father, what he said was, "Jes' ax anybody, Mr. Bronson. They ain't nobody can whips they feets around faster'n me, no matter what that fool train done."

Seth was slight, both shorter and thinner than his wife, what there was of him all sinew. His hue was like Lizzie Maud's, what she called "magonny," meaning that the darkness had in it a tinge of red. His eyes were especially bright, and his every action quick, injured leg notwithstanding. It was as if moving at great speed was what his body was accustomed to doing and it couldn't change.

He very quickly settled into his new job and

became the kind of handyman who looked for ways to be handier. He got change at the bank and went out for "cherry dopes" — cokes with a shot of cherry flavor — for Vedra Broome; on rainy days he walked the lady customers to their buggies or wagons, holding an umbrella overhead, knowing this was a service from a Negro to which ladies wouldn't object.

As the days went on, Seth and my father worked on comic routines. There was a set piece for Friday nights — the night of getting paid. At six o'clock sharp, Seth would announce it "be *Shabbos bei nacht*" and say, "*Nu*, Mr. Bossman, it be time for my *gelt*."

My father would bend toward Seth and inspect his forehead. "Well, look here," he would say. "Darned if them horns ain't just about to break the skin." He would then pull Seth's wage envelope out of the register and hand it over with a *blay gezunt*, a "stay well."

For this Seth would give a *danke schoen* — a "thank you kindly" — and walk out briskly, the limp barely showing.

It was becoming clear, however, that the store could really use another clerk. Carrie MacAllister, now seven months pregnant, could no longer be counted on, even part-time. My father told my mother that he and Vedra just weren't enough.

Between me and her garden and crocheting and edging receiving blankets for Carrie MacAllister's forthcoming baby, my mother didn't want to put in any more time at the store. She suggested Vyvid, Vedra's sister, but my father said this was one case where one bookend was more than enough, thank you.

Whenever my father sought solutions, he would go to the side window and, hands in pockets, would stand looking out, ruminating, as if an answer might pop out from a pinecone. Today an answer came so quickly it was clear he had had it in mind all along: Seth could handle the job. "And very nice," he said to my mother, trying to convince her that Seth was a natural choice.

There was nothing natural about it, and my mother knew it. *"Seth?"* she exclaimed, meaning, A Negro *clerk?*

My father tried to calm her. He wasn't going to announce it from the courthouse tower. "We'll just ease him in so nobody notices," he said.

My mother wondered how Seth would not be noticed. "Like a raisin on top of a cupcake he'll be noticed," was the way she put it.

When my father said finally that they had to do right by this man, my mother felt herself caving in. "Just be careful," she warned.

My father told Seth to wait on trade only when he and Mrs. Broome were busy and to use his head about who would accept it.

Seth was joyful, knowing that not many Negroes got a chance like this. Going to work in a shirt and tie? My father always remembered Seth saying, "Won't I be a sight? Everybody be sayin', 'There go that Sunday nigger.' No sir, I ain't no everyday nigger no more." He was, he said, going to be "one good sal-es-man." Like my father, Seth was a good mimic.

As if to "clap the climax," as we would say in Concordia, some few weeks later Lizzie Maud announced that she too was going to have another baby. If it was a boy, it would be named Aaron Claudius and if a girl, Reba Laverne. Lizzie Maud was unsure about this, afraid it might be something Jews didn't allow. "You like that okay, don't you?" she asked my mother. "I mean it ain't against your religion or nothing, is it?"

My mother ran it through what rules she knew. "No," she answered, "that's one thing that ain't against our religion."

Five months later Lizzie Maud gave birth to Reba Laverne, about one month after Carrie MacAllister delivered Sarah Reba.

I saw Sarah Reba most every afternoon, mainly because my mother and Mrs. MacAllister had taken up painting flowers on dresses. While our mothers worked with brushes and paint pots, Billy Sunday and I played house, with Sarah Reba, blond and bland-faced like her brother, as Baby.

Reba Laverne's first visit came when she was about a month old. Delicately formed and brightly shining, she seemed a creature from a place I could not know.

I allowed myself to touch her, to make the miniature finger curl around my big one, to smooth shut the eyelids, to bend the flower-stem legs. When Lizzie Maud put her in my arms, she lay there light as a feather, small as a pigeon.

Soon I was begging to take her for walks. On one Saturday afternoon I put her in my doll carriage, and Lizzie Maud agreed we could go to the courthouse park to show her off.

My mother walked with us as far as the park and then went on to the store.

At the park Lizzie Maud leaned against a tree and talked to a friend while I promenaded Reba Laverne around the clay walk. The park was cool and green in the late-spring morning, and I was pleased to see a goodly number of Saturday morning bench-sitters — more than usual, I thought.

The bench-sitters said things like, "My, you have a fine-looking baby. Who does she favor?"

"She looks kindly like her sister Sarah Reba and kindly like her daddy Billy Sunday," I answered them.

After a while I noticed there was something new in the park — a wooden platform on stilts, on which a group of men were draping bunting and hanging signs.

I pushed the carriage over to Lizzie Maud. She moved her finger slowly in the air from letter to letter on the topmost sign and made out "CONCORDIA GO-GETTERS CLUB CHARLESTON CONTEST."

To Lizzie Maud the Charleston was a Negro dance. So how was it that "white peoples" were "gwine do the Charleston" out here in the park?

I had no answer, of course, but I knew the Charleston very well. Lizzie Maud had taught it to Miriam, and Miriam had taught it to her friends, and they did it "like mad," as Miriam would say, in our house, making use of any space that could accommodate flying arms and legs.

How Lizzie Maud learned the Charleston was by way of the trail of wagons filled with Negroes continually passing through Niggertown, some going with high spirits *to* Chicago, some coming with low ones *from* it. On Saturday nights it was a thing for Concordia Negroes to do: mix with the transients and learn from them whatever dances, games, or jokes were going on in their towns or in the big city.

And now there was going to be a Charleston *contest*. I begged — nagged — Lizzie Maud to hold me so I could see.

The men finished their hangings and took seats at the rear of the platform. Some folks were now abandoning their benches and moving forward; others were filtering through the streets in the park's direction. Soon a dense semicircle had formed in front of the stage.

Lizzie Maud stood her place at the front, me in her arms, Reba Laverne beside us in the doll carriage. Lizzie Maud knew her rights: A little white girl in her charge was her ticket to standing where she pleased. She could ignore the rule that Negroes must stand to the rear.

I thought Lizzie Maud should be in the contest, but she kept saying she was the wrong color and the wrong age. Wrenching around in her arms, I kept insisting, but she just wouldn't move. She was just so *stubborn*. Couldn't budge her with a stick, she herself would have said. Finally totally provoked with

297

me, she said I was as heavy as a "fifty-cent sack of taters" and dropped me to the ground. "I can't be in it," she said to me. "And you stop."

I ran around the platform to see what was what. Several girls were kicking and twirling furiously. All wore short skirts. All had short hair. Miriam, too. *Miriam?*

Yes, there she was, in a short green pleated skirt and green sweater. But it was her hair that was the sight. It was short like the other girls', with spit curls at the sides of her face, like the tendrils on our painted dresses. I raced back to Lizzie Maud.

Lizzie Maud was horror-struck. She too said, *"Miriam?"*

She grabbed me up with one hand, seized the handle of Reba Laverne's carriage with the other, and we rammed our way through the crowd to the platform's edge. From behind it, Miriam's head was popping in and out of view.

To which Lizzie Maud said, "Lord have mercy, it sure 'nuf be Miriam."

Hadn't I told her that? "And her hair," I said. "It's in a bob."

To which Lizzie Maud said, "And your mama gwine bob her heinie."

Lizzie Maud may have been feeling some guilt over teaching Miriam a "nigger" dance.

"Ain't you or Reba Laverne either one watching this mess," she said to me. "Just you get your little self together and *scat!*"

She began shouting as soon as we got to the front door of the store. Miriam! In the park! Dancing for all to see!

My mother herself loved to dance — at weddings and other family affairs — and not just the traditional circle hora, but also one-to-one with a partner, a man preferably, or, if all the men were taken, another woman. So what was Lizzie Maud telling her? That Miriam was dancing for *strangers?*

My father stayed calm. He touched Reba Laverne on the cheek and pronounced her "sweet as a Hershey's kiss." He wondered to my mother what was so terrible about Miriam dancing. Was she dancing in her underwear? Was she doing the hootchy-kootchy? No? So what was the problem?

My mother had to see for herself, so off we went to the park and rammed our way back through the crowd. Miriam was under way, legs and arms a-sail, the music of a portable Victrola playing scratchily in the background.

She soon went into the Finish, in which you stooped over, put your hands on your knees, shoved them together and apart, and then patted your backside.

A few other girls got up, put on a record,

and danced. Like Miriam they wore sharply pleated skirts that flipped and swung and shoes with little fat heels and perky bows. "Boy howdy, are they ever beautiful," I breathed. When all the girls had had a turn, a big, heavyset man with a perspiring face came forward. Tom Dillon.

He gave each girl a hand, smiling at them as he did. He picked up the winner's loving cup, held it aloft, and announced that the winner was going to be determined by the amount of clapping.

His hand went up over girl number one. Some applause. Each girl in turn got some clapping, and when it seemed too slight, folks ratcheted it up a bit. Then the hand went over Miriam.

I heard clapping, but also something new — cheers and whistles. I knew Miriam had won.

Mr. Dillon beckoned to Miriam, and she moved to stand beside him. He took her hand and held it while he told the crowd the contest was a prelude to the dance that night for raising money to send a Concordia boy to college, and as "your Go-Getters Club president," Dillon was urging the crowd to buy tickets for the cause.

He smiled down at Miriam. "Now here's our little winner. And a mighty nifty little dancer she is, too," he said. He crouched down until he was eye-to-eye with her. "What's your name, little lady?"

"Miriam," Miriam said.

Tom Dillon glanced over to the crowd. "Here's a little girl with no last name." He looked back to Miriam. "Is that right?"

"No, sir," my sister said. "I have a last name."

"Then why don't you let us in on it?" Still squatting, Dillon grinned out at everybody.

"It's Bronson."

"Bronson?" Mr. Dillon rose slowly to his feet. "Are you one of those Bronsons?"

Up there on the platform, Miriam realized soon enough that being "one of those Bronsons" was, in Tom Dillon's view, not only unfortunate but perhaps deplorable. As he plopped the cup in her hands, he informed the men at the rear of the platform, loudly, that they'd let a Jew girl win their contest. He let out a big "Haw," to show the joke was on *them.*

The crowd, having gotten very quiet, heard every word. My mother knew everyone in the crowd, they were Bronson's customers, and they knew she was among them. They were probably split down the middle: Some thought Mr. Dillon was comical as all get-out, and some thought he was a disgrace. In any case, they began leaving, glancing our way, talking softly.

In a very few minutes the only ones left were us. We walked slowly through the park and back to the house. I pushed Reba Laverne quietly, expecting that at any moment my mother would explode at Miriam for bobbing her hair.

To my surprise this didn't happen. It might have been that my mother was actually secretly pleased: If she herself wasn't up to "bopping," she was perhaps glad to see that Miriam was.

About Miriam's dancing, my mother didn't know how she felt. She tried to tell Miriam that dancing in public was for shiksas, not for nice Jewish girls. "Do you understand?"

No, Miriam didn't, not at all. "For pity's sake, Mama," she said, "you and your Jewish. What makes you think shiksas aren't nice girls, too?" She named some who had danced with her in the contest. "Are you trying to tell me they're not *nice?*"

My mother knew them all, some as friends of Miriam's, some from when they came into the store. Yes, she thought, they were nice; they were respectful, polite. She liked them. *Oy,* how to explain? Was it the dancing? Or was it that being made fools of by Tom Dillon made everything good about it seem bad?

302

That night Miriam put the cup on our dresser, and we lay on our bed and stared at it for long minutes. And what a cup it was — huge, the size of Miss Brookie's Chinese pots, which held her aspidistras, and all silvery shine.

Miriam still has the cup. It rests in a big box in her home, along with other mementos and sentimental items from all periods of her life; but most of them, she will say, are from the days in Concordia.

Chapter 19

New York Aunts

I had plenty of playmates and, except for a few inconsequential things they did that I didn't — like going to church — our lifestyles were similar. I was disconcerted — and envious — only when there were visits to or from relatives. It was one thing I couldn't get in on. My family talked a lot about our New York relatives, and letters went back and forth (those that came to us always started, "How are things in 'the sunny South'?"), but I was almost four before I laid eyes on any of them. The occasion was a visit from my mother's sisters, my Aunt Sadie and my Aunt Hannah.

The visit was part of that scenario of my mother's in which Aunt Hannah and Manny Rastow would meet, fall in love, get married, and settle down in Sidalia. Each time she saw Manny, her conviction that this was a wonderful idea was reinforced. She finally broached the subject to my father. "Here's a man would work out perfect with Hannah," she said to him.

My father gave a jokey answer. "You mean they're both so short they could stand on the wedding cake themselves?"

My mother said wasn't it funny that she and my father both had been thinking about them getting married.

"So that's what I was thinking?" my father answered her.

My mother decided to go ahead and write to Aunt Hannah and send money for the ticket. And just *mention* Manny. No fuss about him. And no announcements in Concordia. Her sister was coming and that's all anybody had to know. "Ain't we entitled to a visit from somebody in my family?" she would say.

When word came back from New York, Aunt Hannah *and* Aunt Sadie were coming. My mother said she should have known. And how could she tell Sadie not to come? One word from her and Hannah wouldn't be coming either. "You could believe me," she said to anybody listening.

Oh, boy, my aunts were coming. Nobody else had aunts from New York. And one of my aunts might get married and live here!

The impending visit became the pivot and focus of our lives. Logistics and support apparatuses were worked out as for a World War battle. Sleeping arrangements had my aunts in our room, and us in Joey's room, bedding down on the skinny bed feet to head, as my mother and Hannah had done as girls. This dumped Joey on our sofa. Yes, yet again a sofa for Joey.

If Joey could be relegated to the front room, his erector set, which he and T played with almost daily, could not. In the end it was posted to the front porch.

To honor the aunts Joey and T dedicated themselves to a construction to represent New York and went out onto the cold porch every afternoon to build the old Washington Bridge, which crossed the Harlem River from Manhattan to the Bronx, where, Joey told T, the aunts lived. The geography books from Uncle Philip were brought out, and the bridge pinpointed.

T was intrigued by the name "Bronx," and took it upon himself to research it in Joey's *Book of Knowledge*. Pleased that he was able to impart some "book" information, he told Joey that it had come from a Danish family named Bronck who had owned most of the land. When T spoke of New York matters in his rural Southern accent, it was no doubt marvelous to hear, and on this occasion, T explained that "the Bronx" had evolved from "the Broncks." According to Joey, the way he told it was, "Like as not, them Manhattan folks would say to one nother, 'Y'all reckon we ought to go up yonder and pay a call on the Broncks?' "

Lizzie Maud had been borrowed from Miss Brookie for two full days extra. It had been an awkward negotiation, taking place on the telephone. When it was over, my mother had hung up the receiver slowly, feeling the heaviness in her chest. She'd sat for a moment at the little telephone table and then gotten up and put two begonia plants on the windowsill in Miriam's and my bedroom.

Finally, they were here: Aunt Sadie, her longish nose bridged by rimless glasses, and Aunt Hannah, littler even than my mother. I felt like Erv Medlin: I could scarcely speak, only gaze. These were *my aunts, my relatives.*

Aunt Hannah, full of dimpled smiles, was obviously glad to be with us. *"Oy,"* she said, "how I been looking forward."

Aunt Sadie, on the other hand, let us know that the trip was a burdensome thing for which Aunt Hannah was to blame. "Hannah nagged and nagged," she said to us. "So could I let her come by herself? How she loves to be on the go is nobody's business."

My mother tried to figure out how Aunt

Hannah could be "on the go" when surely she went only to work or to the relatives. Or was it "on the go" to visit the cemeteries in Brooklyn or Queens, a cruel schlep, in which on your day off you rose at dawn, negotiated a maze of subway and trolley connections, milled around the cemetery trying to find the graves, and had time only to glance at them before they closed the gates? Still, with Hannah, you never knew.

Actually Hannah was the family "darling," which was a category. Hannah looked like a darling — small and soft with thick curls the color of new pennies; she acted like a darling, always trying to please, worried that she might *dis*please. Too much worried, my father always said. In the family she was called Hovvah-leb. Hannah-dear.

She was the youngest daughter and, having finished high school, worked as an assistant to a bookkeeper. Still, as with all darlings, her life was her family. She was especially close to Philip, the youngest sibling, and indeed the family called her his second mother. It was a title that pleased her very much.

"Anyway, so here we are," Aunt Sadie said. "But I ain't making no promises."

My mother struggled to project innocence. With Aunt Sadie the modus operandi was never to suggest you had an idea that she didn't have first. "Promises about what?" she asked her.

In answer Aunt Sadie gave a look that said, Are you trying to kid *me?*

The aunts' Gladstone bag — of yellow leather stiff as a wooden crate — held presents: hand-knitted scarves from my grandmother; books from Uncle Philip; boxed chocolates; a whole box of Hershey bars just for me; a string of amber beads for my sister; a gossamer shawl with wide satin ribbon borders for my mother; and, for my father and brother, shiny embroidered white silk yarmulkes, though we all knew that despite my mother's pleadings, they no longer wore caps even on Friday nights.

In our room Aunt Sadie immediately vetoed the begonias ("They smell funny"), and at the first meal, which starred pot roast, Aunt Sadie wanted to know if the meat was kosher.

My mother knew her sister was just "trying" her, as the neighbors might say, since she knew very well it wasn't kosher. She told Aunt Sadie to do as she did, which was not to think about it. "Keep it out of your head," she advised her.

"How can I keep it out when it's already in there? Nu, do you expect me to eat *traif?*" she asked my mother, and gave the word that she and Hannah would eat only dairy. "Just eggs and cheese and whatever else you got in the dairy line," she said, adding serenely that, after all, she and Hannah were not used to eating what we ate, we being "regular *traifnyaks*."

When Aunt Hannah tried to smooth things over, said, "I don't mind, Sadie, whatever we eat is all right with me," Aunt Sadie answered, "And you, you stop jumping up for anything new."

When Sadie said this, my mother, doing her best to stay focused on why her sisters were in Concordia in the first place, brought Manny instantly to mind. Could Manny not be considered new? Of course he could. My mother, unlike her sister Sadie, wished with all her might for Hannah to jump up for this something new. "Jump up, Hannah," she said silently. "Jump up and grab him."

Though Aunt Sadie was a trial — always acting like a boss whose workers were talking strike, my father said — the Bronson aunts ("aints" in Concordia) were instant celebrities. By virtue of living near them, the neighborhood children became celebrities in their own right and visited often to maintain status. They all had aunts of course, but theirs were too much like their own mothers to be intriguing. And, boy howdy, one of the Bronson "aints" (Aunt Sadie) wore black all the time, and they spoke in what could have been tongues.

The neighbors came to call, and after they left, Aunt Sadie would say, "What you see in them ain't worth talking about. They're just so goyish."

What made them so goyish I didn't know. That they said *y'all* instead of *youse?* That they either had very straight hair or got it curled at the Cinderella?

I could not believe that Miss Brookie would not want to meet the aunts from New York, so I ran and got her. She said she had been planning to come. "Think I'd pass up a chance to visit with some New York people?"

My mother was all open arms. "It's been so long," she said to Miss Brookie. My mother thought this was the moment when a peace treaty would at last be signed.

Sadly, it wasn't. Miss Brookie declined to grant forgiveness, just gave my mother a cool "Hey, Reba."

She sailed into the kitchen, joined the aunts in the breakfast nook. My mother put a glass of tea in front of her, and Miss Brookie, no doubt from the years of watching my parents, knew just what to do. Her only misstep was in swallowing the whole sugar cube at once. When she had got the sip down, she said,

"What's doing in New York, ladies?"

Aunt Sadie said, "Same old thing," and gave a shrug.

Miss Brookie said you could say "same old thing" about Concordia but not about New York. She thought New York "totally irresistible." Miss Brookie's "take" on New York, as they say now, was very different from that of the rest of the Concordians, who thought New York was the next worst thing to a sugar ditch.

"Never mind irresistible," said Aunt Sadie, who, though she had always made clear that New York was the only place to live, was not about to agree with Miss Brookie. "I can resist it plenty."

I suppose by now it had come through to Miss Brookie that these were not the "New York people" she had hoped for. She finished off her tea, said, "Have a nice stay in Concordia," slid out of the nook, and, having sailed *into* the house, she now sailed *out* of it.

One night, in an effort to divert our guests, Joey and Miriam and I decided on a soiree like the ones at Miss Brookie's. We would get up acts.

After supper the audience was ushered into the front room, while we prepared. As the youngest performer, I insisted that it was my prerogative to go last.

Joey did his tumbling act first, dashing through the door of the space-heater hall and throwing himself into a contained (of necessity) somersault. He segued into a backbend, and walked a foot or two like an upside-down spider. Everybody applauded.

My sister went out next. She danced energetically to a record on the Vic and, when it came to an end, kept dancing to her own humming and pretty soon was out of breath.

I wasn't ready. Miriam rested a bit and then did some more dancing and, when needed, some more humming.

I still wasn't ready. Joey brought in his bridge model and gave a little lecture. Everybody applauded some more, though the volume was weakening. My father yelled out, "Enough already, Stella Ruth. You got your customers complaining."

I finally glided out. My upper body was draped with the Spanish shawl that had formerly draped Miss Brookie's piano, before being cast aside in favor of one with a more ponderous fringe. A paper rose drooped behind my ear; my mother's fox fur piece, its teeth gripping its tail, encircled my neck; my sister's rhinestone earrings (hitherto hidden from my mother) dangled from my earlobes. Laughter and applause greeted me.

Like the lady I had seen at the recital in Chautauqua, I placed the palms of my hands together and lay them alondge my cheek. I opened my mouth to sing. Unfortunately, the song I had chosen was "Oh, What a Friend We Have in Jesus."

I knew the word *Jesus* was not employed at our house, but this was a *song,* one in much demand at backyard bird interments. On this occasion, however, its opening lines made everything go ka-boom.

My father took the coward's way out and shot out of the room, impacting several chairs on the way. My mother shrieked "Stella Ruth!" and Miriam slipped from her chair to the floor, her dress flying up and bloomers coming into view.

Aunt Sadie jumped up as if a bug had bitten her sharply on her bottom. "Reba!" I heard her shout. "Is this child saying what I think she's saying? Is she? Is she?"

In a moment Joey had rushed up and clapped his hand over my mouth as if to stanch a broken hose. Over his thumb I saw Aunt Hannah hiding a grin and my mother clutching at her heart.

Joey put my shawl around me and dragged me out of the room.

Aunt Sadie stayed on it a long time. "Church songs! Christian hymns! That my ears should hear such things!" There were sudden, similar bursts all evening. "Is this the way you bring up Jewish children? Is this what these children have been learning, Reba? Are you crazy?"

My mother tried to answer with apology, justification, reason. Finally she said, "It's so awful hard down here. You don't know how it is with no nothing Jewish. Can I keep my eyes on them every second? They're out playing. How can I know every little thing they're doing?"

"And who are they playing with? Tell me with who." Aunt Sadie glared. When she had glared at everybody in turn, she stomped off to bed.

Miriam and I made for bed as well. But if the excitement in the front room was over, in Joey's bedroom it was not. No, in Joey's bedroom a little more excitement began when Miriam was undressing on the bed, yanked her dress up over her head, and, with her head completely enclosed, began to sing. And what was she singing, softly to be sure? Nothing other than the first verse of "Oh, What a Friend We Have in Jesus." It seemed to me the most delightful thing in the world, a siren song, so tempting, so inviting that all I could do was pull my own dress up over my head, scrunch over, and join my voice to hers. And what could Miriam and I do but sit with our heads together, dresses up over them, and sing verse after verse and laugh ourselves silly?

It was time to implement the main plot. My mother had made a long-distance call to the Rastows, in which she'd mentioned as casually as she could that she wanted them to come to dinner on Sunday to meet her sisters. When Gladys had asked for some sort of facts about the sisters, my mother had broken it off with, "So you'll come on Sunday and you'll see for yourself." Gladys had said "Delighted" in the way that meant she wasn't delighted at all.

As the visit neared, my mother's hidden agenda was completely exposed. The aunts understood it all plainly, and Aunt Hannah at least had no objections. But she had plenty of questions. "Is he . . . uh, handsome?" she asked Miriam.

"Very," Miriam answered her.

"Handsome" could mean something besides pleasing features, well arranged. Did it also mean Manny was tall?

Miriam had to say that he was not exactly tall, but tall enough for Aunt Hannah.

Aunt Hannah's level of expectation probably took a steep drop. She said in a rueful voice, "A midget in the circus is tall enough

for me. . . . I suppose he has kinky hair, too?"
She was now fearing the worst.

When she heard that Manny's hair, though
dark, was straight and parted in the middle,
she brightened. "Like John Gilbert?" she
asked Miriam.

"You know, he *does* favor John Gilbert."
Miriam wanted Aunt Hannah to know that
Manny was full of fun. "He's just a bear for
cutting the fool," she said.

"Cuttin' the fool?" Aunt Hannah always
tried her best to imitate Southern talk. "Ah
'clare, your Manny sounds *purely scrumptious,*
hear?"

Aunt Sadie had my mother on the stand,
first to find out what kind of living this "boyfriend" of Hannah's made.

"Sadie, stop!" my mother cried. "You
know he ain't no boyfriend!" But she was
happy to be able to inform Aunt Sadie that
Manny made a lovely living from a lovely
store. And in a nice little town. *Nice little town?*
What was she doing, my mother, flopping
around in these strange waters?

Aunt Sadie crinkled her nose, as if getting a
whiff of a thing too long in the icebox. "And a
shul? They got a shul?"

"You know they don't have no shul."

My father tried to float my mother a life
preserver and reminded her of the *mohel.*

317

Aunt Sadie was not impressed. "So a *mohel* comes in, gives the *putzel* a cut, and leaves. And the baby grows up an ignoramus singing Christian hymns."

"Well, at least he'd be singing circumcised," my father said.

It was a snowy Sunday the day the Rastows came. At the door Gladys Rastow immediately took in Aunt Hannah's finger — the third finger, on the left hand — which, my mother said later, must have looked to her as bare as a dogwood branch in winter.

Gladys Rastow greeted both aunts coolly. Aunt Sadie returned the favor. When they spoke to each other, it was as if they were biting off tough crusts of rye bread.

My mother had improvised a table that could seat the whole crowd. When dinner was announced, Gladys rushed to a chair on one side of Aunt Hannah and sent Delores to the other. Manny managed to foil her by seating himself directly opposite Aunt Hannah and not taking his eyes off her.

After things had been passed, Gladys pointed to Aunt Hannah's plate. On it were some lonely-looking garden peas. Gladys looked at them and asked of anyone whose attention she could enlist, "Can it be that these Bronx ladies eat only *peas?*"

It was a remark that led Aunt Sadie to expound a principle: that if you're a Jewish person, you don't make exceptions. After she had expounded it, she said, clearly addressing a lesser person, "That's the way we live, Mrs. Rastow, Hannah and I."

Suddenly all eyes went to Aunt Hannah. As if the copper of her hair had descended into her cheeks, her face was agleam. And then she had bent her head over her plate. She might have been saying, Please God, please make them stop talking.

In another moment she had risen from the table and, murmuring "Excuse me, I got something to do," was running for the front door. I ran after her.

Aunt Hannah and I were sitting on the swing, not talking, just being cold, when here came Manny.

"Such arguing ladies," he said. "They might be having a good time, but believe me they're spoiling my appetite." He sat down across from us. "Yours, too?"

In case he was talking to me, I said yes, and Aunt Hannah said she wasn't really hungry anyway.

Manny ran to his buggy. He grabbed up a blanket from the back seat, brought it back, sat down between Aunt Hannah and me, and tucked the dark green plaid over us. "So you'll warm up a bit," he said.

Aunt Hannah said how surprised she was to find cold in "the sunny South." There it was again: "the sunny South."

He took hold of one of Aunt Hannah's hands, and she didn't take it away. I sat there aware of every nuance of speech and movement, and if someone had asked, I could have said when they used each other's first names and which of their fingers were interlocking. Manny said for Aunt Hannah to wait for him next Sunday. "You hear me what I'm saying, Hannah?" Where they were going was to Deerfoot Lake.

I was delighted. Deerfoot seemed to me ideal for a courtship or, for that matter, for any kind of good time. In summer it served as our spot for picnicking and swimming, although it had ragged gray trunks of trees sticking out of it, reminders that Deerfoot had once long ago been not a lake but a forest.

Deerfoot was good in winter, too. It was shallow and froze fast, perfect for ice-skating. If you fell in, you couldn't fall too deep, and lots of people were there to pull you out.

I pictured Manny and Aunt Hannah driving around the lake, walking on the ice close to shore, holding hands.

They were going to eat in the restaurant at

Deerfoot. "Just the three of us," Manny said to Aunt Hannah.

Me? My heart was beating fast.

Sadly, the three turned out to be Aunt Hannah, Manny, and a widemouth bass. Bass, along with the crappies, flourished in Deerfoot. "Only a widemouth different than the ones in the house, believe me," Manny said.

Gladys Rastow came charging out, Irving and Delores and Sheldon behind. She eyed the blanket, as if the function it was performing was not only unauthorized but illegal. She snatched it up. "We've got to go," she said to Manny.

Manny got up slowly. He bent down over Aunt Hannah. His lips were right on her ear. "Don't forget next Sunday."

Aunt Hannah nodded, and Gladys watched. And so did my mother. And so did Aunt Sadie. Well, so did everybody.

Aunt Sadie spilled out to my mother, my mother used to say, like an open fire hydrant. Gladys Rastow seemed to be her main target. "I wouldn't wish that sister-in-law on my worst enemy, never mind my own flesh and blood. *Oy*, what a yenta." (I always thought Gladys would rather have been called a yokel than a yenta.)

My mother was trying to keep her plan on track. "What are you making such a fuss? Nobody's marrying Gladys."

"And in that little Southern town yet," Aunt Sadie said.

"I'm in a little Southern town and I'm still alive," my mother answered her. "Things ain't perfect, but —"

Aunt Sadie was ready. "But you ain't permanent. That makes the difference, right?"

On Sunday Aunt Hannah awoke in a fever of excitement that heightened as the morning went on. She dressed right after breakfast, even to her green wool tam, stationed herself in the front room, and dashed back and forth to the window. "I could have sworn I heard a buggy," she'd say. She'd sit down again, get up, sit down. As she darted about, the scallops around the hem of her white wool dress caught the light like newly minted silver coins. She looked beautiful.

Around eleven Manny clip-clopped up and in a quick jump was out of the buggy. Aunt Hannah ran back to her chair and sat down, jamming the tam on her head, firmly, as if it were a device to keep her from jumping up again. Miriam opened the door.

In came Manny, calling out greetings, dashing from one to the other of us, being playful as usual, seizing a handful of Joey's curls, bowing to Miriam while he kissed her hand and clicked his heels, pinching my freckles and pretending to hold them in his fist. Aunt Sadie watched from the kitchen doorway.

Manny wondered if Aunt Hannah was going to be warm enough. "Anyways, we got the blanket in the buggy, that big important blanket," he said, smiling at me as if I was a co-conspirator. "So let's go."

Aunt Sadie came walking in. "Don't be so quick, Mr. Buggy Ride. She forgot something." She handed Aunt Hannah a brown paper sack. "This is for you while Mr. Sidalia, Kentucky, is eating in his restaurant." Aunt Sadie referred to Manny only by a made-up name or "he," as if using his real name would make him a real person. "I don't want you should get sick while I'm in charge."

When Aunt Hannah looked stricken, my father took the sack from her hands. "She won't need this," he said, handing it back to Aunt Sadie. "They're not in business to make people sick."

Manny grabbed up Aunt Hannah's coat, and then he took her hand, and pulled her out the door. On the porch they stood for a second while Manny put her into her coat, and then they both laughed and ran to the buggy.

When Aunt Hannah came in, if she was sick, it was more like lovesick. Manny plucked off her tam, and her hair flicked up from the dry air, shooting out a little, as if from the sheer joy of liberation. He unwound her scarf, and told something of how the day had gone, looking all the while into Aunt Hannah's face. Aunt Hannah had apparently done a bit of the driving, and Manny said, "This girl with the reins in her hands — some sight."

"A city girl don't know from horses," Aunt Sadie countered promptly.

Manny said he was a city boy and certainly knew from horses. On his wagon, he said, there had been two horses and six legs: "Him with his four and me with my two."

Aunt Sadie grabbed the scarf and tam from Manny's hands. "So thanks for the buggy ride. Hannah enjoyed."

Manny laughed. "Looks like I'm saying good-bye." He touched Aunt Hannah on the arm, his fingers lingering. "I'll be seeing you. Soon."

Aunt Hannah nodded. "Yes, Manny. Soon." After Manny left, she stayed looking out the window for long minutes.

"See?" Aunt Sadie muttered. "Now we got *some* job to do!"

Aunt Hannah may not have even heard. She had grabbed up the tam and scarf, plunked the tam on Miriam's head, and flung the scarf around her own shoulders. In a moment she was pulling Miriam around the room in a movement half dance, half ring-around-the-rosy.

Aunt Hannah's eyes squeezed shut, then flew open. She took Miriam close in her arms. "Oh, baby girl, you should have been there! Everything so quiet! And the snow white, white, white!"

She swung Miriam into a twirl, and Joey began singing a current tune, one that might have been written for the occasion, promoting as it did buggy riding over automobiling: No smell of gasoline, just an old-fashioned team," it went, and further told of the "wonderful treat to hear the pat of horses' feet." As Joey caroled, my father clapped along.

I could resist no longer. I wedged myself between Aunt Hannah and Miriam and started twirling with Miriam. Then Aunt Hannah grabbed Joey. In a moment she and Joey snatched up my mother and they became a twirling threesome.

That left my father and Aunt Sadie, but there was not going to be any twirling *there*.

Aunt Sadie said to Aunt Hannah, "Sure, go on and dream yourself into a nightmare."

Everybody at last stopped dancing, and Aunt Sadie wanted to know where it went from here.

"Back to the lake, I hope." Aunt Hannah closed her eyes.

Aunt Sadie told her to save her jokes. "And for God's sake, keep your eyes open already."

Well, Manny was coming to Concordia tomorrow afternoon.

"He don't go to work on Mondays?"

Well, he did, but he would be taking off early.

Taking off early? Aunt Sadie smelled something. So what was so important he had to take off early?

Manny wanted to talk to my father.

To who? You could see Aunt Sadie feeling insulted.

My father maintained his calm, perhaps not wanting to get into a competition with Aunt Sadie about who had family authority when. He said the thing to do was to let Manny talk, and if Manny was serious, he'd just tell him to talk with my grandfather in New York. "You think he's serious?" he asked Aunt Hannah.

Aunt Hannah said, yes, she thought he was serious.

If this was harmonious music to my ears, to Aunt Sadie it was discordancy. "Just hold your horses, everybody," she said. "Hannah ain't really thought about this thing."

Uh-oh.

Aunt Hannah stared at her. "You got something against Manny?"

Aunt Sadie took a seat in the nearby chair and leaned close. "It ain't him," she said, in a lowered voice, as if they might hear her in Sidalia. "Though what's so hot about him, I ain't sure either." There were, apparently, plenty of other things to worry about.

The other things, Aunt Sadie said, "began at the beginning," when my mother came to the South. According to Aunt Sadie, perhaps forgetting that it was she who had fought tooth and nail to keep my mother from doing it, my mother had to come. "Her place was with her husband," Aunt Sadie said to Aunt Hannah. "But you ain't in that kind of predicament."

It was when Aunt Sadie went on to say that Aunt Hannah would meet a nice boy in New York and settle down like "a normal Jewish woman" that Aunt Hannah burst into tears.

How could Aunt Sadie make my pretty, everybody-loved-her Aunt Hannah cry?

My father at last opened up. He said that Aunt Sadie did not have the last — or best — word on everything. "Do what you want, Hannah," he said. "You want Manny, so tell him. You don't have to do everything Sadie says. Be your own person for once."

Could my Aunt Hannah act on what my father had said? No. Defying Sadie was something outside her experience, and she was at this point totally confused. She asked through her tears, "But what's wrong? Wasn't this what we all wanted?"

"Not all of us," Aunt Sadie answered her. "Only Reba and the rest of the *Southerners*."

My mother was darting from Aunt Sadie to Aunt Hannah. "Wait! Wait! In the morning we'll be calmer," she pleaded.

"*You* may not be calm," Aunt Sadie answered her, "but *I* am. Like a cold potato I'm calm." She crossed her arms and sat motionless. "There's things Hannah should think about before Mr. Horse-with-Two-Legs comes back tomorrow."

Aunt Sadie looked to my mother. Hadn't my mother been telling her how her heart ached to see her mother and father, her "Ma and Pa"? Did my mother wish this on her baby sister?

My mother's face drew in like a pricked balloon. "Hannah," she said, "Hovvah-leb. Maybe you should listen. You're so young, you don't how it is to live among strangers."

"But I'll have you! Since when are you strangers?"

There was a long silence while my mother wondered if she could chance it. Could she say, with my father sitting right there, that we wouldn't be in Concordia forever, that we were tem-po-rary? She couldn't help herself; she said it. And then she asked Aunt Hannah, "And what will you do then?"

She would have Manny, Aunt Hannah said. "Don't that make up for everything else?"

And Aunt Sadie said promptly, "Not everything." What was Aunt Hannah going to do when she had a family? "Then what?" Aunt Hannah asked her. *Then,* according to Aunt Sadie, Aunt Hannah would be like my mother, living in a goyish world, not knowing what to do when it was time for her son to become a man.

It was Joey's cue to bolt out of the room. And my father's cue to really get into it. Aunt Sadie had finally said too much. "That is our business, not yours," my father told her. "So just butt out." To Aunt Hannah he said, "How can you listen to Sadie and her bogeyman stories?"

This gave Aunt Hannah a bit of spunk. She raised her chin and said to Aunt Sadie, "I think I can manage."

But Aunt Sadie had an ace in the hole, the coup de grace: "Have you figured how you're

going to leave Philip?" she asked Aunt
Hannah.

And, of course, Aunt Hannah cried out,
"Philip! *Oy*, Philip! Don't say Philip!"

Aunt Sadie cried right back, in a voice as
loud as I had ever heard, "Why shouldn't I
say Philip? I got to say Philip!" Her groans
filled the room. "So she thinks she's found
Mr. Happy-Ever-After! A Jewish girl don't
have no business to cut herself away from her
family for that! Is she a cripple she has to
marry the first man who asks? There are
plenty of men looking for wives, believe me!
My Izzy can bring them home by the dozens!"

The thought of the men my Uncle Izzy
could bring home by the dozens, the men
from the immigrant pool, switched my
mother to the other side. My mother said that
by this point she was "so much to-ing and
from-ing," she was dizzy. But how could she
not speak out when Sadie was comparing
such men to Manny? "Sadie, listen!" she
cried. "You'll still see Hannah. You'll come
here! You can come here when you want!"

Aunt Sadie ceased all motion and sat staring at the opposite wall as if reading a legend
written thereon. "No, I ain't never coming
here again," she intoned.

"Oh, Sadie!" Aunt Hannah cried, and her
sobs once more filled the room.

My father, perhaps, like me, feeling overwhelmed by all the emotional firepower, agreed with my mother that it should be left for the morning. "And maybe whatever disease Sadie is suffering from," he said, "will change its mind by then."

"Don't count on it," Aunt Sadie answered him.

All through the night the house stayed awake. My mother slipped in and out of her sisters' room. Toward morning Aunt Sadie came out and bedded down on the bentwood rocker. The crying from Aunt Hannah never stopped. In the morning she emerged from the bedroom silent and pale, stood at the kitchen door, and said, "I hate to be here when he comes." Then she sat in the breakfast nook and stared at her coffee cup.

The day passed in silence.

Finally Manny arrived. He came around six, just as the early darkness was setting in, and was out of his buggy in a great leap. Aunt Hannah went to meet him in the front yard.

Manny took her hands in his and smiled into her face. As she spoke, the smile faded until it disappeared altogether. In the next moment he had broken away and was striding into the house.

He sat down on the sofa and shook his head

when my mother offered him tea. His dark skin seemed to have gone lighter, though his eyes were darker than ever. No, there would be no playfulness from our playful Manny today. I pushed up against the wall on the other side of the room to distance myself from this stranger.

Manny finally spoke, to say he was waiting for my father. "I need to talk to Aaron. I got to get put straight," he said, sitting with his coat on, holding his hat in front of his knees.

Aunt Hannah sat on the other end of the sofa, silent, tears always just about to spill over.

My father came home, mad at Sadie, mad at my mother, and having to face Manny. He hooked his coat and hat on the rack. "Well," he said to Manny. "Well, well."

Manny jumped up. No "hello," no "*Nu*, so how's business?," just bewilderment, asking my father, "What's all this, Aaron? What's all this Hannah is telling me?"

My father had no answers. He had nothing to offer that could possibly comfort. He said, to say something, "Ladies cut off their noses to spite their faces."

Manny pushed his face up to my father's. "It ain't up to the *ladies!* It's up to Hannah. That's all who it's up to!"

My father tried to tell Manny about

Hannah, about who Hannah *was*, but Manny wouldn't listen. "These sisters of hers have turned her so she don't know which way is up no more," he said.

Manny looked to my mother. "How come you did this thing?" he asked her. "I'm really surprised. I always thought you liked me, Reba."

My mother felt a hard blow to her heart. "As much as a brother I liked you!" she cried out to him.

"So now you don't like me no more? So now all of a sudden I'm maybe a murderer or a thief?" Manny's eyes were dark as night. "For God's sake, so what's wrong with me?"

My mother used to say, in one of her most memorable mixed metaphors, that she was reaching in the barrel and finding there not a leg to stand on. What was wrong, she said to Manny, not really believing it, not really *dis*believing it, was that she now foresaw no bed of roses for Hannah. "Let it be, Manny," she said. "I beg you let it be."

Manny would not let it be until he had heard again from Hannah. He touched Aunt Hannah on the cheek. "Tell me what you want, Hannah. Don't be afraid." He had it right. Aunt Hannah was afraid. Afraid of sister Sadie, afraid of leaving Philip, afraid. Aunt

Hannah said she couldn't leave her family. "It's not in me," she said to him.

Poor Manny. He had had the misfortune to fall in love with a family darling.

Chapter 20

The Bar Mitzvah Question

If the Manny and Hannah story seemed enough misadventure for one day, there were misadventures yet to come.

After Manny had left, all of us, except for Aunt Hannah, moved into the kitchen. The meal began as a silent one. My father was angry, but as I knew so well, he would not stay that way for long. When my mother was angry, she could persevere, but my father had no fortitude for this. His anger always had only a brief stay, and when it was gone, it was gone.

He had done his best with Hannah, but he had figured all along that she would not listen to him. Although he thought she was a very foolish girl, a noodle, well, if she preferred something else to Manny, it was up to her. Her reasons were her own. Ah, women, he would have thought, go figure.

At the table he pretty soon brought out a story from the store, about a customer who

335

had grudgingly allowed Seth to wait on him and ultimately had bought not only the shirt he had come in for but also two ties. "What did I tell you?" my father said. "The man's a born sal-es-man." For Seth's show of enterprise, my father had put him on commission.

My father had instituted the practice of commissions some time ago. Not only would it give the clerks an extra incentive but would also allow them a share in the store's prosperity. Vedra Broome was very much in favor and rushed around the store, as my father noted, "going like sixty," as we said in the days when sixty miles an hour was a blazing speed. The commission added two percent of sales to seven-dollar-a-week wages.

My father's offer of conversation went unaccepted. All heads stayed bent over the soup.

After supper, Joey and Miriam left, and my mother brought over the glasses of tea. For me there was my usual: a small amount of tea and a large dollop of jelly.

Aunt Sadie gave a look to my mother, left her tea standing, slid out from the nook, and went into the front room. This was all very portentous. It was obvious that my mother wanted to talk, and to talk *serious,* as she would say, to my father. I scrunched into a back corner.

The aunts were leaving, we all knew that.

Though most of us were going to at least miss Aunt Hannah, my father was not going to miss either one of them.

Even my mother found it hard to regret Aunt Sadie's upcoming departure. Most of Sadie's complaints she could put up with, but on the subject of the bar mitzvah, Sadie had been a "torn" in my mother's side. Run from Sadie though my mother did, run from *herself* though my mother did, Aunt Sadie always managed sooner or later to catch up and pile on the guilt. As to Joey already being almost thirteen, the magic age, Aunt Sadie said Joey was a smart boy and with double Hebrew lessons "could do it easy."

On this night my mother introduced the bar mitzvah discussion with a reminder to my father that her sisters would be leaving soon. He said he'd try to survive. "But some job I'll have to live through it."

"And Sadie and I have been talking."

My father gave my mother one of his fake looks of disbelief. "You and Sadie been *talking?* Remind me to tell it to the *Sentinel*." He took a long, noisy sip of tea. "I ain't exactly in the mood for no more talking from you and Sadie." And worse, my father knew exactly what was on my mother's mind.

My mother tried for a way to say it. She started with the thought that there was nothing in Concordia for the children, but she always said she knew immediately it had come out all wrong.

It certainly sounded all wrong to my father. "Nothing here but family and friends," he snapped. "Nothing here but what to make them happy." He was waiting for my mother to say that Joey should go to New York with Sadie. When she didn't say it, he said it for her. "Is that what you mean, Reba?"

I held my breath for the answer.

My mother didn't say yes or no. She just said it was a chance for Joey to go with somebody looking after him.

So who had decided that Joey was going in the first place, my father wanted to know. "When did we decide this? Do I remember deciding this?"

"We all know what has to be," my mother said to my father.

My father just turned and yelled for Joey to come into the kitchen. He wanted to hear from the horse's mouth, as he said, if we all knew it had to be.

My brother came in. He too knew what it was about.

Straightaway my father asked, "You want to go to New York and be a bar mitzvah boy, Joey?"

Joey didn't say yes or no either. Joey has always said that at that moment he was too full of my father needing him on Saturdays, full of school, full of Concordia. No, he didn't want to go, he didn't want to go in the worst way. He said to my father, "Mama wants me to."

It sounded awful to my mother. "It ain't like we want you to go away!" she cried. "We don't! We don't!"

My father would have none of this. He told my mother to tell it right. "And how it is, is you want him to go. Otherwise, why are you making all this fuss? You want him to go, ain't that right?" My mother couldn't understand this fine point. Of course she wanted Joey to go, but of course she *didn't* want him to go. Why was my father saying it like that?

My father persisted. "Say it, Reba, say it. Say you want him to go."

My mother finally said it. "All right already. I want him to go. He's a Jewish boy, and a Jewish boy has to have a bar mitzvah."

"Tell me, Reba," my father said, in a *very* quiet, ominously quiet, voice, "is it right that a bar mitzvah should break a little boy's heart? And his mother's and father's, too?"

My mother answered that sacrifices had to be made, that they had to be good Jewish parents. She said, "Aaron, don't you see? We have to do right!"

"Right by who?"

339

"Right by God," my mother said, as if finally stating a something no one could argue with.

She reckoned without my father. "What God? Who God?" he cried out to her. "What God do you know? You only know people who say they speak for God. Can't you see that?"

My mother was scarcely listening. By now she was only trying to pacify. She already had Joey in cheder. "He'll be back before you know it," she said.

My father knew better. It would be almost a year before Joey would be back, and it would seem a very long time indeed. He glanced over at me. "The little one will have a hard time remembering she's *got* a brother by the time he comes back." He looked at Joey and said, "No, Joey, I don't have no way to explain. It don't make no sense to me neither."

And, as he pushed himself out from the table, my father was saying, "So that's how it is. And how it is is how it is."

The next day my mother went with my brother to withdraw him from school. I went along. Going to one of the "real" schools was to me an adventure not to be missed.

"We've so enjoyed having Joseph with us," said Miss Ada, the principal of the sixth-through twelfth-grade school. She could have been a twin to Miss Mattie: hair done up over a similar rat, same protruding shirtfront suffering from starch overload.

Miss Ada pulled out Joey's records from a yellow oak file cabinet. "These will show what a good pupil he's been," she said as she handed the papers to my mother. She hoped they would take time to appreciate him in "that great big school he's going to." "Lord knows," she said, "he's been pure inspiration around here."

My mother went home with the papers, and Joey and I went around to T's classroom. We waited in the hall for recess. When the class came out, Joey caught T by the arm and pulled him over to the wall. "Got something to tell you," he said.

T wanted to know if Joey wasn't going to recess.

"Nope," Joey answered him, "I'm going to New York."

"On a visit?"

"Nope, I'm going to school there."

"You folks moving?"

"Nope. Only me's going."

T did his thing of flicking his eyes up. "You telling me a story?"

"Nope, I got to go to study for my bar mitzvah." Joey has always said that at that moment, he "wished to his soul" (an expression from Concordia that he still uses) that T could go with him. How could he go to the home of "the Broncks" without T?

T hit the wall softly with his fist, turned back, and said to the air, perhaps to the world, "This is so sorry, there ought to be a law."

The records were given to Aunt Sadie. Joey was to live with our grandparents, and Aunt Sadie would enroll him in the nearby public school. "It's a lovely school with a lovely playground," she informed him.

Miriam said Concordia had a lovely school with a lovely playground.

Aside from hostile exchanges between Miriam and Aunt Sadie, in these last few days there was little else in the way of talk. Aunt Hannah neither asked a question nor answered one. She did her packing by dropping things haphazardly into the Gladstone bag, after which she would sit on the front porch.

My father was almost as silent, though on one memorable occasion, he lashed out at Aunt Sadie. "Why did we need you anyway?" he asked her. "We had a nice family in a nice little town with a nice business. Who needed you to come here and turn everything into I don't know what?"

Though it was obviously a rhetorical question, Aunt Sadie's lips gathered together, made a little knot in her face, and she said, "I'm only looking out for the family, like always."

To which my father replied that so far, with her looking out for the family, everybody was miserable. "Hannah ain't happy, and ditto for the rest of us." He gave her a look. "Okay, you win. Pack up your soft-boiled eggs and go on home."

My mother, according to my father, was also to blame. "Look what you done, Reba. And for what? For who?" For the first time in my life, I was seeing my father *furious* with my mother, not joshing her, not teasing her, but mad and meaning it.

With my father's anger so intensely upon her, my mother's already shaky confidence all but collapsed. She was suddenly aware of a longing for bed, for green eyeshades.

The train was an early-morning one. Only my mother and I were with Joey at the depot. My father was not there, no reasons given. He had simply gotten up before sunrise, readied himself for work, and gone silently out the door.

My sister was not there either. Although her teacher would surely have excused her for such important family business, she had nonetheless grabbed up her satchel and headed off for school, yelling as she went, "Will somebody please *explain* this to me?" Seth took us to the depot in the wagon.

Even though I had been to our outdoor depot many times, today everything about it seemed strange. There was no real light, and shadows fell in curious angles.

My mother was straightening Joey's collar, fussing with his tie, pushing at his hair. "If you've forgotten anything, I'll send it right away," she was saying.

T came into the depot, alone, no Erv. "I had to see for my own self that you was truly going," he said to Joey. He stubbed hard at the concrete floor with his black hightop shoes. "You coming back?"

"Sure. Soon's I finish everything."

"Lord, that's a long time off."

In a moment there was the chugging, snorting, and clanging of an arriving train. Then it had stopped and was exhaling giant white puffs. The Negro porter came along and grabbed up all the bags on the platform and swung them into a car. "Whoever belongs to these here bags best come along," he called out. "This here train's raring to go, like a hound dog after a rabbit." I had often heard the porters say exactly this, and I had always laughed, but today it didn't seem much of a joke.

Aunt Sadie shouted to Aunt Hannah and Joey, and Aunt Hannah finally moved up the steps, Aunt Sadie shoving from behind.

Joey wasn't moving. There was a problem: My mother was holding him around the arms, and I by his legs. He finally wriggled free from my mother's grasp; I was still wound around.

He bent down and spoke into my ear. He wanted me to do him a favor. He wanted me to wave good-bye to him like Raggedy Ann. "It'll make Mama laugh," he whispered to me.

I unwound. I put my hand up and let it flop around crazily in a rag doll's version of a wave. Though it brought no laugh from my mother, I felt entitled to a quid pro quo, and I told Joey he had to bring me back a present.

Joey agreed. "A sweet to eat and a toy to enjoy. Promise."

Aunt Hannah appeared once at the train window, did a small flutter, and went back out of sight. Aunt Sadie gave a few business-like nods. Joey was leaning out the window waving to us as the train pulled out.

Afterwards T split off in the direction of school, and my mother and I turned the corner toward the wagon. A plump lady was rounding full tilt from the other side. "Did I miss him?" the lady asked, struggling for breath. It was Miss Brookie.

My mother nodded.

Miss Brookie said, "Damn! Double dog damn!" and blamed the stove for making her late. "Wouldn't you know that on this particular morning, it would decide to take its own sweet time?" She held up a cardboard box. Inside was Joey's favorite coconut cake. She had wanted to give it to him. "So he won't forget us," she said.

"Forget us?" My mother hurtled into alarm. "Why should he forget us?"

No doubt sensing that at this moment my mother needed all the support she could get, Miss Brookie showed some signs of softening in her feelings toward her. "Why, I might have sent him to New York, too," she said to her.

My mother brightened a bit. "You would? You would have sent him?"

"Yes, I might have." But Miss Brookie could reassure no further. Certain principles could not be violated. She plunked the box into my mother's hands and said, "But, mercy, your reasons and mine? As different as billy goats and bananas."

We started on our way again. My mother was now carrying the cardboard box, though it took a moment for her to be conscious of it. Then all at once the presence in her hands of a lard-laden cake, given to her by a lady who chided and scolded her, meant for a son to whom she had just said a tearful good-bye, seemed just one burden too many. She settled the box on top of a nearby ligustrum hedge.

And the day was not over: At the end of it, there was my father moving out from the bedroom behind the French doors and into Joey's room. What he told my mother was that he didn't feel too good about things. "I don't even feel too good about me," he said. "Maybe I need to be by myself for a while."

At first we all missed Joey very much. We each had our own way of missing him, but we all missed him. Of course, with time these feelings subsided, and it wasn't long before everything closed over like grass over a bare patch in the earth, though, it must be reported, my father continued to sleep in Joey's bedroom.

My memories of Joey were like scenes from old picture shows, and they no doubt receded more quickly for me than for the others. It wasn't long before I had to work hard to bring him to mind. In short order I couldn't recall what he looked like; and then I had no memory of his ever having lived with us. As my father had predicted, in a few months, as I was very young, I forgot Joey just about entirely.

Chapter 21

Gentiles

Though the passing years were bringing their share of changes, there was one constant: the long, boring Sundays. I had taken Joey's place in the casino games, but Miriam would play for only a short while before quitting. If we didn't say as Miriam used to, "I hate Sundays!" the sentiment was there.

The Rastows were never Sunday visitors anymore, and news of them was scarce. Sammy Levine had nothing to report until one day he told us that Manny had married a local Sidalia girl. My mother used to say that the news was a "lump" in her heart.

So on the Sunday I saw Seth walking up to the back door (in "good darky" fashion), I thought that here at last was rescue. I anticipated cat's cradles with the length of wrapping-counter string Seth always carried in his pocket.

He came onto the little back porch smiling funny. He told me to run fetch my daddy. Nothing else.

My father came right out, and Seth stood stiffly in his Sunday clothes and said he had something to tell him. "Something mighty important," Seth said.

My father went to one of the private jokes he and Seth shared. He said to him, "With all that Jewish blood you got in you, nothing but money can be that important. How much you need?"

It wasn't money. It was that he had "done bad." Mr. Lassiter had told him so. Lassiter, the man who delivered coal.

"Lassiter? What's he got to do with the price of eggs?"

It was not eggs but Seth's clerking that Lassiter had made his business. He had told Seth that clerking was not for niggers, even if they only sold to niggers. "He say I dassent sell at Bronson's no more," Seth told my father.

My father immediately pinned it on the Ku Klux Klan. Seth's news had caught him off guard, as he had somehow managed to forget about the Klan.

Trying to project an air of confidence, he managed a little — a very little — smile. "Where is it written that we're on this earth to keep Everett Lassiter happy?"

Seth confirmed it was the Ku Klux Klan. He pronounced the first word "Klu," as did the rest of Concordia, black and white. There

349

had, Seth said, been talk of marching. "It mean a cross-burning for sure. Maybe worse."

My father could not allow himself to think what "worse" could mean. What he *could* think was that this all came from Vedra Broome. She had been unhappy when Seth had been put on commission, and this was the result. "I think I got the picture," my father said to Seth. "You leave it to me."

When my father told my mother, he said, "I ought to fire Vedra so fast her curls would open up."

But it wasn't that easy. First of all, my father didn't believe in an eye for an eye. "You do that," he once said to me, "and pretty soon you got a town full of blind people." Anyway, firing Vedra had to be weighed: It was not something you could do without considering ramifications. It was Seth who would have to go. He could not even go back to old handyman's job, not with Vedra in the store.

My father felt responsible for finding something for Seth to do, and, as usual, he wandered over to his regular post for problem solving, the window that overlooked the sward of grass between our house and the Overbys' about thirty feet away. He gave some thought to talking to somebody high up in the Klan, reasoning with that person, maybe even buttering him up. He decided against it. What that man needed was not a false kiss but an honest slap, and he was in no position to deliver it.

As he stood there gazing absently, he ran through Seth-type job possibilities. He had about exhausted them when the Studebaker swam into his line of vision.

He stared at the car, fast turning into a heap of rusting metal since Joey had left. My father had not followed through on his vow, after Joey's departure, to learn to drive. Whether he had declined to learn because cars had a lot of mechanical failures and it was necessary to be able to do some repair work at home — something, my father thought, that was definitely for Gentiles (my brother's affinity for car repair was considered aberrational) — or because cars were becoming associated with traveling salesmen, it didn't matter. Perhaps it was both reasons. At any rate, the car had become useless.

He watched a bird fly into an opening in one of the isinglass windows where a snap had given way. "The world's most expensive birdhouse" was the way he always described the car as he saw it at that moment. Still, it gave him an idea: Seth would be a chauffeur. "I guess that's nigger work, ain't it?" he said to my mother.

My mother praised him for working something out.

"Didn't take much brains," my father answered her.

Recalling an old saying of her mother's, my mother said to my father, "The highest wisdom is kindness."

"Ah, I did only what I had to."

"No, you didn't *had* to. But you did," my mother persisted. She spoke to her invisible third person. "That's because not everybody's a mensch like my husband, you can't tell me no."

And on that night when it came time for bed, instead of giving a curt nod and making for Joey's room as he usually did, my father decided he'd had enough of the skinny bed and "bunking" his head on the shelf, and asked my mother, "You figure you got room for a mensch behind them French doors?"

For a time afterward, my mother tried hard not to speak much to Vedra. Vedra had betrayed them, in a way that to my mother was not much different from the way of kulaks. On ensuing Saturday mornings when she came to the store, she gave no greeting, just materialized. But, upon catching sight of her, Vedra Broome would launch into a wild welcome, and my mother would mutter *schmeichler* — flatterer — under her breath.

My mother's resentment of Vedra somehow carried over to Carrie MacAllister. It was Carrie MacAllister's misfortune to have the burden of representing for my mother all the Gentiles of the world. On this occasion my mother was so mad at Gentiles she gave up the flower-painting-on-dresses sessions with Carrie.

My father was puzzled. "What happened with the painting ladies and all the lilies? Mrs. Mac don't want to do it no more?

"I don't know what she wants," said my mother, hoping to convey that she didn't *care* what Mrs. Mac wanted.

My father took this not at all well. He liked "Mrs. Mac." He reminded my mother how Carrie had wanted the store to do well and how she had named Sarah Reba after her. "Don't that tell you something?"

"It tells me she used to work for us and might want to again."

"Now you're talking crazy."

"Mmmm."

My father told her not to "mmmm" him when he was "talking a tip-top lady here," one who could also take a joke. "Remember that time with the borscht?" he asked my mother.

We all remembered that time with the borscht, when Mrs. MacAllister had laughed until the tears ran upon learning that what she had done — plunked her shmaltz herring into her borscht — was not the custom after all.

"Taking a joke ain't everything," my mother said.

"No, but it's something."

My mother would not be convinced. "Deep down," she said, "who knows? If we do one little thing they don't like, right away they say, 'What can you expect from a Jew?'"

Chapter 22

Joey's Homecoming

The time was approaching for my mother to concentrate on my brother's homecoming, when she would no longer have to depend on letters, though it's true that letters had been a great help to her. She would read them over and over and say, "Look how good Joey is doing. All A's. And doing good at cheder, too."

My father would overflow with pride when it came to Joey's public schooling, but when it came to Hebrew school, praise from him was conspicuously lacking.

As for the actual bar mitzvah ceremony, my mother thought she had figured it all out: It would be during a slack business time, my father could safely leave, and off they'd go.

My father said off my mother could go without *him*. He said to her, "Are you *meshuggener?* Let people congratulate me on something I didn't want nohow?"

"We got to go," my mother wailed. "We got to."

"So go," my father said, some of his old mad returning.

In the end my mother would not go without my father. She asked Aunt Sadie to have a party for Joey after the ceremony. "Make it nice," she wrote, and enclosed money for it.

Aunt Sadie explained, in a letter written by my cousin Benny in the name of his mother, that without my father there, there could be no party. "If the father was dead," the letter said, "that's different. But with the father alive and not here . . ."

So the bar mitzvah was a simple one, nothing like my mother's dream. Our grandfather took my brother to shul on a Saturday morning, and with Uncle Meyer and Uncle Philip assisting, the deed was done.

All at once Joey's homecoming was down from months to days, and then it was the very morning, and my mother was merely counting hours.

She woke the family early. I said to myself, It's your brother — your brother Joey, remember? But I didn't remember. And I certainly didn't like all the fuss. I had called and called my mother, but never once had she come. When I yelled, "Mama! Mama! I need you!" all I got was my mother yelling back, "Get dressed, get dressed!"

My mother at last came into the room, threw a sweater in my direction, and left. The sweater fell on my lap. I looked down at it and decided it was not only repulsive but possibly dangerous. I wondered how my mother could expect me to put on the awful thing when my blouse wasn't even buttoned yet.

I was on the verge of blubbering when my mother came back. "What's the matter with you?" she asked me. "Miriam's already in the car with Papa. Seth's waiting for us, and in the middle of everything, you decide to just sit. What's wrong? Don't you want to see your brother? Stand up and button your blouse." She went out the door.

I hung my head, and the tears popped out. Through the fat globs I tried to make out the buttons. Those rocks, those huge, craggy rocks, could they possibly be buttons? I made a grab for them and tried to shove them into their slots. They wouldn't go. They were the stubbornest things I had ever seen. I finally cried out, as loud as I could, "They won't go, they won't go!"

No one answered my cries, and pretty soon I gave up expecting anybody. I picked up the sweater and dragged it along as I went out of the house. The car door was open and I crawled through it. I was a stupid worm shoving my own self into a bait can.

At the depot everybody was talking and laughing. Seth had moved to the waiting-room wall and under the overhang was talking to a friend. Each time he laughed, I took it as a cue to jump with both feet on a crack.

In what seemed a very short while, here came the roar, and I covered my ears with my hands. Not yet! Not yet! I cried out to myself, though even if I had yelled it out loud, no one would have heard me.

The train whooshed to a stop, the bells clanged, and the porters in their shiny black coats and brimmed caps jumped off and, lightning-fast, put the little steps under the train doors.

My father walked quickly up to the train, my mother and sister half-running behind him. I hung back with Seth and kept my eyes on him.

Seth was looking toward the train. I saw a smile overtake his face, and I shifted my gaze. What I saw was a tall boy with black curly hair and a freckly face. He was holding a paper sack and was at this minute hugging my parents and my sister.

That's Joey, I said to myself, your brother. I grabbed at Seth. But Seth had no time for me.

"Mr. Joey, Mr. Joey," he yelled, and ran to the boy.

They laughed with each other for a moment. I saw Joey look around and heard him ask, "Where's Stella Ruth?"

I didn't move. My mother turned toward me and motioned "come" with her head. Still I hung back.

My mother came over. "What's the matter with you?" she said, and shoved me forward.

Joey knelt down in front of me. "Hello, you silly girl. Don't you remember me?" He put down the sack to hold me by the shoulders. "How'd you get so big anyway?"

I stared at him.

"I know something to make you talk." Joey reached into the sack, drew out a plump doll, and put it in my hands. A second thrust into the sack produced a lollipop as big as the moon. He held it in front of me. "Don't you remember what I promised? 'A sweet to eat and . . .'" He stopped, waiting for me to finish the jingle.

I said nothing.

"Don't tell me you've forgotten?"

Without looking I turned the doll over in my hand. I felt the hair. It was straw-stiff, sticky like the excelsior stuff in the store boxes. The dress was just as scratchy. I went on fingering. The lace down the front was hard and scabby, like a two-day-old knee scrape.

Everybody was smiling at me, waiting. They didn't know I wasn't going to speak. They didn't know that what I was going to do was run. I told myself what a fast runner I was and that if I wanted to, I could outrun them all.

I snatched the lollipop out of Joey's hand. Lollipop in one hand, doll in the other, I darted down the platform.

I was running toward the train engine, running with all my might, faster than I had ever run before. As I ran, the doll dangled upside down. "I hate you! I hate you!" I cried, and with all my strength hurled the doll to the side of the engine. Its head fell off; body and head bounced to the platform. I picked the body up and flung it once more. I threw down the lollipop and trampled it into sugary clumps.

Then I was running again and shrieking, "No, no, no!" When I was finally out of breath and not sure of what else to do, I sat down, dug my face into my knees, and let the crying come.

In the first weeks, when my brother was around, I stayed pretty quiet. There was this stranger called "Joey," and I was at first strongly disinclined to admit him as part of the family. It was a feeling that wore off, to be replaced by shyness, which in turn yielded to curiosity, and soon I was asking questions and Joey was answering. When he described the big whale at the American Museum of Natural History or told about climbing into the arm of the Statue of Liberty, it seemed I was hearing of a dreamworld.

But Joey never talked for very long, not to me, not to anybody. He always said he had to get back to his book. When my mother went to his room to try to get him to come out, he would say "later" and then read on until she came again.

T came over, but after he and Joey got out the erector set, they did no projects with it. They played some checkers and chess, but there was no longer any joshing and pretend accusations of cheating. Joey occasionally took the car out, but he went alone. When he was asked where he had gone, he headed for his room, saying, "Out in the country somewhere."

My mother at last realized that he was lonesome. She said to my father, and was surprised by what she was saying, "He's lonesome for New York."

My father agreed. "Sure he is. He's been doing New York things, and he's missing them."

My mother wanted to know what he was missing. Standing at Joey's door one Saturday morning, she spoke to him as he lay on his bed. "So what did you do in New York you can't do here? What's so different?"

Joey shrugged. "It's fine here, Mama. Don't worry."

"I can't help but worry. You ain't the same. Missing something a little bit I can understand, but to be homesick in your own home I never heard of." Maybe he wanted to go to the Saturday serial?

He had seen it in New York, and he was going to the store later.

"Papa don't need you that bad. Go see the picture anyway."

"I've seen that already, too."

"So see it again, like always. Or go call T and go somewheres with him. And for a cherry Coke afterwards. Or maybe a cherry *smash* like you once had. Wouldn't that be nice?"

Joey just looked at her.

My mother was trying to understand. "You went to lots of places Saturday mornings in New York?"

"Yeah, I guess so."

"To museums and operas and things? With Uncle Philip? You like that kind of thing?"

"Sure." Lest my mother get the idea that he

just went in for the higher things, Joey also mentioned the New York baseball teams, especially the Yankees, since the Yankees played in the Bronx. We had a cousin who lived in an apartment building that overlooked Yankee Stadium, and sometimes, Joey said, they'd watch a game from the rooftop. "Best seats in the house," he said.

Baseball was nothing my mother was prepared to discuss. "When school starts, you'll find more to do what you like," she said to Joey.

When school started, the principal called my mother on the telephone. "Joseph" was too advanced for his class, and she wanted my parents' permission to skip him to the next one.

"Yes, fine," my mother told her. "Joseph will be glad."

Well, Joey wasn't quite as glad as my mother had thought. Concordia classes ran in years, not in half years as in New York, so Joey was skipped a whole year. At the end of the first week, he came home with another problem: The class thought he was too young for them. T was in the class, but, Joey explained, T had other friends, and you couldn't expect T to be just with him.

My mother wrung her hands. "Now *this* is wrong! Something's always wrong!" She kept trying. "So you'll make friends later. Right now you'll learn."

This didn't work either. "That's just it," Joey protested. "I'll be wasting my time. If I was in New York, I'd be learning a lot more a lot faster."

My parents went together into Joey's room to talk it over with him. Since it was definitely a family matter, Miriam and I pushed in with them.

My father thought it was the Rapid Advance thing that was bothering Joey. Rapid Advance was a New York City program to which Joey had been assigned, one designed to move motivated pupils ahead more quickly. My father said to nobody in particular, "He feels like he's being cheated since he was supposed to go." He looked at Joey. "Ain't that right, my boychick?"

Joey's face was bright for the first time since the day of his return. He talked about the school he would have gone to, one with a library and laboratories. And every day an art and music lesson. Uncle Philip had gone with him to look it over, and, Joey said, "Boy, were we impressed!"

Miriam thought maybe Joey also had a sweetheart he was missing. Miriam wanted to talk not about educational programs but about courtship customs. She pursued the subject, doing serious research. "What on earth do y'all do when y'all have sweethearts? Are there football games?"

Joey shook his head.

"Do y'all have *dates?*"

Joey finally obliged her. "We don't call it a 'date.' We call it 'taking a girl out.' " When he took a girl out, he said, they went to the pictures, to a theater downtown, or to the Paradise on the Grand Concourse. Afterward they got an egg cream — which, as I found out, mysteriously contained no egg and no cream — on the way home from the subway. Joey said "THEE-a-ter," not "thee-AY-ter," the way we did.

My mother took Miriam's subject to heart. As she saw it, there was nobody in Concordia for Joey to take out, meaning, of course, no Jewish girls.

Pretty soon the old discussion began, only this time both my parents, if not delighted that Joey would have to leave, were accepting.

Joey went back to New York, to my grandparents' apartment, before the year was out. Afterward, we saw him in summers when he came home for vacation. While he was with us, he played a little chess with T and guessed, with the rest of us, at the number of beans in the jar in the U-Tote-'Em window — an enduring summer contest in which a boy might win a baseball and a girl a box of bath powder — but the truth was we all treated him as a visitor and a guest.

Chapter 23

Miriam's Romance

Miriam's social life was exceedingly active. Besides the piano lessons and chats at Miss Brookie's, there were football games, Saturday afternoon bridge parties, after-school gatherings at Tippett's Drug Store and Ice Cream Parlor. But the social week marked time until the Saturday Night Party.

The Saturday Night Party was a tradition in Concordia, and Miriam's crowd had arrived at the age when the mantle had fallen to them. The party was held at the home of one or other of the girls, and when Miriam said it was her turn, my mother did not demur. As with anything, she felt a responsibility to pay back. She only wanted to know who to invite and how many.

The gang, Miriam said, so about twenty in all.

And with the parents?

Parents? "What parents?" Miriam asked my mother.

"You can't give a party without inviting the mothers and fathers!" my mother cried. "I never heard from such a thing." She started, "In New York —"

Miriam wouldn't let her finish. "Oh, New York!" she said, as usual dismissing New York and its "tacky" ways. "We don't need *chaperones*," she said. "After all, we're not *children*." And not only that, none of the other parents were ever there.

My mother was truly shocked. She looked, according to how Miriam has told it, as if she had ventured into "a nest of wicked old fire ants."

My mother was adamant: There would be no party without her being there.

Miriam gave my mother an accusing look. "You don't trust us. Just go on and admit it."

My mother tried to give Miriam an honest answer. "I don't know what I do. I hear the way you girls don't talk about nothing but boys. I see the way you dress for them. I ain't afraid to say I don't know what to expect from nobody. What do I know from these people?"

In the end Miriam said, "All right, be there if you want to. But I completely *despair* of you."

The party was on. Twenty-two teenagers were invited. My mother was surprised that T

368

was one of them. T didn't go to parties, and he was older than Miriam. "Even if he does act younger," my mother said.

"Act younger?" It was Miriam's turn to be shocked. "You haven't noticed him lately if you think that."

My mother probably *hadn't* noticed that T had grown very tall, and had acquired a way about him that all the girls found "dead attractive." He seemed to be everybody's crush, though, the girls wailed, he paid them "no mind atall." Miriam said she had to practically *order* him to come to the party.

In another year T was going to college, to "U.T." — the University of Tennessee — with Miss Brookie in full support, including financial. When he had told my parents that he was planning to study agriculture, my father said, "You mean to say, Mr. T, you can go to college to learn how to be a *farmer?*"

"Yes, sir, Mr. Bronson. There's a whole school of agriculture in Knoxville specially for us bumpkins who want to learn the best ways to run a farm."

But didn't T already know how to run his father's farm?

Of course, he did. But he was aiming for more. "I'm fixing to run a big farm someday and learn about government programs and whatall. Hicks like me are going to do big business on the farm one of these days, wait and see."

My father had at last started to understand — putting business practices to farming made sense to him — but my mother had gone on scoffing, convinced it was just another bizarre Gentile plan. "You want to farm," she said privately, "you put some seeds in the ground and wait till they come up. Or you get a bucket and go milk some cows. But a farmer going to college? Can one *tokhes*" — one backside — "sit and stand at the same time?"

"Mama, for pity's sake!" Miriam would say. "You think all anybody should be is an old doctor or lawyer!"

My mother tried to deny this. After all, she would say, Joey wanted to be an engineeer, and had she told him no? And "Bertha's Murray" (my first cousin, once removed) was going to be an accountant, and "I'm not stopping him neither." She thought to close it out. "Farmers going to college! Foolish!"

But Miriam was the one who had the last word. "You won't understand anything in a million years! You just keep thinking everything has to be the way it is with *Jews!*"

In preparation for the party, the front room was stripped down to essentials. Rugs had been rolled up and carried to other rooms and

370

furniture had been relocated, so except for the radio and Victrola, the front room was bare. When grape juice punch and sandwiches and cookies had been set up on the table in the breakfast nook and my father had retreated to Joey's room, the house stood ready.

Having been warned to make my presence all but invisible, I stationed myself — along with T-Dog, the puppy T had given me from his Peggy's litter — just inside the hall. From there T-Dog and I could peek out and watch the "flappers" and the "sheiks."

I had learned from Miriam that the word *flapper* came from the fad of wearing unbuckled galoshes, so that when the girls walked, their galoshes "flapped" around their ankles. When I asked about *sheik*, she said, "Think."

I thought. "Rudolph Valentino!" The sheik!

"I 'clare if you ain't the smartest thing!" Miriam said, already putting on her party personality.

As my mother had predicted, the girls were dressed "fit to kill," as the lingo in Miriam's crowd would have it. Their frocks were mostly of silk, though sometimes of chiffon, georgette, or satin. Beads, feathers, and ribbons perched on heads, encircled hips, cascaded down fronts, balanced on shoe toes. Bronson's notions counter — and no doubt

Dalrymple-Eaton's — was always picked clean by Friday afternoon.

Though nobody asked me, I decided Miriam was the most "smashing," the current word for truly outstanding. This was not surprising, as Miriam was still going to St. Louis and returning with all the latest. On this night she was wearing a yellow silk dress with spaghetti straps and a beaded bodice and a very short, very swoopy hem. "The bees' knees," she had pronounced it.

The only fashion Miriam resisted was that of the flat bosom. Whereas most of the girls who had anything in that area swaddled themselves to give that day's desirable boyish look, Miriam would have none of it. She lectured often on "bazooms," the word shortened among her friends to "zooms." "Tacky," she pronounced. "It's downright tacky. I'd never wear an old bedsheet around my zooms just to be a slave of fashion. Lord, if you have the brains of a squash, you know that boys like girls whose zooms do something, not just lie there like some old cow flop."

Party procedure was ritualized. The boys threw their hats on a bedroom dresser, advanced into the front room, stood in a clump across the room from the girls, and snickered. When one of the boys finally broke ranks and asked one of the girls to dance, the party began.

It surprised me not at all that the boys fought over the next dance with Miriam, as she had a reputation as a wonderful dancer. She had begun bringing dances home from St. Louis, and she and Lizzie Maud always exchanged what they knew.

One interesting thing about the Saturday night parties was what the attendees did with the Vic. They'd wind it tight as it would go to produce rhythms so dizzying that the dancers would fall down just trying to keep up. This happened more and more as the night went on.

While I was stashed in the corner of the bathroom, I found out why. One of the girls came in and said that somebody had spiked the punch, and another said yes, she had seen Earl Hedrick with a jar of white lightning. "Reckon he made some Purple Jesus," she said, "Purple Jesus" being what grape juice punch spiked with moonshine was called.

When Miriam came in, I informed her that somebody had spiked the punch. Miriam already knew. "And don't you dare tell Mama," she told me.

I went back to my observation post. I looked at T and tried to see him as the other girls did. He seemed definitely handsome though too fair and snub-nosed to be a true sheik. Also, true sheiks danced, and T didn't. Tonight he was either fooling around with the radio or reading one of Joey's *Popular Mechanics*, which was still being delivered to the house. Then I saw Miriam go over to him and order him to dance.

T stopped what he was doing. There was a shyness about him that I had never seen before. "Reckon I don't know how," he said.

"Then I'll teach you," Miriam said.

"You don't want to take time to do that," T said. "You'll send all these boys into a fit."

Miriam laughed and said, "They'll bear up."

T put his magazine down on the radio table and put his arms out. Miriam called out for somebody to put on something slow and took his hands.

"Box step," Miriam said to T, propelling him around to a record of someone singing, "Because of you/The skies are blue/Be-loved, Be-lov-ed . . ."

T was holding her as if she were a china doll. Miriam looked at the space between them and said, "I'm not going to shatter."

I watched while T brought her to him. And I watched while he brought her closer and closer until he had her tight in his arms. And then Miriam put her head on his shoulder.

When some boy came up to cut, she shook her head.

Miriam had stopped propelling him around and just went where he went. Her head never left his shoulder, except when they had to separate at the end of a number; and when another began, T took her in his arms again. They were still dancing after everybody had gone. It certainly looked to me as if Miriam and T had become sweethearts. But this was something else I kept to myself.

My mother noticed on her own. That following Monday morning T came to the house and walked Miriam to school. Soon he was doing this every day. It got so that instead of being with the gang, he and Miriam came home by themselves and stayed on the front porch or took a walk after T's football practice. On Saturday afternoons, they went to the picture show by themselves.

My mother finally asked Miriam, "You got no friends but T?"

"I have plenty of *friends*, Mama. If you're asking me do I have any other *beaus*, the answer is no."

My mother looked as if she wanted to say something, but she didn't say it.

My mother stayed acutely aware of Miriam and T. There was no way to miss what was happening. When T went away to college, every day a letter came in from him for Miriam, and every day a letter went out from her.

One day in the kitchen my mother looked at the calendar with the picture of the little girl with eyes as big and dark as mud pies over the words TRAYNOR'S HARDWARE, EVERYTHING FROM A WASHER TO A WHEELBARROW, and saw there an encircled date. She was sure it had to do with Miriam. More important, did it also have something to do with T?

She came into our bedroom to find out. Miriam was writing. "Who you writing to?" my mother asked Miriam, already knowing the answer. Who did Miriam write to if not T?

Miriam didn't look up from her letter. "T, of course."

"What do you have to tell him you write so many letters?"

"Oh, you know, Mama. We have lots to tell each other. You know, odds and ends."

"You write so much odds and ends, what about your homework?"

This was not quite fair. My sister had never been keen on homework, and her new relationship with T had little to do with whether she was more or less keen. "Mama, what on earth are you fussing about?"

"I'm *fussing* about the mark on the calendar." What was so important that Miriam had to remind herself so early?

376

It was a party weekend at the University of Tennessee. And it *was* important, at least to the girls who had been invited and perhaps even more important to those who *hadn't*. "It's something at U.T.," Miriam said. "A couple of the girls are going."

"So?"

"So I'm going, too."

My mother assumed battle posture. "Girls fourteen years old going by themselves? And boys and their *dates* there all alone? I never heard from such a thing."

"I know you haven't. But I want to go."

"What you want and what will be are two entire different questions," my mother said, sounding just like my Aunt Sadie.

As the U.T. weekend approached, there was open warfare — shouted words and slamming doors. My mother's resolution hardened. In the kitchen fixing biscuits one day, she hoped she was saying the final word: "You're not going and that's that."

"Why can't I?" Miriam shouted. "Give me one good reason! That's all I ask — one good reason!"

"One good reason is I say so! That's good reason enough!"

My father probably had paid little attention to the clashes that had been taking place in our house. Remembering the battles among the *mishpocheh* he had lived with in the Bronx, he would have dismissed it as simply what families "do." And of course it *was* an example of what families "do," except that with my mother and Miriam there was always something extra. Was it generational? Geograpical — Russia pitted against America? New York versus the South? Religious — Jewish versus Name It? Whatever it was, my mother didn't go to my father with this latest complaint.

But a case could easily be made that my mother was more worried about Miriam (and me) "dating" Gentiles and then *marrying* them than she had been about Joey being bar mitzvahed. Bar mitzvahs came and went, but marriages came, didn't go, were always on view and open to judgment. People should see that one of her daughters was married to a *Gentile? Sadie* should see? My mother carried with her the memory of the Jewish girl in her shtetl who had wanted to marry a Russian. She always remembered the cries of "Over my dead body!" and "I'll see you dead first!" and the other alarums in which the ultimate penalty was always invoked. And *oy,* the talk that went on. There had also been the Jewish boy in her Bronx building who had actually *married* his shiksa. Hadn't the family carried on like people gone crazy with grief, to the extent that a kaddish, a prayer for the dead, had been said in shul for the son? My mother remembered it all.

Chapter 24

Aunt Hannah's Wedding

As for Seth's successor in the store, it was Mary Hyams, who had worked in the Oliphant store. Mary Hyams was relaxed and jolly, a good thing in a person who had to put up with Vedra Broome butting in on sales and claiming half-commission.

On her part Vedra confided often that Mary was not up to snuff. My father listened, nodded, and went on undisturbed. Business was so good, he had no time to worry about Vedra Broome and her "cockamamie stories." My father said, "She's like a *grager*, that one."

As I found out, a *grager* was a stick attached to a toothed wheel. It could make a terrible noise. During the holiday of Purim, the children took them to shul, and in the reading of the Book of Esther, whenever Haman the Wicked was mentioned, they would go into impassioned *grager* twirling. Yes, Vedra Broome was a *grager*.

My father was indeed too busy to bother with Vedra's grievances. Times were good, Bronson's was flourishing. The factory men came in regularly to pay their bills, and the farmers did the same. If some were short because of other, more important bills — the doctor or the farm-supply store — my father waved them away and said they were good for it.

Occasionally my father nudged, and once he dunned. This happened with an old landholder living way out in the country who had made his only purchase early on, airily calling out afterward, "Just send me a bill." Although my father didn't send out bills, he humored the old recluse, only to learn that it was the man's custom to heap all his bills in a top drawer of a chifforobe and each month fish one out randomly for payment. When Bronson's bill never came up a lucky pluck, my father went out to see him. On this one and only visit, the man greeted him by waving his fist and shouting, "You listen here to me, Bronson, if you don't stop your all-fired pesterin', I ain't goin' to put your goddamned bill in the goddamned drawer atall!"

My father laughed and walked away. What was one crazy deadbeat, this ultimate "slow-pay"? Times were good, customers came aplenty. If he didn't right out say that life was a bowl of cherries, it certainly described how he felt.

My mother thought of the good times as "helpful." They canceled worry about money, and, almost as important, they enabled her to have a car, and a car could take her out of Concordia occasionally. The car was at her disposal, Seth was at the wheel. She could go on an excursion anytime.

We took out-of-town jaunts every Sunday. Sometimes we just drove out onto dirt roads in the country, into the dense woods and around the little lakes. (The big lake — Deerfoot — was off-limits, my mother's memories of Hannah and Manny and that body of water still painful.) Sometimes we went to a nearby town.

My mother tried hard to get Miriam to go with us, partially, it has to be said, to distract her from dwelling on T. "Come, darling," my mother would say, "come. Come see something different. We'll take a ride and have some ice cream after."

Miriam would always shake her head and say, "Just go on."

My mother was sure Miriam would go with us when we learned from Sammy Levine that *The Jazz Singer*, the first "talkie," was playing in Paducah. "It's a picture that's got singing and dancing," my mother told her, and anyway, why should Miriam stay home all alone?

When Miriam answered, "I won't be alone. T's home for the weekend," my mother sighed, "T, T. Always T."

This time my father said, "She don't want to go, so she don't want to go," and suggested we ask the MacAllisters.

For my mother the trip abruptly lost appeal. Since Vedra had done her nasty deed, my mother hadn't gotten back on track with, um, *Gentiles*. And as to Sylvan MacAllister, he never said boo, my mother told my father, so what good was he? Anyway, *The Jazz Singer* wasn't a picture that had anything to do with the MacAllisters. "It's about a Jewish family in New York. So why should they care about it?"

"A Jewish family, a *family*, what's the difference?" my father answered. He offered an inducement: They could show off Al Jolson as a Jewish boy who had made really good. "We got the car," my father said. "For the same money they can come with us. So ask them already."

The MacAllisters came with us. Seth drove and stayed with some Paducah cousins until it was time to come back and get us.

My mother cried through the whole picture. The tears showed up at the very beginning, when the mother was torn between her son's ambition to be a jazz singer and her rabbi husband's wish for his son's beautiful voice to be put in the service of the shul; escalated through the son's leaving to join the show world; and climaxed when the son came to his father's bedside on the eve of Yom Kippur to tell him he would do the singing of the Kol Nidre, the prayer asking atonement from God for the sins of the past year.

In the car going home the picture stayed with her. She sat thinking of a particular Yom Kippur service in her neighborhood shul when a celebrated cantor had been a guest singer. When his voice had broken under the heavy emotion of the Kol Nidre, the whole congregation had burst into wailing. How *joyful* it had been, and how joyful afterward had been the mingling with the *mishpocheh*, everyone holding their hands over their hearts to show how deeply they had been moved.

From the front seat my father turned to talk. "So everybody enjoyed? What did you think of it, Mrs. Mac?"

"Real good," Carrie MacAllister said. She offered that there was a lot in the picture to think about. "Lord, I like to cried my eyes out," she said. "I sure had me a good time."

So occupied had my mother been with her own tears, she had taken no notice of Carrie's.

"If crying is a good time, I guess you could say we had the time of our lives," she said, and gave Carrie a little smile. It meant something to her that Carrie had cried, so much in fact that all at once her anger went up in smoke. "I hope you had plenty of handkerchiefs," she said to Carrie, and laughed.

"Used up the two I brought and then went down to my petticoat," Carrie answered her, and laughed back.

Sylvan MacAllister was a blond, open-faced man, the physical pattern for his children. He was staring out the isinglass with a look of turning things over. In the theater he had watched the screen as if observing creatures on another planet who by some miracle had been caught by the camera.

Since Sylvan was so reserved — he never introduced a topic and rarely participated in one already introduced — my father thought to start things off by asking him something with a simple answer. "Has that Al Jolson got talent or what, Mr. MacAllister?"

To my father's surprise Sylvan took his time, as if the question needed thinking about. "Some, I reckon," he finally said. Al Jolson, it seemed, didn't "do a colored" as well as some he'd seen. (With Seth in the car, Sylvan perhaps thought to substitute "colored" for the usual.) "He made himself up good, but he don't have the ways coloreds have. Take the Knights of Americus minstrel shows, for example. Lord, they got end men so good at being coloreds, you just bust out laughing. That Jolson fella's got to practice some." This was the Sylvan MacAllister who never said boo?

As to Al Jolson's blackface act, my father always said he himself was perplexed over it, though the jury is still out on whether this perplexity came then or in later years. Still, I want to take him at his word and believe that even at that moment he found it hard to defend Al Jolson. Those thick white lips, the coal makeup. Was it not too much? To make fun of people already so *auf tsores*, already so full of woe?

He didn't go on with it with Sylvan MacAllister. He addressed himself instead to Carrie. "Like you said, Mrs. Mac, there was a lot in that picture to think about."

In June of that year my mother had a plan for a longer excursion. Where it would take us was to New York, to Aunt Hannah's wedding. If I was ecstatic, she was surprisingly not. She was in a dither about her garden. Here it was the middle of the gardening season, everything planted and growing, and where would she be when it came time to pick and put up? In New York, that's where.

I didn't care about my mother's garden; I cared about *finally* getting to go to New York, to see all the relatives, to experience *New York*. I could think only *Please, Mama, please!*

And, of course, my mother decided she couldn't *not* go. My father said he was not going, and "that's that," and when my mother said she definitely wanted Miriam to go with us, Miriam just as definitely wanted not to. T was going back to school in the fall, and Miriam wanted to be with him as much as she could.

My mother sighed, T again, and then a letter came to Miriam from Aunt Hannah asking Miriam to be there. It was a plea Miriam couldn't refuse.

Aunt Hannah was getting married to Ezra Goldstein, the son of the furrier just moved in around the corner from my grandparents' apartment. Officially Ezra was a "cutter" in his father's shop, but in truth he was only an unskilled "nailer." What he did was nail the customer's selected skins to the boards on the basement wall and trace out the pattern.

He and Aunt Hannah had met when his father had stopped her as she walked past their shop window. "Ezzy, come up," Mr. Goldstein had yelled into the bars of the basement window, according to how Aunt Hannah told the story to us. "I got a girlfriend for you. A real *schaineh maidel.* If I didn't have Mama already, I'd marry her myself."

Soon afterward Ezra had a talk with my grandfather, asked him if he could take Hannah out, and got a yes.

My grandmother had expressed doubts: The boy had no pep. My grandfather's answer was that Ezra was the son of a boss and the son of a boss didn't need as much pep as the next one.

After we got to New York and met Ezra, Miriam told my mother, in the contentious mode she had adopted for the visit, that thin, quiet Ezra was certainly nothing to get "all hot and bothered about."

"I declare," she said to us, "when I think that Aunt Hannah could have had Manny, I could just weep."

My mother told her not to mention Manny anymore.

On this visit I met all my relatives and was dazzled by all of them, by all these people who were *not* dazzled by New York — who accepted casually life way up high in a tall building, who rode the subway as if there was nothing strange about traveling under the ground, who simply raised their voices to be heard over the uproar "downtown."

We stayed in my grandparents' apartment, and I made a viewing spot of the fire escape just as Joey had. I didn't play stickball in the streets, but my cousins had roller skates and my mother bought me some, and we went roller-skating on the sidewalks (we skipped the light fantastic on the sidewalks of New York?) or in the big asphalt-paved school-yard. Although there were sidewalks in Concordia, they were narrow and had grass growing through the cracks.

The wedding was big, attended as it was by the whole of the New York family plus the contingent that had defected to Boston. A little orchestra played, everybody danced, and my Uncle Meyer, red-faced with drink, danced with me and all the other children. All the women said that at these affairs he always drank too much so he could forget he had an Austrian-Jewish wife who looked down on Russian Jews, that he had a fat son (my cousin Morty) who was never interested in anything he couldn't eat — a *gruber yung,* they called him — or that he was a door-to-door cemetery plot salesman; and maybe that was true.

After the newlyweds left, to honeymoon in the Catskills, we stayed on in my grandparents' apartment, Miriam still prickly as a sandspur.

"So what's wrong with your daughter?"

Aunt Sadie asked my mother. "She don't like being with the family?"

My mother tried to think of something in a hurry. "No, what it is, is she's homesick." Would this go down?

It wouldn't. "Homesick for what? For that hilly-billy place? That's a place to be home-sick for?"

Joey tried to entertain Miriam by taking us to the downtown department stores, and our cousin Eddie worked especially hard, only to have his efforts fail every time. He finally asked her, "What's wrong with you anyway?"

And Miriam answered him, "I don't care to discuss it."

"Why not?" Eddie considered Miriam for a long moment and snapped his fingers. "I got it. I know what it is. You got a boyfriend and he's down there and you're up here."

Miriam did a flounce. "So?"

"So you miss your boyfriend, that's all."

"We don't call them *boyfriends*," Miriam said, summoning hauteur. "We call them *beaus*."

"Well, anyway, you got one, right?"

"Maybe I do."

Eddie opened his eyes wide. "You got a *Gentile* boyfriend? A *shaigetz*?"

Miriam and Eddie exchanged glares as the word hung in the air.

★ ★ ★

If Aunt Sadie was disdainful that Miriam actually *wanted* to go back, she was thunderstruck when my mother announced she was ready to go as well. "Your husband can't make out without you?" she asked my mother.

"You know he ain't no helpless man. It ain't him only."

"So what is it?"

My mother hesitated. Her answer would go over with Aunt Sadie like a plate of hog jowls. She steeled herself. "It's my garden, Sadie. I hate to think how it must be. Nothing picked, everything overgrown."

"A garden ain't family," Aunt Sadie said to her.

"No, it ain't. But try to understand," my mother answered, herself not totally understanding. All she knew for certain was that her garden needed her and that *she* needed *it*. "You ain't never had a garden, Sadie, so you can't know."

When we came home, my father asked, "So why are you home so soon? You missed me so much?"

My mother laughed. "You and my garden. Don't ask me which comes first. You at least I knew would be all right. But *oy*, my garden!"

My father winked at me. "Well, what do you expect? You left it to run itself. What can it be but terrible?"

"I hate to take a look."

My father's advice was that when there was something to do that you didn't want to, best to do it right away and get it over with. "So why not go out now and take a look?" he asked my mother.

She held back. My father gave her a push. My mother tried not to look as we went out the back door and into the yard.

Now I knew the reason for my father's wink: There was nothing rotting, nothing in ruins, just plants looking as they should look after the season — stripped clean.

And when we got back on the porch, my mother saw the jars — the shelves and shelves of jars and jars.

It was the neighbors, my father explained. "They came over and picked the place bare."

Then they had put everything up. "Some hard job they gave themselves," my mother said. "*Oy*, such a hard job." And no, nobody, she said, could have done anything nicer.

And here we have an "upsy" in my mother's "upsy-downsies" with Concordia, when my mother first allowed the word *home* to take a place in her thoughts. And what this meant was that if the Miriam-and-T thing hadn't been fluttering around, "tem-po-rary" would be hanging on for dear life.

Chapter 25

Concordia's Savior

In the fall of that year, 1929, the business picture was, as usual, exceedingly bright. My father had no significant debts, the Nashville men and my grandfather having been paid off long ago. My father was feeling himself at last to be a businessman of consequence.

And it was at this particular time, at this blissful time, that it happened. On a day when my father felt confident — why should he doubt it? — that business would proceed in a routinely perfect way, the black hole that had, unbeknownst to him, been out there all the time opened up and all but swallowed him.

On that day my father had picked up the paper before he went off to the store, feeling that the usual cursory glance at the morning's news would be sufficient. What could the paper tell him except that there was nothing to worry about, that people had faith in business, that stocks were rising? Did he need the paper to tell him what he knew from his own little Jew store?

He therefore paid scant attention to the headline before him as he sat with the paper on this particular Wednesday morning. But something caught at him. So before proceeding elsewhere in the paper, he stopped, went back to the headline, and read it again. When he did, when he could finally focus fully, what the headline was telling him was that the stock market had crashed.

It almost sent him from his chair. If the headline had said that a meteor was heading for earth, it would have been no more of a blow. His senses reeled, and when they at last slowed down, the questions came. How much exactly did it have to do with him? He tried on a couple of things. As one who never played the market, was it possible he was immune to a market failure? Or maybe a countrywide catastrophe would take a long time to reach a little town like Concordia?

Both fantasies had brief lives. In what seemed just weeks the factory men showed up with promissory notes in their hands. They said the shoe factory had run out of money.

All night every night my father's eyes stayed open — his eyelids seemed to be held fast by thumbtacks — while he worried about what would be. (The only sure thing he had in his head was that my mother must not know the scope of the trouble.) It stayed with him all day as well. When he couldn't stand it any longer, he would suddenly bolt out of the store, to go see what the other stores were doing, to just walk up and down First Street, to talk to somebody. He decided one day to go out and have a talk with Roscoe Pinder. My father had resisted having any real conversation with Pinder since the day my mother and I had gone out to the factory, but now that episode seemed very small potatoes indeed.

He found the factory owner at the desk in his little office. The dish used as an ashtray was overflowing with cigarette butts. Pinder had always been spare, but, as my father liked to say, on this day he had the look of a yardstick.

"Yeah, I want to talk, too," Pinder said. "Maybe not to you in particular, Bronson."

My father took no offense: The man was hurting. "We're all in this together," my father said to him. "So talk, I'll listen."

My father recalled Pinder opening up with, "Hellfire, Bronson, did you come all this way just to aggravate me? Are you telling me my factory and your little Jew store have the same stake in this?"

My father brought out an old saying: "Look, Mr. Pinder, if there's a fire at your neighbor's big house, ain't your little one also in danger?"

Pinder shrugged, as if it didn't really matter. The problem was, he finally said, that orders had just slacked off. "You'd think nobody was wearing shoes no more." He must have known that his problem wasn't the competition from up North, but he seemed not to be able to resist saying to my father, "You and your goddamned Yankees."

Being called a "Yankee," with or without the prefatory "goddamned," always made my father feel misunderstood. Who? Him? A Yankee? Who said so?

If my father had come out to give him sympathy, Pinder said, he should save it until he had heard it all: There was a matter of a forty-five-thousand-dollar note coming due in the next week.

My father was dumbfounded. "Forty-five thousand! My God! An old customer like you? They absolutely positively got to treat you right! They got to give you at least an extension!"

Pinder said to tell that to that "son of a bitch," the president of the bank, Ernest Fetzer, who appeared to have another way of looking at the problem. "He says the whole economy is a piece of shit and he ain't runnin' a shithouse." My father knew little about

Ernest Fetzer. He had only noticed that no-body ever called him "Ernie."

My father was puzzled. Even if what Pinder said was so, what good would it do Fetzer to foreclose? Why would anybody want to take over the building?

Pinder had a surprise answer: If Fetzer had to take back the building, it wouldn't "piss off that fox atall." What he "suspicioned" was that Fetzer had somebody eager to move in, somebody who hadn't felt the Depression and maybe never would.

And who might that be?

Well, there was talk of the government looking for a place. For a chemical plant. For making chemicals for war. "But don't get your hopes up, Bronson," Pinder said. "Chemical plants don't hire big. All you get from them is a big smell."

But would that bother Ernest Fetzer? Not according to Pinder. "Fetzer wouldn't care a monkey's patootie if the town turned into one big stink," he said to my father. He gave it a thought. "No sir, he'll be downright pleased if I can't meet the note."

My father said that at this point Pinder cupped his hand to his ear and said, "You hear that, Bronson? That sound is from a piece of machinery that *I* had specially made at the tooling plant, that *I* stood a man behind

and taught how to use, that *I* kept tip-top."
How did my father think it felt to know he was
about to lose all that?

And the men. They had learned a trade;
they took pride in being skilled workers.
"What about *them?* Lord knows I got good
men here. The men had apparently said they
would tough it out. But," Pinder said,
"they're depending on me to make things
right. . . . Lord, the whole town's depending
on me."

My father felt deeply for the man. That
such a thing could happen, that what a man
had built up for so many years should come to
nothing. What was needed was some hope.
My father recognized the moment as one in
which a plan must be devised, and he set himself to devising one. And then, ah, he had it.

Pinder, however, not only didn't want to
listen, he didn't even want my father to *be*
there. And who could blame him? My father
didn't want to be there either. What he
wanted was for something to pick him up and
deposit him in the middle of the store on an
ordinary day, everybody busy with customers
or, if it was a slack time, everybody joking. His
eyes suddenly filled with tears. *Oy,* he said,
when the heart is full, the eyes overflow. Another saying in a day made for sayings. "Mr.
Pinder," he said, and now he said it firmly, "I

want you should listen to me."

Pinder, my father used to say, was like a man who had been running for miles and could just barely manage to stay alive. "Okay, I'm listening," he said finally.

My father's idea was for a meeting.

"I've had meetings," Pinder answered him.

Yes, he no doubt had had many meetings, but none like the one my father had in mind. My father had in mind a *town* meeting. "We'll invite everybody. The whole town," he said, and waited for a reaction.

None was forthcoming. My father began to sell, hard. "It'll work, Mr. Pinder. We'll turn them out like family at a reunion."

Pinder finally reacted: He gave a grunt. And then he said, "Or like family gathering for the viewing. Or more likely out of pure morbid curiosity, to see how I'm bearing up under the passing."

He asked my father if he had a miracle up his sleeve. "You think you're Abraham? You fixing to talk to God?"

My father certainly wasn't thinking of talking to God. Could he guarantee Pinder the money? Of course not. But what he *could* guarantee was that he could sell the town on the idea that if they wanted the factory to stay open, they had to at least come to a meeting.

Pinder continued to resist. How could a

town meeting help? He needed money, and he needed it fast.

To which my father said, "Well, I always brag about being a born sal-es-man, Mr. Pinder, and this is one time where I got to put *tokhes ahfen tish*."

My father said Pinder's eyebrows went up, so he explained, "It means I got to put my rear end on the table."

And when Pinder's eyebrows stayed up, he said, "I got to put up or shut up."

When my father came home from his talk with Pinder, it was at last time to fill my mother in. "So what do you think, Reba?" he asked her.

My mother went wide-eyed. The factory was in trouble? *Oy*, and *oyoyoy*. "So tell me what you're telling me," she said to my father.

It was no time for dissembling. "Trouble, trouble, trouble in spades," my father answered her. Trouble in spades was an old pinochle term meaning that when spades are trump, all gains or losses are doubled.

"No need to get excited," my father told my mother, while his own heart bumped away in his chest. He tried to infuse his words with re-assurance: The factory was not going to close, if they did the right thing, which, he said — albeit with only a little conviction — was to have a town meeting.

My mother wanted to know if Roscoe Pinder had agreed to it, and my father had to say, "Not 'agreed' exactly. Just didn't say no."

On that day my mother recalled a saying, too: "He's maybe like a drowning man grabbing even for the point of a sword," she said to my father, and felt a chill as she said it.

My father was full of assurances and guarantees, too full. When he was like this, my mother knew, it usually meant he was only hoping for the best. So she cried, "Wait! Wait!"

"Tem-po-rary" had gotten off the ropes and was staging a comeback. It all at once seemed very logical to my mother: If there was a perfect time to leave Concordia, it was now. There was still money in the bank, and, though she didn't mention this to my father, we could go before Miriam and T got anything really serious into their heads. "Look at it this way," she said, "we came in with a letter and a wagon and we could go out comfortable. Ain't that something to think about?"

"No," was my father's prompt answer. No, we had to help out. "We can't just go and make believe we was never here."

"But if we stay and there ain't no living?"

My father answered that we would cross

that bridge when we came to it.

He was already making plans. We would announce the meeting by knocking on doors, going out in the fields to the farmers, getting the preachers to announce it in church, put it in the *Sentinel*. "And then they'll come," my father said to my mother.

"Yes, maybe." And, my mother wanted to know, if and when everybody came to the meeting, so what then?

"What then?" my father answered her. "After everybody gets to the meeting, I'll think of something, that's what then."

As my father had predicted, everybody came to the meeting. It was held in the school auditorium; and even that capacious space, balcony and all, was barely up to it.

Miriam was in many ways responsible for the turnout. She had rallied her friends, and they had knocked on doors and yelled, "Town meetin', seven P.M., Saturday night, high school auditorium! Don't y'all dare not come, hear?"

Now, with the other girls, she slipped into the row behind my mother and me, toward the back. My mother and I had an empty seat between us for my father.

Though the auditorium lights were on, their effect was negligible. The room remained gray, as if lightly veiled. Only the stage, because it had its own lights, was bright. On each side of the stage the long purple velveteen curtains hung in heavy folds, the dust on them showing up under the lights as a silvery patina. Above center stage, at the top of the proscenium, was the chipped plaster shield representing a coat of arms. Carrying out the school colors, gold letters on a purple background spelled out LUX FACIT VERITATEM, which I took to mean, "Always wash with soap." Well, I would think, sometimes I did, but not *always*.

Chairs had been set out on the stage. When I asked who they were for, my mother said, "For the big shots."

There was surprisingly little laughter among the crowd. Greetings were exchanges of solemn stares and head shakes. The children were lively at first and kept the auditorium churning by hopping from row to row, but their parents soon issued a warning. "Ardell," one mother called out, "this ain't no church social. You quit cutting the fool and sit down and offer up a prayer."

I resisted joining the row hoppers, although I watched them with some envy. I felt somehow that I must stay with the family. We were deeply involved, I knew that: We had talked about nothing but the meeting for days, and my father had remained serious the whole time.

At last onto the stage, from the wings, moving in a loose body toward the table, came Roscoe Pinder, the Reverend Charles Boomer Jones — Brother Jones — and Mayor Canaday and Ernest Fetzer.

That was when my father came to sit in the vacant seat.

Wasn't my father a "big shot"? Shouldn't he be up there on the stage? I checked with him. "Ain't you a big shot, Papa?"

"To be a big shot you got to make a big noise," my father explained. "I'm getting my ammunition together."

The place was growing quiet. Soon it was hushed enough that the swishing sound of the auditorium door could be heard, and when I looked around, there was Miss Brookie coming through, pushing into the last row, squeezing into a seat.

And then a truly heavy silence fell upon us. As the mayor walked to the lectern, there was the clear squeak of floorboards rubbing together.

The mayor thanked us for coming, saying we all knew why we were there, and that we had some business to discuss. But first the preacher would lead us in prayer. "Brother Jones," the mayor said, making way for him.

The preacher said, "Let us stand and pray," and I wobbled upward next to my mother and half-lowered my head, listening out for "In Jesus's name" to tell me the thing was over.

The preacher retreated, and Roscoe Pinder moved forward. He explained about needing a loan of forty-five thousand dollars to keep the factory open, though, he said, "Y'all must know I ain't feeling too hopeful at this point."

To which my father muttered, "With *zutz* like that, he'd have a hard time getting a dog to give up its fleas. This crowd wants to be pepped up, not laid out."

Mr. Pinder sat down and the mayor got up again to give a rundown on how important the factory was to "our town." He too looked joyless, though he had a new thought — that we didn't "want the shame and disgrace of knowing our people had to move away to find jobs." He concluded with, "Let's be good citizens and support this cause."

Now to the front came Ernest Fetzer, a heavy man, with a heavy man's walk, and looking as if he were there as a favor to everyone. He took off his glasses, blew on the lenses, polished them with a handkerchief pulled from his pocket, put them back on. Taking his time, being important. He gave the audience a long look, grasped the sides of the lectern, and at last was ready to speak. He began with a grievance. "I reckon y'all think this is my fault," he said. "By damn, everything's always the banker's fault."

"Listen to who thinks he's the injured party," my father grumbled.

Mr. Fetzer went on in the complaining tone. "I'm here to tell y'all that Ernest Fetzer ain't nobody's sucker." He paused to give the crowd time to appreciate his remark, though the snicker that it brought was ambiguous. "If somebody don't like me, well, I won't expect his vote in the next popularity contest."

"You got it right this time," my father said sotto voce.

When Mr. Fetzer left, Mr. Pinder returned. He stood with his arms crossed and looked uncomfortable. "If y'all come up with some money, that's fine. If you don't, that's your privilege, and we'll all go home."

"Send in another quarterback," my father said over his shoulder to the girls behind us, football fans all. "This one's out of plays."

When Mr. Pinder asked, "Has anyone got any spare cash?" Mayor Canaday got off his chair and said he'd give a hundred dollars, "to start the ball rolling."

"The ball will roll about three inches," my father said.

Eaton of Dalrymple-Eaton's Department

Store rose up to pledge a hundred dollars as well.

"Thank you," Mr. Pinder said. "I appreciate your generosity."

"That's about as generous as a size-five shoe fitted to a size-ten foot." My father bounced around in his seat, grumbling, mumbling, hooting about these "phony-baloney" pledges. "They're handing Jack Dempsey a powder puff and telling him to go knock somebody out," he growled to my mother and me.

One of the factory hands stood up. He said that none of the factory men had much but if the plant closed, they wouldn't have anything. He pledged twenty-five dollars and said he hoped some of the other men would see fit to do the same.

A farmer rose and, with his voice shaking as if he were riding in a wagon, pledged two acres of cotton, redeemable when he got paid for it. "In about two months, I reckon," he said.

There was a brief spate of clapping. A few other farmers made offers: a couple of acres of corn, an acre of tobacco, part of a steer, a pig.

The pledges started dying away. When it happened that whole minutes went by between pledges, everyone in the room knew that there were to be no more.

Mr. Pinder jerked his head from one side of the auditorium to the other. "I ask one more time: Any pledges?"

The question hung in an auditorium gone quiet, as if it had suddenly emptied. Then in the silence a strong voice was heard. "Attention!" the voice said. "I want everybody's attention!"

It was my father's voice. He was standing at his seat, his hands cupped around his mouth.

In a moment he had all eyes. "Bronson's Low-Priced Store pledges five thousand dollars!" he shouted, and pushing past my mother, he shot down the aisle and raced up the stage stairs to the lectern, yelling, "Let's get this thing going!"

The crowd came alive. There was jumping up, cheering, whistling. My father held his arms out and grinned hugely, as if welcoming an old customer who had been laid up for a while. He had the key, the grin seemed to say, the one that would unlock the treasure. *"Sha,"* he said at last, *"sha,* let's talk."

The crowd laughed and moved to sit back down. "Okay, who's gonna come up with another five thousand?" my father shouted.

"I will!" came an answering shout. Miss Brookie, way in the back, was struggling to her feet. Once there, there was a moment of hesitation before she spoke again, before she said, "Or rather, I *might*."

She spoke loudly to Roscoe Pinder. What she said that was she would meet my father's pledge if Roscoe Pinder would meet hers.

Mr. Pinder shared a look — a half smile — with the crowd, the one that said we all knew that Miss Brookie could be very harebrained indeed but was owed the courtesy of a hearing.

I was like T: I never read anything harebrained into Miss Brookie's ideas. And there was certainly nothing harebrained about this one. It was not complicated, not abstract, not irreligious. It was very simple: If the townspeople were being asked to came through for Mr. Pinder, then he ought to be able to find his way clear to coming through for them. "What you need to do is stop hiring children," Miss Brookie told him.

I thought of what Miss Brookie had said that day when we had gone to Mr. Pinder's office, about how you never knew what kind of dance would take place when "the fiddling got to going." Were the fiddlers playing? I thought they were, and it was a tune Miss Brookie had called. I waited for the dancing to begin.

My father contemplated Mr. Pinder, and Mr. Pinder contemplated back. "Miss Brookie thinks you got to help the town," my father said.

Mr. Pinder said that working to keep his plant open was "help aplenty." And how many people wanted him to stop hiring children anyway?

My father looked out at the audience and asked if anybody shared Miss Brookie's thought.

To my surprise, and most certainly to her own, here suddenly was my mother rising. She stood at her seat, and then in a very small voice, she said, "*I* do. *I* share her thought."

In the end there was a show of hands. When those opposed to children working showed the most, my father said to Mr. Pinder, "I guess Concordia don't want to be known as a town where children work in a factory."

Mr. Pinder was trying to hold to the principle that it was his plant and he ought to be allowed to run it the way he saw fit. He looked around at the others on the stage, as if calling upon them to affirm this. "I got that privilege," he said.

Miss Brookie for one did not believe he had this "privilege." "Not if you want my five thousand, you don't," she yelled.

"It's your call," my father told Mr. Pinder.

Mr. Pinder waved a hand, as if resigned to dancing to Miss Brookie's tune, and said,

411

"Bronson, if you ain't the limit."

Miss Brookie's five thousand could be counted on, but more was needed. "Now who else?" my father asked the crowd.

No answer. My father undertook a survey of the audience and spotted Mr. Spivey down front. "Look here, Mr. Spivey, I got a proposition with your name on it: You put up five and I'll match it with another five!"

The crowd waited.

Mr. Spivey got to his feet and said he wanted to "understand" what my father had said. "You'll match my five thousand with your five?"

"You bet!"

"A five with a five?" Mr. Spivey smiled his little smile, as if about to make my father miserable. "How about more?"

My father hesitated only a second. "Yessir! Any amount!"

The hint of pleasure on Mr. Spivey's face went away. "Ah, all right then, I'll pledge . . . well, I reckon I'll pledge three . . . yes, three's about right."

"Glad you could see your way clear, Mr. Spivey." It gave my father an idea: If that's what it took, he'd match every pledge. "Who else? Come on, take my money! What Tennessee yokel wants to see the color of Jew money?"

At this the audience roared its delight, which Ernest Fetzer did not share in. He had come to the lectern with advice for my father, to tell him to stop leading everybody astray. He asked Tom Dillon's set question: "Lord, what did Concordia do to deserve Jews?"

My father made a joke of it. "I'll tell you, Mr. Fetzer — the only place you won't find a Jew is in a Christian cemetery."

The crowd laughed at this, too, and Ernest Fetzer sat back down.

My father went back to exhorting, pleading. "Do it for Concordia. Do it for yourselves. Do it for your children." He grinned. "Do it for me." He grinned wider. "How am I going to make a living if this thing don't come out right?"

The crowd guffawed once more, and my father said, "If you can't help your friend with money, at least help him with a sym-pa-thetic groan."

At this the crowd emitted a loud, fake groan and laughed loudly at its own drollery.

My father teased, "What're you going to do with all the money you got, you folks? Ain't you never noticed that shrouds don't have pockets?"

Amid the laughter, my father found Dalrymple, the other half of Dalrymple-Eaton.

"Mr. Dalrymple? Ain't you got something you want to do?"

It seemed maybe Mr. Dalrymple did. He got to his feet and cleared his throat. It appeared his partner, Mr. Eaton, had "underestimated the need" and he, Dalrymple, was "pleased" to make it five thousand. He sat down, got back up. "We'll want to take back the other pledge, of course."

My father laughed and said, "What can I say? It's a deal." Now who else wanted to see "a tightwad Jew" spend his money?

Pledges came in: a thousand from the drugstore, another thousand from the U-Tote-'Em. All the merchants pledged something, and if they hung back, my father heckled them until they came forth. "Don't be shy," he might say. "We ain't in church. It ain't no sin to discuss money matters in here."

Each new pledge was greeted by a wave of cheering, even after the pledges began to come in smaller — hundred-dollar ones, ten-dollar ones, children's single-dollar ones.

Finally my father held up his hands. "*Sha, sha,* hold your horses." He turned to Mr. Pinder, to find out where things stood.

Mr. Pinder waved the tally sheet. The money was there.

And now the crowd truly erupted. They stomped their feet. They clapped their hands

414

over their heads. They put two fingers in their mouths and whistled. A few pushed into the aisles and danced. Mothers held their infants up so they could say in later years that they too had been in on that night — that glorious night when Concordia had been saved.

The crowd walked my father all the way home and came on in. It was like the aftermath of a football game or a music competition when Concordia had won.

Late that night, when we were finally alone, even with all the praise and all the excitement, my mother, maybe not completely *modren* but certainly practical, wondered how much it was going to cost us.

And of course my father had it all in mind. If his figures were not down to the penny, they were down to the hundred. He figured he had pledged twenty-two thousand dollars. Of course, Pinder had promised to pay back all pledges, but who knew? "It's worth every cent," my father said to my mother. "For how good we did the town, it's worth every cent."

My mother thought it was worth it, too: On the way home Miss Brookie had called her a mensch.

Chapter 26

Miriam's Rescue

Of course, before too long the euphoria of "the night Concordia was saved" played itself out and was replaced by the reality of hard times.

Very quickly the whole country was down with the Depression disease, and Concordia was deathly sick with it. The shoe factory, though able to stay open, was operating with a skeleton workforce, and farmers were all but giving away their crops. The Negro women who worked as domestics opened their hands on payday to find there even fewer dollar bills. Some found no dollar bills at all, just maybe twenty-five cents. Some found nothing. "You'll have to wait til next week" became routine. Even totin' privileges were carefully monitored. Those whose wages went unpaid for weeks at a time might finally arrange a trade of some sort — work exchanged for a couple of home-put-up items or a dress just run up by the mistress out of fabric that had been put by perhaps years before.

When the stores on First Street started closing, my mother was newly alarmed with each GOING OUT OF BUSINESS sign. And when Mary Hyams had to be let go, she was icy with fear. My father tried to reassure her and said over and over that we could tough it out, that we had the kind of prices people liked. "But," he would add, "I wouldn't want to be in Dalrymple-Eaton's shoes, no sirree." And as if in confirmation, in a couple of months Dalrymple-Eaton's closed.

My father would tell my mother to stop thinking about going to New York (for he knew that's what she was thinking), that now was no time to be in New York. Up there they were selling apples from behind a little box on the street, didn't she know that? "Is that what you want me to do?" he asked her. No, my mother did not want my father selling apples on the street, but couldn't we sell the store and live on what we got for it?

"So who's going to buy a store in times like these?" he reminded my mother. Nobody, she had to say, nobody would buy a store in times like these.

My mother was beginning to wring her hands over Miriam. If the Depression would just be over, we could leave in time for Miriam to meet some nice Jewish boy in New

York. (She, of course, had me in mind as well, but Miriam's needs were imminent.) She crossed her fingers that it wasn't too late. And if it was? She couldn't even think about it. The truth was that she was getting very fidgety indeed.

In the middle of all the gloom there came a ray of sunlight: Miriam had been picked as Concordia's representative in the annual county high school music competition. It was a big honor. The competition sparked intense rivalry, and participants became famous countywide for their instrument playing, much as county football players were celebrated for their broken-field running.

Despite the hard times, my parents at last thought about giving Miriam her own piano. My mother had convinced herself, privately, that it was in a good cause — that making it easy for Miriam to practice might cut into her time with T. At any rate, my father went over to Venable's Music Store and bought one, an upright so big it stretched across a whole wall and then some.

Miriam and Miss Brookie had decided on "The Golliwog's Cakewalk" and the Minuet in G, and Miriam spent a lot of time practicing her pieces. And this meant, as my mother had hoped, that when T was home, he and

Miriam were not always together.

One Saturday afternoon, Miriam said she was going to Miss Brookie's to spend the day practicing over there.

My mother said, "Already something's wrong with our piano?"

No, it was that the competition was on a grand, and Miriam wanted to practice on one.

My mother was going to the store and, as Lizzie Maud no longer came on Saturdays, she told Miriam to take me with her.

When we got to Miss Brookie's, nobody was home. The house was empty, quiet. And hot as blazes.

"Wonder where she's got to," Miriam said, putting her music on the rack. "Reckon she's down at the mayor's, blessing him out for this hot weather." She settled herself on the piano bench.

I wandered around the house. I went up to the bedrooms where we had once stayed, came back down. I opened the icebox, took out the pitcher of tea, poured some into a glass, replaced the pitcher. I checked the harp to see if it still played, and Miriam told me to hush.

I thought about going outside, but I had noticed on the way over that the sky was turning dark, and ever since that awful time in the

Broomes' storm cellar, I definitely had no use for storms. There seemed nothing to do but to lie down on the Victorian affliction divan. I listened for a moment to Miriam pounding away, and I began to get sleepy. I could hear a drop or two of rain coming down on the front porch, and I wondered if there was going to be a thunderstorm. Then my eyelids closed, and I was adrift.

I was not quite tight asleep when I heard the squeak of the front door. Miss Brookie, I thought, and hoped she wouldn't talk too loud. The voice I heard, however, was a man's voice, and it was very loud indeed. It was saying, "Well, well, what have we here? I do believe it's the Jew babies." There was a laugh. "Tell you what's the truth, you never know what you're going to find at Brookie's."

I turned over into a sitting position. Mr. Dillon.

Miriam had stopped playing. Her mouth was shaped into a stiff little smile. "Miss Brookie's not here, Mr. Dillon. I declare I don't know where she is."

There was silence. Miriam went on in her role as substitute hostess. "She'll be mighty sorry to have missed you."

"You let me decide that, little lady," Mr. Dillon said. "You don't know if she'll be sorry or not." He gave Miriam a sort of teasing smile. "Now do you?"

"No sir, I guess that's right." Miriam began to fool with the music on the rack.

"See how it is, you dassent go around talking for other folks. Especially Jews talking for Christians. Jews and Christians don't think alike, you know that?"

"I hadn't thought about it all that much," Miriam said, turning pages swiftly.

"I'm talking to you, girl, so pay attention. You may have call to remember what I'm saying someday," Mr. Dillon said.

He crossed the room to the nearest chair — one of Miss Brookie's *un*easy ones and inappropriate for a man of his size — and sat down. Pulling a cigarette pack from his shirt pocket, he extracted a cigarette, then withdrew a box of matches and struck a match into flame with his thumbnail. After lighting up, he threw the match on the little table beside him, put one leg over the other, and let out a great cloud of smoke.

Miriam spoke into her music book. "If you're going to wait on Miss Brookie, I reckon we'll just go along. You won't want to hear me practicing." She stood up and walked around the piano. "Come on, Stella Ruth."

I got myself up, glad to be rid of the prickly red plush and all the sweaty spots.

Suddenly Mr. Dillon was pointing at Miriam. "Hey. Hey, wait a minute," he said to her. "Ain't you the one who won our Charleston contest that time?"

"Yes, sir." Miriam pulled me by the hand.

"Well then." Mr. Dillon bent forward. "Don't you see? That makes us friends. Sit back down and we'll have us a little conversation." Mr. Dillon's look took in Miriam from top to toe. "You still know how to dance?"

I guessed they were going to have a chat. I went back to sit on the divan.

Miriam plunked back down on the piano bench.

"Tell me about it, big sister," Mr. Dillon was saying.

Miriam looked over at me, as if asking me how she should answer. I wanted her to say, "I'm the best dancer in town next to Lizzie Maud," but she just said, "A little."

Mr. Dillon's eyes were tightly focused on her. And doing the crinkling thing. "You still dance better than any girl around, you know you do. Ain't that the truth?"

Miriam said, "I don't know," and looked at me again.

I was tired of all the talk. I considered nagging Miriam to leave, but I had gotten too many blessings out for this habit of mine. I leaned back on the sofa, feeling again the need to sleep. It was so *hot*. My eyes began to close.

"Little sister?"

I realized Mr. Dillon was talking to me.

"How about it, little sister?" he was saying. "Don't big sister here show them a thing or two about dancing? And don't the boys flock around?" He returned his look to Miriam. "Course they do, like flies around a ripe peach."

I wondered if he really wanted an answer. Just in case he did, I nodded to the back of his head.

"Let's see can we get big sister to dance for us. Like she does for the boys. Shall we ask her?"

I couldn't help it, I had to say, "Go on, Miriam, dance. Mr. Dillon wants to see you dance."

"Hush, Stella Ruth," Miriam said. "You just hush."

Mr. Dillon was looking at me, intently, as if preparing to say something important. "Why don't you just go on out and play, little sister?" He waved a hand toward the outside. "You won't have no fun sitting here while us two old friends get in some chatting, now will you?"

It was Miriam who answered. "Stella Ruth doesn't want to go out, Mr. Dillon. It's fixing to really pour, and if there's anything she hates, it's a thunderstorm."

"There you go talking for other people again," Mr. Dillon said to Miriam. "I got to break you of that habit." He took time out for some rough, raspy coughing.

The coughing subsided, he laughed, and an ash fell off his cigarette end and onto his shirt front. "All right, that's fine. Baby sister and I will just sit right here. And you, you pretty thing, get on up and dance for us."

"I just can't, Mr. Dillon."

"I vow I never knew Jew folks to be so bashful. Next to niggers, Jews is the worst for calling attention to themselves." Mr. Dillon laughed and coughed, coughed and laughed. "Now tell me why you can't dance for me."

"Because I don't think my mama would like it. She might wear me out."

"Don't you worry none about your mama," Mr. Dillon said. "You just leave your mama to me. Fact is, she wouldn't want you to disappoint old Tom Dillon." He put his cigarette out in the ashtray on the near table, got up, and went over to the piano. He leaned toward Miriam, and his bulky body blocked my view. Though he talked low, I could hear him plainly. "Lord, a pretty thing like you ought not to be hiding behind that piano," he was saying.

I watched as he moved around to the piano

bench. "Come with me, pretty thing," he said to Miriam. "You and me'll dance."

He grabbed Miriam up, and she stood there, her hand in the man's grip. But instead of dancing, he just stood there looking into Miriam's face, saying the same words, mumbling them over and over, "Come on, pretty thing" and "You get on up here with me," although Miriam was already up. Then, before I could turn my eyes away, he had his mouth on hers.

Miriam's head jerked away. "Please, Mr. Dillon! Please, please! Don't do this! Please don't do this! Stella Ruth and I have to go home!" The voice didn't sound like Miriam's. It sounded like some lady's in a picture show. She was swinging her head and ducking. "Stop this!" she was saying. "Please stop this!"

And then Miriam was screaming at me. "Stella Ruth! Get somebody! Hurry!"

I was already at the door when I heard the last of her words. I knew what I had to do: I had to get to Miz Earp's. I darted to the front door, preparing to run across the strip between the two houses. But when I pushed open the screen and stepped out, there was the rain — pelting, pounding, battering. I had a moment of wanting to draw away, to go back into the house, to lie down and close my eyes. Oh, I knew I needed to make the run, but when I looked out into the yard, into the fury of the wind and rain, I couldn't. I could only cry out for the rain to stop.

Then all at once a figure was running up the walk and bounding over the porch. It was T, already snatching open the door.

"T!" I cried. "Hurry!"

In the house T was holding Dillon by the collar, shoving him forward. "You crazy old coot! I got a notion to wring your neck!" he was saying.

"Listen, Medlin," I heard Mr. Dillon say, "I was just messing around."

"Messing around? What right have you got to mess around with Miriam?" T tightened his hold. "If I had good sense, I'd bust your head wide open!"

And then Mr. Dillon was out the door and rushing through the rain to his car. When I turned back, Miriam had sat herself on the divan. There were no tears, just big eyes and a pale face. With both hands she was shoving her hair over and over behind her ears.

We sat down on either side of her, T and I. T's breath was still coming hard. "That danged fool!" He looked at Miriam. "You hurt?"

Miriam shook her head.

"What on earth got into that weasel?" T had apparently not been going to come, but then he "got to thinking" that maybe he could walk Miriam home.

Miriam sighed. It wasn't the sigh we all knew so well — the one that told us my mother was *purely hopeless* — but one that came from a far deeper place. She lifted her head and tied the ribbon around her hair. "Listen, y'all," she said.

We waited.

"Listen, y'all," she said again. "This is important." What was important was that we couldn't let our mother know about this.

"Not tell your mama?" T was bewildered.

Miriam shook her head. "She'd kill me."

T still couldn't understand. "But why? You didn't have nothing to do with it, nothing atall!" T might have been surprised, but I wasn't. I was used to Miriam keeping secrets from my mother.

"Yeah, I know," Miriam answered T. "*I* know and *you* know. But Mama always knows something different." And if my mother was told, Miriam said, we'd be leaving town "on the next thing going out."

Then surely, T was saying, Miriam must tell our father. "Lord," he said, "if 'twas up to me, I'd run tell your daddy this minute."

Not our father either, Miriam said. "If Papa knew, he might get it in his head to agree with Mama."

She took our hands and made us swear. "Y'all swear never to tell Mama. Or Papa, either one." She squeezed our hands hard. "Cross your heart?"

"And hope to die," we said.

Miriam didn't feel like practicing anymore and she didn't enter the piano competition. She said one of her fingers wouldn't move right. I assumed it was a story she had made up, but when I watched her move her hand, I saw it was true: The forefinger on her right hand just stayed stiff, its only movement a kind of flutter. She would stand over the piano and plunk with one finger, but that was all.

I wanted to know if it had happened when she was wrestling with Mr. Dillon, and Miriam said no, her finger just decided on its own that it wouldn't move right.

For a while she didn't have a whole lot of fun. She didn't even go on the fall buying trip with my father, and my father said to her, "How you going to be a clotheshorse if you don't gallop around the wholesale houses once in a while?

"Who would have thought?" he asked my mother. "That little finger. Who would have thought?"

"She'll get over it," my mother answered

my father. "We all have to get over things."

She did get over it, and her finger returned to normal. And when she got over it, she was more in love with T than ever. Whenever T was home, they were together day and night, and in summer he was always home. During the day T did chores at his family's farm, but every night he and Miriam would go sit on the grass of the vacant lot across from our house (still there, still vacant) and Miriam would play her ukelele. This plot of ground (which had seemed as spacious as a meadow when I had played in it but, on my revisit, turned out to be just a builder's-sized lot on which, in all those years, nobody had built) was where the neighborhood children chased fireflies in the summer twilight and where after dark the older brothers and sisters brought whatever stringed instruments they had and sat together and played. There was only one banjo, for banjos were expensive, but several ukeleles, which weren't. There was also a zither, whose sound lingered longer in the warm air than any of the others. And it was here, on the grass, in my meadow, that Miriam and T sat and strummed and talked the summer nights away while my mother watched.

Chapter 27

Push Comes to Shove

My mother's dream that the Depression would be short-lived, and we could go to New York, remained a dream. The Depression lingered and lingered. Still, our store remained open and even made a little living, and the shoe factory limped along.

A couple of years went by in this way, and then Miriam was seventeen, and everything came to a head. It happened at the moment when Miriam asked my mother for permission to spend a weekend with T in Knoxville.

Miriam thought to broach the subject in the kitchen while my mother was fixing cole slaw. As Miriam never watched my mother cook, never just sat in the kitchen and chatted, *schmoozed*, as my father would say, when Miriam came in, I knew something was up.

Miriam sat in the nook and plunged right in. She told my mother that she would take the train to Knoxville. "Goodness knows I'm old enough," she said, an unsure quality in her voice. "After all, I'm seventeen."

Exactly, my mother was thinking: *Seventeen* is exactly the problem. Hadn't she herself been seventeen when she got married? Chopping furiously at the cabbage, she gave a curt no.

Whenever Miriam could see that my mother was in a mood where no amount of wheedling would help, she could be counted on to say absolutely the wrong thing, and she did it then: She told my mother how "important" T was to her.

"What are you saying?" my mother asked her. "A boy means so much to you?"

Apparently Miriam still wasn't thinking. "Yes," she said.

My mother finished chopping. She grated the carrot and onion (her addition to traditional cole slaw) and went to the icebox and brought out the mayonnaise (the mayonnaise issue having long ago been settled in favor of the mayonnaise). She was saying nothing, seemingly just going about her business. I knew better.

Like everybody else in Concordia, Miriam rushed into all silences. "I'm thinking how T's way over there," she said, while I cringed, "and I'm over here and how much I love him."

Was my mother swayed by Miriam's evocation of romantic love?

She was not. She said, "We all want things we can't have, Miriam. It's time you learned that."

Miriam was not through. As she said later, "Mama always thought T just hung the moon, so I just *knew* she'd give in when I reminded her how *smart* and *considerate* he was."

My mother said she didn't have to be told how good T was. But did Miriam have to be told that T was not a Jewish boy? "You're altogether too serious about T," my mother said to her.

Miriam, now desperate, said the worst possible thing: "If you don't let me go, I'll just run away!"

No surprise here, my mother could also say the wrong thing. "So run," she said. After which she left her cutting board and went to her bedroom with a headache.

Miriam did not run away after all; she ran over to Miss Brookie's. I ran with her.

We rushed into Miss Brookie's house, Miriam already crying out for relief — from all the abuse she had endured, from all the *unfairness!* What do you think, Miss Brookie? Mama's just so *unyielding!*

Miss Brookie astounded both of us. She did

432

not immediately settle into her usual half-humorous, half-serious comments on my unbudgeable mother. Her opening remarks were something quite different and quite unexpected: She talked about what she called "blighted love." I was stunned, and Miriam was as well. What did Miss Brookie know about love, blighted or unblighted? As it turned out, Miss Brookie knew a quite a lot.

It seemed that Miss Brookie had experienced a "blighted love" of her own. My Miss Brookie? My round Miss Brookie, my unstylish Miss Brookie, my Miss Brookie who, as far as I could tell, disdained all feminine stratagems? Where? When? Who? In Chicago was where; when was the time she had visited with the Landaus; and Jack Landau was who.

The story poured out of her, as if, I thought, she was telling it for the very first time. Had the story always been a secret? I've always hoped that perhaps in later years, she was able to tell it to T.

She and Jack Landau had wanted to get engaged, but — "Wouldn't you know it?" — Miss Brookie's father "just wouldn't hear of it." If Miriam's "blighted love," was due to my mother, Miss Brookie's was due to her father. He had been just like my mother on the subject, Miss Brookie said — "rigid as a steel flagpole." And what had Jack's German-

Jewish folks thought of it? Well, they thought "the planet would keep on rotating," as Miss Brookie put it. But in the end, her father had been so "downright apoplectic," Miss Brookie said, that Jack just stopped trying. When she told us the story she took her glasses off, as if to return to the days before she wore them.

As to what Jack Landau looked like, he had black curly hair "like Joey's." (We've often thought that Joey's hair may have been one thing that tipped Miss Brookie off that first day that we were Jewish.) And as she would have it, he was the "perfect image" of the David of Michelangelo. Yes, Miss Brookie could have romantic dreams, too.

But what could Miriam do about her plight? Miss Brookie's advice — and this was also surprising from one so independent — was that if Miriam were older, she could follow her heart's "yearning." But Miriam was so young, too young to make a decision that might deprive her of her family. "You don't want to get yourself into that wicked fix," she said to her.

But, I remember thinking at the time, Miss Brookie *had* been older; and this was apparently on Miss Brookie's mind as well. "You could say I deprived *myself*," she said. "I often think what a ninny I was."

Miriam wasn't interested in being told she was too young. She wanted to be told that everything was my mother's fault. If my mother would only understand! Couldn't Miss Brookie do something with her?

Miss Brookie said no, she couldn't. "Your mama's come a long way, Miriam, but this is one threshold she won't allow herself to cross. And no amount of yawping from me is going to change that."

Push was coming to shove. For my mother this last go-round with Miriam was also the last straw. It was time to leave. She started her campaign slowly, as my father had done when he was trying to get my mother to leave New York. That night when she spoke to him, it was only about Miriam wanting to go to Knoxville.

My father asked what Miriam was going to Knoxville for.

"To see T, of course," my mother answered him.

"So? So she'll give him our regards."

My mother blazed. "She's going out of town to see the boy she's in love with and you say 'give him our regards'? And who is she in love with? A *shaigetz*, that's who!"

My father waved a hand as if to swat away an idea that had no right to be in the same room with sane people. "Are you trying to tell me them two babies are in love?"

"What else am I trying to tell you?" my mother answered. "And Miriam's no baby!"

My father continued to scoff: "Tell her it's enough already with T," he said to my mother. "Tell her she should have more than one boyfriend."

And who would another *boyfriend* be, if my mother could ask. "It could only be another *shaigetz*," she answered my father, "or ain't you noticed there are no Jewish boys in Concordia?"

My father was not really in the dark; he knew what my mother was up to, and that she had thrown down the challenge. So he said, "Aha, so now we finally at last get to the point."

The point was, of course, that my father was being called upon to make a decision: whether we would live on in Jew-less Concordia or move to Jew-full New York. Push had come to shove. He could no longer keep the problem in it-will-never-happen land.

He tried to shake my mother's determination by reminding her of what Miss Brookie had said about the azalea that had suddenly appeared in my mother's garden. "If we leave," he said to her, "we'll be like the little azaly. We'll be volunteers. And turning up our toes, like Miss Brookie said."

"So we'll turn up," my mother answered him.

My father wanted time to think it over. Did my mother expect him to just "pucker up the lips" and blow a kiss good-bye?

If in New York my mother had lain in bed and pondered going to the South, my father now lay in bed and pondered leaving it. What made it so hard was that my father thought of Concordia as his home.

On the face of it, Concordia as "home" seemed inappropriate, just this side of un-thinkable. My father was not an old-timer, much less a native, and he was a member of almost every possible minority: a shopkeeper among factory workers and farmers, foreign-born among American-born, a Jew among Gentiles. Even as a white, his majority status was doubtful, for a proper census might have revealed that not whites but Negroes made up Concordia's majority. So, to face facts, the Democratic party was the only majority membership he held. Still, he asked himself, so where else was more appropriate for him to call home?

The place in which he had been born was certainly not home. There he had come into the world a stranger, and from all signs he had been going to stay one. And though Savannah and Nashville had been promising, his stay in those places had been too short to make a real judgment.

If Concordia was my father's home, the store was the essential element in making it so. In twelve years Bronson's Low-Priced Store had become so much a part of First Street that it was hard for people to remember when it hadn't been there. Its success had given my father confidence, and on at least one (memorable) occasion he'd used it to help out the town. So, he figured, if Concordia needed him, and he needed Concordia, why not call it home?

My father guarded against sentimentalizing Concordia, going "too easy" on it, as he said. He reminded himself that it was not a place of uniformly soft hearts and warm spirits, a place where the inhabitants were partial to Jews. He wasn't a fool; he knew Concordia wasn't that way. But the way it *was* was okay by him. And why not? Having in Russia been tormented, chased, and attacked by Cossacks, having in New York been insulted and ignored, whatever maltreatment he had endured in Concordia was minor league. The Ku Klux Klan? Their threats had not materialized, though my father did not kid himself. "It wasn't because they loved me so much," he would say.

No, it was more that having experienced a Jew store, they were now convinced that having one in Concordia was a good thing.

He did not have to ponder long whether Miriam and I thought of Concordia as home. That was a given.

But my mother, my mother. My mother had bent but never truly bowed to the idea that Concordia was home. She could not comply when my father used to say, "Know when you're happy and the rest is easy." It was good and useful advice, but given as my mother was to standing on one foot and then the other, she never knew if she was happy or not. There was always something missing, something that if she only had it, her life would be complete.

Beginning at the beginning — with Miss Brookie — my father thought of all the Concordians who had helped us, wished us well, wanted to be our friends, and he wondered if my mother could leave them as easily as she imagined. And the neighbors? Why, in this, the summer season, their yards were dense with growing things that were the very progenitors of my mother's growing things.

All in all, discounting some occasional unpleasantnesses (and where was that place so dedicated to providing the milk of human kindness that the milk was ever-protected against turning sour?) and my mother's uncertainties, my father concluded with some confidence that Concordia had brought more than a modicum of contentment to the Bronsons.

And so it followed that one morning as my father lay in bed thinking these things, so cooled was he by the overhanging trees in the side yard, so delighted by the fragrance of what he called "Mama's Abie's Irish Rose bushes," a euphoria overtook him. What would be so wrong, he asked himself, if we brought Gentiles into the family? Ask my mother, point blank, why Miriam should not marry T? What would be so wrong?

Oy, with my mother, what would be so right? She would say, "That's your answer? That's what you'll say to your daughters? That it's all right to marry a *shaigetz?*"

Well, my father wondered, was it all right, *really* all right for us to marry a *shaigetz?* In facing the possibility — no, the *probability* — that if we stayed in Concordia, Miriam and I would do just this, he had to face what would happen if a Concordia boy brought home the news that he wanted to marry one of the Bronson girls. Accept us though Concordia did, call me a Concordian as it would, my father knew it was with a gingerliness, a reservation. In their eyes we were different in a way important to them, and Miriam and I would doubtless be thought not quite right for their sons. (Still, it could be said that we had gone a long way toward convincing them that Jews were not sent from the devil.)

On our side, if we married local boys, my father envisioned something worse: my mother avoiding us. Maybe there would be, with the birth of a grandchild, an uneasy reconciliation. What was the good of this? As my father saw it, there was not much good in it at all.

And if we stayed and tried hard to turn up some Jewish boys? In later years my father used to say that in this particular scenario, he pictured us scouting around in a couple of Tennessee counties, whacking at bushes, climbing trees, peering through binoculars, in which case we might flush out one or two (not Sheldon Rastow, nobody would have tried to flush out that pest Sheldon Rastow), but even my mother would have thought it unfair to have such a small pool to choose from.

And the "lists," those famous lists my father knew from the Savannah days, which cataloged all the Jewish eligibles for miles around? Where were they when we needed them most? They had thus far not come to our little dot on the map and showed no promise of doing so. Perhaps the compilers of

441

the lists were not as interested in attracting girls as boys, and it was true that though most any Jewish boy was on the list, faraway Jewish girls were there only if they came from wealthy families. And a wealthy family we were not.

Send us to New York? My father himself scotched that idea. We live in New York while he and my mother stayed on in Concordia? The family divided like that? Like what happened with Joey? *Oy*, whenever he thought this, he always asked himself, What could compare to a family being together?

Still, the notion of dwelling in a place with a heart as hard as iron and a spirit as cold as ice, *oy!* And with the Depression holding everything in its grip, what, my father wondered, would he *do* in New York? Especially what would he do if he could not sell the store, which he saw as likely? Again he did not kid himself. Sale or no sale, my mother knew as well as he that we could still make it: What with the money that was still in the bank, what with the factory continuing to pay back (if only in small amounts), we could live out the Depression for a few years without my father joining a breadline or — almost as despised a thought — clerking for somebody else, if, as was doubtful, such a job could be found. Since in these days a little money went a long way, and my mother was skilled in making money go as long a way as possible, the family would survive.

And if the store by some miracle was sold? Well, my father figured, in that case there was a possibility of getting something in New York. It wasn't out of the question. During the Depression, people were willing to deal down, down, down. "Down to where they paid you to take it off their hands," my father used to say.

He saw what this decision must be: If my mother couldn't yield, he could. We would abandon Concordia, abandon the store. So on the last morning of contemplation, and with the bedroom no longer cool and fragrant but sticky hot and musty, my father turned to my mother in bed beside him and said, "So you want to try some gardening in New York? So we'll go there and see."

It was left to my father to break the news to Miriam. "She'll take it better from you," my mother said to him. "From me she'll be like a wild animal."

She didn't take it very well from my father either. "What do you mean *moving to New York?*" she asked him, eyes dark.

"I mean moving to New York," my father answered her.

Miriam's response was to fling herself at my

father's feet. "Take it back, Papa!" she cried, her toes kicking against the floor. "You can't mean it! We can't move, we can't!"

Though he was far from calm himself, my father tried to calm Miriam. He looked down and spoke to the back of her head. "Sweetheart," he said to her, "you'll see. It might be a hard fit at first, but we'll use a nice little slipper spoon and you'll slip in easy."

"I don't want to slip in! I want to stay here!" Miriam screamed. "You can't take me away!"

"We have to go," my father said to her.

"But why? Why? Just tell me why, that's all I ask!"

Of course it was not all she asked, and the answer would not satisfy her. And my father's answer — that we couldn't afford to take risks — did not. "But you're always taking risks, Papa!" she cried. "You're not afraid of anything."

To which my father said, as if to himself, "And that's what you think."

On the floor Miriam lay hoping she was having a nightmare. And like my father, she had idea after idea: We would go and she'd stay alone in the house; she'd stay with a neighbor; with one of her friends. She'd stay with Miss Brookie.

My father wouldn't answer, wouldn't listen. And when he had finally had enough, he

444

reached down and dragged her to her feet. To my surprise he was very angry. My father? Angry with Miriam? He was *never* angry with Miriam.

"I've had enough of this," he said to her. "Enough to last me a lifetime. It's time for you to realize you're a member of this family and you'll do as we tell you."

And Miriam, perhaps as surprised as I was, said no more.

Of course, I didn't much want to go either. The next year I was destined for the big school (for grades five through twelve), and I had a lot of plans. I had already been thinking ahead to college and had made no secret of it. The teachers, no doubt excited by my enthusiasm for college, gave me special attention. Miss Nonie, the adviser for the *Annual*, had told me she would be "tickled" to have me work on it, and I was definitely looking forward to *that*. And what would happen to T-Dog? To Willy? To *everything*?

How to leave? A going-out-of-business sale? My father dreaded the thought. There would have to be an advertisement in the paper and signs plastered on the store windows. My father shrank from this vision. What kind of thanks was that for a store that did by us so good?

It didn't occur to my father to call on his good luck. He had been thinking lately that his good luck must have grown old and feeble and gone into retirement. Still, the store was saved from humiliation by something, because it turned out that a buyer was not as unlikely as my father had thought: Out of the blue the One-Stop people came by one day and made an offer.

On that day my father came home in the late afternoon and sat down full of weight on the divan. He sat inspecting his hands in the way Manny had done on that last day with Aunt Hannah. "All right," he said.

"What's all right?" my mother asked him.

"Nothing is."

"So what are you talking?"

He was "talking" that One-Stop representatives were looking to expand from Kentucky into Tennessee and had come into the store and made him an offer, and he had accepted. My father said, "They got their teeth all set to gobble us up." Glad as he was not to be forced to have a going-out-of-business sale, it was the only thing he *was* glad about. The moment of truth had arrived.

My mother was stunned. "Expanding in these times?" she asked my father.

I knew that even though President Hoover had been insisting that prosperity was "just around the corner," my father always said, "A lot he knows about it." But now with President Roosevelt newly elected, I wondered if maybe the Depresssion had already started to go away.

No, my father said, it was just a new concept in business that enabled the One-Stop to expand. One-Stop was a chain, like Woolworth's. "With so many stores to stock," he explained, "they can buy cheaper." He didn't want to go into it any further. He saw chains as the new way of doing business, and not his way at all.

It was not too long before the *Sentinel* had the story:

MERCHANT TO LEAVE CONCORDIA

Mr. and Mrs. Aaron Bronson of Fifth Street, proprietors of Bronson's Low-Priced Store on First Street, have announced their intention to leave Concordia and to return to their home in New York City. According to Mr. Bronson, the move will be within the next month.

The Bronson family have been residents of Concordia since 1920, having come here from Nashville, where they had gone after arriving in New York City from their native Russia. They have oper-

447

ated a successful business here since that time.

It was a very long article, pointing out all the details of our lives in Concordia: my father's role in the saving of the shoe factory, my mother's standing up for Miss Brookie, Joey's success in school, even Miriam's withdrawal from the piano competition, which, it said, was due to "an untimely accident." And, it added, "Stella Ruth, the youngest, is a native of Concordia, having been born in our town in 1922." It ended with, "The Bronsons leave many friends in Concordia. The *Sentinel* wishes them well."

My father cut out the item and tucked it into his wallet.

The buzzing was all over town: "Did you hear tell of the Bronsons? They're *leaving!* Hellfire, just picking up and hightailing it out of here! Lord, lord!" People called at the store. One old farmer told my father that he didn't sleep "a lick" all night. "What's a fact is we was beginning to think of y'all as kin," he said.

Even if this wasn't strictly the truth, my father thought it took something for the old man to say it. He thanked him, and said, now easy with Southernisms, "And for our part we'll carry a heap of Concordia away with us."

Those closest to us wanted to blame somebody, so they blamed my mother, and of course they were mostly right. T came to the house, Erv along. Miriam was not at home. My mother and I were packing that day, and Miriam was taking no part in the packing, not even her own.

We were in the front room, my mother and I wrapping things in newspaper, stashing them in crates, she impatient and in no mood for argument. T had questions. Did she want to leave? No. Did she have to? Yes. She tried to explain to T in the easiest way. "Look, T," she said, "don't you see? Down here we're like jelly in iced tea. It just don't go."

T jumped on what he saw as a flawed premise. Arguing with T had always been difficult, and my mother again found herself being pulled up short and held to reason, by that way of T's that always reminded me of Joey's. "There ain't nothing against jelly in iced tea, Miz Bronson," T said. And I thought, well, what is there against jelly in iced tea?

We never doubted that T knew the real reason we were going, but if he had been told by Miriam or had just "suspicioned" it, we weren't sure. At any rate, he saw the future somewhat differently from my mother. What he saw, he said to her, was a future in which we stayed and became kin. Hearing this, my mother wrapped and stashed ever more furiously. Finally, T, perhaps realizing it was hopeless, stopped saying anything, turned to Erv, and told him to tell us good-bye. "See can you do it," T said to him.

Erv prepared his little speech by working his lips in and out. "Good-bye," he said at last. "Good-bye to you Jews. Having Jews here was the best thing Concordia ever done." Was my mother going to correct Erv? No, she was not.

Lizzie Maud wanted to know what got into my mother that we "gwine go away." She stared at my mother, *glared* at my mother, arms stuck out on her hips like doughnut halves. "Shucks, you ain't gwine like it up there no way, no how," she said to her. "All them peoples, all them big buildings, all them trains!" She shuddered at the vision she had projected. "And ain't I reckoned you be one of us by now?"

Miss Brookie knew the specific thing to blame it on — "the religion hokum," as she called it — and offered my mother an out. "If it's religion you're hankering for, why, you don't have to go an inch." She suggested we just stay right in Concordia and "partake" of hers.

Religion? Miss Brookie had a religion?

Yes, she said, she did, and one that was a

"heap sight" better than most. Hers was doing for other people, people who couldn't do for themselves. Slipping into her sociologist mode, she said, "Powerless people."

My mother was bewildered. What kind of religion was that? She was in for more bewilderment when Miss Brookie said that my mother was a member in good standing.

"Remember when you joined?" Miss Brookie asked her.

Though my mother shook her head, I knew what Miss Brookie was talking about. And when my mother thought about it, she knew as well. As she often said, how could she forget a moment of such joy?

Miss Brookie said, "Oh, Reba, I could just shake you for making us all so unhappy." And when she said this, a barely there smile slid off her face, like icing off a too hot cake.

Before we left, Miriam was already homesick. She told me she felt like a dog during dog days. I didn't even like to think about dog days, that August week when stray dogs suspected of having rabies were rounded up and towed through the streets by a rope attached to the dogcatcher's wagon. Was that how Miriam felt? Like a dog being dragged down a gritty dirt road? She certainly looked forlorn. Her hair seemed to have darkened, or maybe her skin had paled. And her cheekbones stood out more than ever on her too thin face.

There was no ceremonial leave-taking from the store. On the Sunday before the Monday takeover my father and a representative of the chain would take inventory, on which, my father said, he was going to get "a big twenty cents on the dollar."

On the last Saturday, he made no fuss about the closing, just followed his routine: He showed up early, stayed late, and in between good-byes did some selling.

At midnight, in his customary way, he stood at the door to give a last inspection. When he was satisfied, when he saw that the muslin was completely over the counters, that no boxes were in the aisles, that stools and sticks in the shoe department were where they ought to be, he turned out the lights, went outside, locked the door, put the keys in his pocket, and began to walk.

On the sidewalk, he walked past the bank, past the feed store, crossed the cobblestones to the empty store that had been Dalrymple-Eaton's. He did what he always did at this point — looked back at the store for his final glimpse of the day, at what the windows said (in two places and in gold): BRONSON'S LOW-PRICED STORE.

When he came home, he said to us, "So I

said good-bye to the store. And on Monday it belongs to somebody else."

And so we left. T-Dog went with us; Willy stayed and returned to Miss Brookie's backyard. Some things went, and some things stayed.

We rented an apartment in the West Bronx, one that affirmed what my father had said about everybody being willing to deal down, down, down in these times, as the apartment came with two months' free rent — a concession, it was called. And my father took a little money from the sale of the store and bought a garage. Joey, unable to find an after-school job (he was in college now), worked there repairing cars, thereby totally astounding my mother's family. My father didn't much like his new business — "What kind of business is a garage for a sal-es-man?" — but then he went out and "sold" contracts to taxi-fleet owners, which made him feel better and enabled him to make a kind of cold peace with New York. Still, he would often pull out the clipping from the *Sentinel* and read it, to company, to us, no doubt to himself if nobody else was around.

For a long time (for her) Miriam stayed submerged in depression. She had no use for food and went to bed right after supper. She had energy only for writing to T, reading his letters to her, and hugging T-Dog. My mother worried that Miriam might turn to green eyeshades.

But in the fall of 1933, when school started, Miriam began slowly to improve, no doubt helped by all the attention she was getting from the high school boys, a lot of whom offered to be her beau from the moment she enrolled. For most of them it was their first encounter with a Southern belle, and they seemed not able to get enough of Miriam's accent, which, it must be said, got ever thicker, until it was as thick "as weevils on a cotton boll," as Miriam herself would have described it.

Before too long she had turned into her old self again, and when she did, the letter writing slowed, and then stopped. The letters from T did the same. But, as Miriam will say to this day, her memories of T have stayed with her vivid and sweet.

My new school was not a four-room schoolhouse but a four-story one, and I came to it underprepared in fractions and over-prepared in Tennessee geography. The teachers made a fuss over me, not, as in Concordia, because I had made a declaration for college, but because they too were smitten by

Southern accents. Still, they felt duty-bound to ensure that I spoke mainstream (read New York) English and sent me to speech therapy, where I sat with other foreign arrivals — Chinese, Poles, Romanians — and was taught to say "chawklit" for "chocolate" and to hang on to my final *g*'s.

In certain ways my mother's dreams did come true. Miriam soon married a Jewish boy and Joey a Jewish girl.

When I was ready for marriage, I married a Jewish boy, thereby ensuring peace with my mother, though it could have been just coincidence. And though it has never been a secret that my husband is and always has been more a member of Miss Brookie's congregation than of anything else, my mother didn't question my choice: He was born Jewish, and my mother, like Miss Clara, subscribed to "born a Jew, always a Jew," though she wouldn't have said it quite that way.

I wonder what would have happened if I had married a Gentile — a dreaded *shaigetz*. Would I have been disowned by my mother? Disavowed? Disemboweled? There's no knowing. But I do know that with my husband's and my decision to live in the South, my mother had no quarrel.

I think that of all of us, she was the one who most missed Concordia. Though there were things about it that she did not miss, there were many more things that she did. As she grew aware of this, she would say, "Go know the upsy-downsies of things."

As for me, while I lived up North, I did not spend my time yearning for Concordia or for the South; it was more subtle than that, more like a gravitational pull. I confess that, like Miss Brookie, I have moments when I pine for the attractions of the big city, but when I do, unlike Miss Brookie, I can just get on a plane and go there. And I have never come back home without being glad that this neighborly land is where my home is.

I sometimes try to hear what my father would say about my life in the South. When I do, there his voice is, where it has been all the time, I guess, tucked away in my head somewhere, telling me that old saying of his — and I don't deny that he may have made it up himself: "Know when you're happy, and the rest is easy."

And yes, I still see Jew stores. Whether the townspeople call them that, I don't know; but in small Southern towns there is the occasional sign that says MANDELBAUM'S FAMILY STORE or SCHECTER'S DRY GOODS AND READY-TO-WEAR, unmistakably Jew stores left over from the golden age of Jew stores. It occurs to me to wonder how they managed to make it. Did they have the same Sturm und Drang over bar mitzvahs? Did they not have daughters?

When I see these signs and these stores, my feeling of connection is very strong, and I try to imagine how my life would have proceeded had our store been among these survivors; and I think how close it came. Somehow I have the feeling that if my father's shove had managed to outmuscle my mother's push, Bronson's Low-Priced Store would still be on First Street, and the letters on the windows would still be shining forth.

The employees of Thorndike Press hope you have enjoyed this Large Print book. All our Large Print titles are designed for easy reading, and all our books are made to last. Other Thorndike Press Large Print books are available at your library, through selected bookstores, or directly from the publishers.

For more information about titles, please call:

(800) 257-5157

To share your comments, please write:

Publisher
Thorndike Press
P.O. Box 159
Thorndike, Maine 04986